# THE NOVELS OF HENRY JAMES

## LITERATURE AND LIFE SERIES
## (Formerly Modern Literature and World Dramatists)
### GENERAL EDITOR: PHILIP WINSOR

**Selected list of titles:**

SHERWOOD ANDERSON  *Welford Dunaway Taylor*
JAMES BALDWIN  *Carolyn Wedin Sylvander*
SAUL BELLOW  *Brigitte Scheer-Schäzler*
ANTHONY BURGESS  *Samuel Coale*
TRUMAN CAPOTE  *Helen S. Garson*
WILLA CATHER  *Dorothy Tuck McFarland*
JOHN CHEEVER  *Samuel Coale*
JOSEPH CONRAD  *Martin Tucker*
JOAN DIDION  *Katherine Usher Henderson*
JOHN DOS PASSOS  *George J. Becker*
THEODORE DREISER  *James Lundquist*
T. S. ELIOT  *Burton Raffel*
WILLIAM FAULKNER  *Joachim Seyppel*
F. SCOTT FITZGERALD  *Rose Adrienne Gallo*
FORD MADOX FORD  *Sondra J. Stang*
JOHN FOWLES  *Barry N. Olshen*
ROBERT FROST  *Elaine Barry*
ELLEN GLASGOW  *Marcelle Thiébaux*
ROBERT GRAVES  *Katherine Snipes*
ERNEST HEMINGWAY  *Samuel Shaw*
CHESTER HIMES  *James Lundquist*
JOHN IRVING  *Gabriel Miller*
CHRISTOPHER ISHERWOOD  *Claude J. Summers*
SARAH ORNE JEWETT  *Josephine Donovan*
JAMES JOYCE  *Armin Arnold*
KEN KESEY  *Barry H. Leeds*
RING LARDNER  *Elizabeth Evans*
D. H. LAWRENCE  *George J. Becker*
C. S. LEWIS  *Margaret Patterson Hannay*
SINCLAIR LEWIS  *James Lundquist*
ROBERT LOWELL  *Burton Raffel*
NORMAN MAILER  *Philip H. Bufithis*
BERNARD MALAMUD  *Sheldon J. Hershinow*
MARY MCCARTHY  *Willene Schaefer Hardy*
CARSON MCCULLERS  *Richard M. Cook*

*(continued on last page of book)*

ii

# THE NOVELS OF HENRY JAMES

## Edward Wagenknecht

FREDERICK UNGAR PUBLISHING CO.
New York

In memory of EDITH RICKERT, the most
brilliant teacher I ever had, who introduced
me to Henry James.

**Library of Congress Cataloging in Publication Data**

Wagenknecht, Edward, 1900–
    The novels of Henry James.

    (Literature and life series)
    Bibliography: p.
    Includes index.
    1. James, Henry, 1843–1916—Criticism and
interpretation.   I. Title.   II. Series.
PS2124.W28      1982      813'.4      82-40280
ISBN 0-8044-2959-6

# CONTENTS

# 1
# Biography

The novelist Henry James was born at 21 Washington Place in New York City on April 15, 1843, the second of the five children of Henry James, Sr., and his wife, Mary Robertson Walsh James, and the junior by little more than a year of his brother William, the philosopher and psychologist to be. The parents were of Irish and Scottish extraction. Grandfather William James had deserted County Cavan, Ireland, toward the end of the eighteenth century, for Albany, New York, where he piled up a fortune in mercantile pursuits, leaving his unworldly son free to neglect money-making and devote himself to his "ideas."

A writer and lecturer on theological and philosophical subjects, Henry James, Sr., was strongly influenced by Swedenborg and, to a lesser extent, by Fourier. When William James edited his father's *Literary Remains* in 1884, he defined the single theme of all his writings as an affirmation of "the true relation between mankind and its Creator."[1] Of the mother, Henry later wrote that "she lived in ourselves so exclusively, with such a want of use for anything in her consciousness that was not about us and for us, that I think we almost contested her being separate enough to be proud of us—it was too like being proud of ourselves."[2]

The writer's childhood was spent in New York,
Albany, and Newport, and there were many visits
to Europe (from one, almost in infancy, he retained,
or fancied he retained, an impression of the Place
de Vendôme), to say nothing of excursions to summer hotels, where, characteristically, he saw the
"large, defensive verandah" as a barrier between
himself and the high tide of "the ugly and the grace-
less." But none of this weakened the close ties of
family affection; he found his peach garden "tasting
of many-sized uncles, aunts, cousins, of strange, legendary domestics, inveterately and archaically
Irish," and he loved them all.[3]

Having eschewed established paths in his own
thinking, the father was no less mistrustful of them
in the education of his sons, which was so haphazard
and unsystematic that as he grew older, Henry
James was quite unable to remember at how many
private schools he and William had been entered;
they couldn't have changed more often, he thought,
if their presence had everywhere been objected to.
He was never to forget that he had been oppressed
by "the dreadful blight of arithmetic," but he is not
specific about concrete benefits received. If, in maturity, he was not unaware that he had been reared
in educational anarchy, he still found himself unable to see how he could have "done" with more.

Religious training was equally unsystematic.
There was plenty of instruction, charming and familiar, and the spiritual world was as freely alluded
to as "the prospect of dinner or the call of the post-
man." But there was never the "shade of an approach to 'keeping Sunday,' " and the discovery of
the clergy in the pages of George Eliot and Anthony
Trollope would come as the "disclosure of a new
and romantic species." When the boys were puzzled
about what church they "belonged" to, the father

would say "that we could plead nothing less than the whole privilege of Christendom, and that there was no communion, even that of the Catholics, even that of the Jews, even that of the Swedenborgians, from which we need find ourselves excluded."[4]

The James ideal in education was very different from that of most fathers of sons. The philosopher was concerned only that life should be "interesting" to his children and not at all that it should "pay." "Success" was simply not discussed; the whole emphasis was upon perceptions: "everything that should happen to us, every contact, every impression and every experience we should know" was to contribute to the building of a consciousness the measure of whose value was to be its ability to feel life.[5]

Thus the inner world early became and ever remained more real and significant than the outer. The hotel infant saw the piazza crowded with "human appearances in endless variety," and the child gave himself up to supposing.

I at any rate watch the small boy dawdle and gape again . . . and, feeling him foredoomed, withhold from him no grain of my sympathy. He is a convenient little image of warning of all that was to be for him, and he might well have been even happier than he was. For there was the very pattern and measure of all he was to demand, just to *be* somewhere—almost anywhere would do—and somehow receive an impression or an accession, feel a relation or a vibration. He was to go without many things, ever so many—as all persons do in whom contemplation takes so much the place of action, but everywhere, in the years that came soon after, and that in fact continued long, in the streets of great towns, in New York still for some time, and then for a while in London, in Paris, in Geneva, wherever it might be, he was to enjoy more than anything the so far from showy practice of wondering and dawdling and gaping; he was really, I think, much to profit by it.[6]

The "literary tone" was there from the beginning. There was the vast, beneficent, overshadowing influence of Dickens; there was the theater before whose billboards the entranced boy might stand as he would later stand before the great canvases of the Louvre; and there were the celebrities one met, as, for example, Thackeray, who said, "Come here, little boy, and show me your extraordinary jacket!" thus inevitably making that little boy forever after hate that jacket. The ideal of representation was never far away; when, on one occasion, the child was told not to "make a scene," a seed was planted in his consciousness that would flower at last in the great scenes of his novels. But "in the house of representation there were many chambers, each with its own lock, and long was to be the business of sorting and trying the keys. When I at last found deep in my pocket the one I could more or less work, it was to feel, with reassurance, that the picture was still after all in essence one's aim."[7]

The years 1855–1858 were spent largely in Europe—in Geneva, London, Paris, and Boulogne-sur-Mer—where the boy suffered a severe attack of typhus. While the peculiar James variety of educational experiment was continued, the Louvre and the Luxembourg gave more than the schools, "and it was to this time," wrote Percy Lubbock, "that Henry James afterwards ascribed his first conscious perception of what might be meant by the life of art."[8]

In 1858 the family settled in Newport, but the next year they were back in Geneva, where Henry, "under a flattering misconception of my aptitudes," was entered at the Institution Rochette, a place of torture designed for those who aspired to such "grim ordeals and pursuits" as those of mining and civil engineering. This of course was "hard and bitter fruit and turned to ashes in my mouth."[9] But the next summer, when, together with William and Wilky, he was a private pupil at Bonn, a sense of relief supervened.

In 1860, William having declared his intention to become a painter, the Jameses returned to Newport, so that their firstborn might become a pupil of William Morris Hunt. By the summer of 1861, William had turned from art to science and transferred himself to the Harvard Scientific School, but the interval in Hunt's studio had sufficed for Henry to establish a friendship with John La Farge, who stimulated his interest in both art and writing and introduced him to Balzac and other important masters.

He translated Prosper Merimée's *La Venus d'Ille* and Alfred de Musset's *Lorenzaccio*, and Thomas Sergeant Perry remembered much later that "he was continually writing stories . . . mainly of a romantic kind. The heroes were for the most part villains, but they were lambs by the side of the sophisticated heroines, who seemed to have read all Balzac in the cradle and to be positively dripping with lurid crimes."[10] Although James himself was later of the opinion that he had never been guilty of even the mildest flirtation with the muse of rime, Perry recalled, or thought he recalled, a narrative of this period, not now extant, in the manner of Tennyson's "Dora."

Meanwhile, of course, the Civil War had begun. The two younger sons, Wilkinson and Robertson, were both in it; the former, an adjutant in Colonel Robert Shaw's Fifty-fourth Massachusetts, was seriously wounded at Fort Wagner, and both lives were ravaged by the conflict. William and Henry escaped the war, possibly with some qualms of conscience on Henry's part, for in his autobiographical writings, he seems to have predated the disabling back injury actually not sustained until October 1861. But though by this time he was sure that he desired nothing save to be "literary," he felt the need, amid the general stress, of deliberately "selecting" something, whereupon, in 1862, he entered Harvard Law School. Even here, however, it was "vision" that he sought. The set courses were of quite secondary interest; the great Chaucer scholar and ballad collector Francis James Child was more interesting than anybody on the law faculty, and Maggie Mitchell in *Fanchon the Cricket* at the Howard Athenaeum was more interesting still. "To get somehow, and in spite of everything, in spite especially of being so much disabled, at life, that was my brooding purpose."[11]

In 1866 the James family moved its base to Cambridge. William was at Harvard Medical School, and for Henry these were the years of literary beginnings. In 1864 Charles Eliot Norton had admitted him as a literary critic to the *North American Review*, and shortly thereafter E. L. Godkin opened the door to the newly established *Nation* and W. D. Howells to the not much older *Atlantic Monthly*.

In 1869 James made his first adult trip to England as "a passionate pilgrim." Landing at Liverpool, he went on to London, Oxford, and Cambridge, thence to Switzerland, Italy, and Paris. "Outside of Italy you don't know how vulgar a world it is."[12] But it was in English air that he thrilled to the inexplicable sense of homecoming he describes at the beginning of his unfinished memoir *The Middle Years*. He felt like "a person abruptly introduced into a preoccupied and animated circle and yet so miraculously aware of the matters conversed about as to need no word of explanation before joining it." The only difficulty was that people applied to him for the elucidation of things American. "There were, it appeared, things of interest taking place in America, and I had had, in this absurd manner, to come to England to learn it."[13]

In the late spring of 1870 he was back in Cambridge, where he settled down to two years of short stories, sketches, and reviews and his first novel, *Watch and Ward*. Increasingly, however, Europe seemed to hold out the stimulus his imagination craved, and in 1872, fortified by a commission from the *Nation* for a series ultimately reprinted as *Transatlantic Sketches*, he went abroad for two years, during which, in Florence, he began work on *Roderick Hudson*. Late in 1874 he returned home, but the next year he made his decision: he went to Europe to live. Although other considerations were involved, the decisive factor seems to have been his conviction that it was the stimulus of an old civilization he needed, for, as Gamaliel Bradford was to remark, "he was a man whose whole life was in art," a man who "lived and thought and felt to write great novels,"[14] and if great novels could be written in Europe and not, by him, in America, then to Europe he must go, and the fact that he happened at the same time to be a passionate pilgrim was only a happy fortuity.

He established himself first in Paris, writing (neither to his satisfaction nor to theirs) Parisian letters for the New York *Tribune*. Although he associated freely with the leading French writers, he soon decided that the Parisian atmosphere was not right for him and therefore removed himself to London, where, except for innumerable short trips to the Continent and what must surely have seemed to most writers (as indeed it did ultimately to him) a surfeit of social life in England, he settled down to the close application which, between then and

1881, produced, in addition to many short pieces, *The Bostonians, Confidence, Washington Square*, and *The Portrait of a Lady*.

In autumn 1881 Henry James returned to America, where *Daisy Miller*, which had been rejected by a Philadelphia editor as a libel on American womanhood, was giving him his first, and nearly his last, taste of popular success. In January 1882 his mother died, and the novelist consequently prolonged his American visit until May. In December he received a message announcing the serious illness of his father, who died, as Henry believed, before his son could reach American shores simply because he could not face the prospect of going on without his life's companion. Business affairs kept James in the United States until August, when he returned to England and did not see America again for twenty-one years.

Between 1890 and 1895 James gave much time and energy to an attempt to master the technique of the drama. He went at the thing with his usual complete devotion to the task at hand, and before he finished, he thought the battle had been won. "My books don't sell, and it looks as if my plays might. Therefore I am going with a brazen front to write half a dozen."[15] Probably the longing for a wider audience was at the bottom of the experiment. For a time he was enthusiastic about the new departure. "The strange thing is that I always, universally, knew *this* was my more characteristic form—but was kept away from it by a half-modest, half-exaggerated sense of the difficulty."[16] Yet, in the very same letter to Stevenson in which he proclaims his pleasure at having "at last *found* my form—my real one—that for which pale fiction is an ineffectual substitute," he must add, in the very next sentence, "God grant this unholy truth may not abide with me more than two or three years—time to dig out eight or ten rounded masterpieces and make withal enough money to enable me to retire in peace and plenty for the unmolested business of a *little* supreme writing, as distinguished from gouging— which is the Form abovementioned."[17]

The "unholy truth" was not destined for long abiding. A dramatic version of *The American* was moderately successful, and four plays were published in the two volumes called *Theatricals*, but when, in January 1895, on the first night of what he clearly regarded as his major dramatic effort, *Guy Domville*, James was exposed to the catcalls of a barbaric gallery, he learned that the theater was not for him. "And yet I had tried so hard to meet them! But you can't make a sow's ear out of a silk purse."[18]

Even so, relinquishment was hard. He accepted Ellen Terry's invitation to write her a one-act play to be produced during her forthcoming American tour. She paid him £100 but never produced *Summersoft*, and he turned it into "Covering End." Then, in 1908, at the request of Johnston Forbes-Robertson, the story became a full-length play, *The High Bid*, for him; the actor tried it out but soon dropped it in favor of what turned out to be his greatest popular success, Jerome K. Jerome's *The Passing of the Third Floor Back*. There were other experiments even later, but the hopes James had entertained were never realized. Nevertheless, his theatrical efforts were not wasted; if it is impossible to prove that his dramatic experiments carried over into the great "scenes" of the later novels, it is equally impossible to doubt it.

The *Guy Domville* trauma behind him, James entered upon his greatest period as a writer of fiction. *The Spoils of Poynton*, sometimes taken as marking the beginning of his "later manner," was closely followed by a more developed study, *What Maisie Knew*. In 1897, the same year that saw the publication of these books, he secured the tenancy of the charming eighteenth-century Lamb House, at Rye, in Sussex. Later his by purchase, it became (though he did not wholly cut himself off from London) his home for the rest of his life and remains the place most closely associated with his memory. Between 1899 and 1904 he produced five novels— *The Awkward Age*, *The Sacred Fount*, and his three greatest, *The Ambassadors*, *The Wings of the Dove*, and *The Golden Bowl*—two top-flight collections of short stories—*The Soft Side* and *The Better Sort*— and a two-volume biography of the sculptor William Wetmore Story. For quality and quantity combined, it would be hard to match this record in the output of any other writer.

In August 1904 James left Rye for a year in America, where he saw the West for the first time, going clear to San Diego. He had wished not merely to see the country but to assimilate fresh experience. "I am hungry for Material, whatever I may be moved to do with it; and, honestly, I think, there will not be an inch or an ounce of it unlikely to prove grist to my intellectual and 'artistic' mill."[19] His impressions of the East have been preserved in a very distinguished travel book, *The American Scene* (1907), but the proposed continuation, which was to have dealt with the West, was never written. Nor, though American scenes and themes appeared in much of what he wrote during the rest of his life, did he find it possible to complete what might well have become a major novel based upon his renewed contact with America, *The Ivory Tower* (the fragment was published posthumously, together with another uncompleted work, *The Sense of the Past*, in 1917). It is clear, however, that he did accumulate impressions with amazing vividness and showed himself marvelously open to new impressions for a man of his age. Yet perhaps the most amazing aspect of the American junket was that for the first time in his life, he undertook public lecturing and, what was more, found himself enjoying it. His two lectures, "The Question of Our Speech" and "The Lesson of Balzac," were published together in a little volume in 1905.

In 1910 William James and his wife came to England to visit the ailing novelist, but William was considerably sicker than Henry was, and shortly after they had all gone to America together, William died at Chocurua, New Hampshire, on August 26. "I sit heavily stricken and in darkness," wrote Henry (their brother Robertson had died shortly before, and their only sister, Alice, in England, after a harrowing illness, in 1892), "for from far back in dimmest childhood he had been my ideal Elder Brother, and I still, through all the years, saw in him, even as a small, timorous boy yet, my protector, my backer, my authority and my pride."[20] Henry James stayed in America for another year, receiving an honorary degree from Harvard in the spring of 1911 (there would be another from Oxford the next year), after which he went home to write the autobiographical works sparked by William's death: *A Small Boy and Others* (1913), *Notes of a Son and Brother* (1914), and the fragment *The Middle Years* (1917). He had already used up much time to prepare the collected (though not complete) New York Edition of his fiction which Scribners published in 1907–1909, for which he revised all his early novels and wrote eighteen elaborate prefaces. The beginning of *The Ivory Tower* waited therefore until 1914

and was ended, as it seemed at the time as if everything might be ended, by what happened in August
of that terrible and demented year.

There are curious contradictions in James's attitude toward the war, which completely absorbed
his last months and almost certainly hastened his
death. It is not true, as has often been said, that he
had never been interested in public affairs before;
he was, for example, pro-Dreyfus, and, like William,
was opposed to the Spanish-American War. What is
odd is that he should have seen the conflict in terms
of unrelieved black and white (for once, surely, his
subtlety deserted him) and that, feeling its horrors
so keenly as he did, he should still have backed
England to the hilt in augmenting and continuing
these horrors and even become impatient with his
native land over her delay to plunge into the abyss.
"The rate at which they are taken is appalling—but
then I think of France and Russia and even of Ger-
many herself, and the vision simply overwhelms
and breaks the heart."[21] At first he tried to cling to
the hope that he might "*make* a little civilization,
the inkpot aiding,"[22] but literature proved tame beside life, and seclusion impossible. He left Lamb
House for London, and there he stayed until the
end. At his age and in his state of health, he could
not, of course, contribute to the destruction, but he
did visit soldiers and comfort refugees to an extent
that nobody could have believed was within his capacity, and spiritually he was, as he himself might
have said, very definitely "in it."

It was under the stress of wartime emotion that
James performed the most spectacular action of his
life by renouncing his American citizenship and becoming a British subject. To be sure, this was partly
a matter of convenience, for living as an "alien" in
wartime England presented difficulties. But he also

wished to "rectify a position that has become inconveniently and uncomfortably false" by offering his "moral support with a perfect consistency" to the country and the cause with which he felt so "absolutely and ardently."[23] His action exposed him to considerable criticism from those who had always vaguely felt that he was "un-American," it being one of the quaintest vagaries of the American temperament to regard those who renounce their allegiance to another government in order to embrace the United States as having manifested a superior brand of virtue while all who move in the opposite direction must rest under the suspicion of moral degradation. Unfortunately, however, James was not permitted to serve his adopted country in any capacity long. On December 2, 1915, he suffered his first stroke. With the new year, Lord Bryce brought the Order of Merit to his bedside, and on February 28, 1916, he died.

# 2
# Theory

James was the very type of the deliberate, intellectual, self-conscious novelist who creates according to definitely formulated and clearly apprehended convictions of what fiction ought to be. Before proceeding to survey his production, we ought therefore to understand his theory.

The first step is the choice of a subject, and no naturalist could contend more uncompromisingly than James that the artist must be accorded complete freedom in making that choice. At the same time, he was convinced of the importance of choosing wisely, "and if I might put up a prayer, it would be that artists should choose none but the richest."[1] As we shall see, he follows Turgenev in maintaining that the author should begin with the characters and not with the plot, yet it is clear that for him the beginning was often not a character in the narrower sense but an idea, "the exhibition of a case." Thus Frank Saltram in "The Coxon Fund" was suggested by Dyke Campbell's idea of Coleridge, but for James "the S. T. Coleridge *type*" was even more interesting than Coleridge himself. Nevertheless, the characters must themselves be important. "We care, our curiosity and our sympathy care, comparatively little for what happens to the stupid, the coarse, and the blind, care for it, and for the effects of it, at the most as helping to precipitate what happens to the more deeply wondering, to the really sentient." His search for the superior case would seem to have led him more often to women than to men, but he welcomed the opportunity to do a man of imagination in *The Ambassadors*.

The original suggestion was often slight. Thus *The Spoils of Poynton* originated at a dinner party in an anecdote about "a good lady in the north, always well-looked on, [who] was at daggers drawn with her only son, ever hitherto exemplary, over the ownership of the valuable furniture of a fine old house just accruing to the young man by his father's death," and James was on pins and needles fearing that the narrator might go on to supply the details which he must work out in his own imagination if the suggestion she had given him was to be fruitful. Similarly, *What Maisie Knew* sprang from "the accidental mention . . . of the manner in which the situation of some luckless child of a divorced couple was affected . . . by the remarriage of one of its parents." But *The Tragic Muse*, formidable as it is, began with nothing more concrete than the desire to "do something about art" and to develop the contrast between art and the world.

This matter of suggestiveness varied enormously. Sometimes, as with "The Private Life," the barest idea would come along, crying, "Dramatise it! dramatise it!" and giving him no rest until he had done just that, or a young man might sit down on a bench near him in Kensington Gardens, and the whole of "Owen Wingrave," plot and characters, would be there. This last is an excellent example of what in one of his great critical phrases James calls "the suddenly-determined *absolute* of perception." *The American*, too, was born thus Minerva-like; the vision of the "case" came to James while riding in a horse car, and when he left the vehicle he was in full possession of what he needed.

But development did not always follow hard upon perception. Its idea always present in some form, *The Tragic Muse* still waited long for treatment, and *Poynton*, too, lay dormant until the day when James woke suddenly to the realization that "the thing had 'come,' the flower of composition had bloomed—all in the happy dusk of indifference and neglect." Nevertheless, the predominant impression that remains is that of work, heroically difficult work, controlled by determined willpower and consciously and deliberately directed toward its defined end.

From his point of view it was all worth doing; no refinement of ingenuity, no excess of precaution could be resented in the effort to secure variety of effect. Of course there were difficulties, but what would the craft be without them? "Now to see deep difficulty braved is at any time, for the really addicted artist, to feel almost even as a pang the beautiful incentive, and to feel it verily in such sort as to wish the danger intensified." When they are past, an author cherishes the memory of such difficulties "as some adventurer in another line may hug the sense of his inveterate habit of just saving in time the neck he ever undiscourageably risks." Meanwhile, there is the high excitement of fitting the story together, which no pursuit of hidden slave with bloodhounds had ever, for excitement, surpassed; and as for the accruent reward, why should the artist be concerned overmuch with that?

Much rather should he endlessly wonder at his not having to pay half his substance for his luxurious immersion. He enjoys it, so to speak, without a tax; the effort of labor involved, the torment of expression, of which we have heard in our time so much, being after all the last refinement of his privilege. It may leave him weary and worn; but how, after his fashion, he will have lived!

Of the development of his theme, which went on in James's mind between its conception and the day he first put pen to paper, he does not tell us much except that diligent notetaking was always inevitable. The whole problem was how to convey to the reader what the writer had seen and felt. Nobody ever realized the difficulty of doing this more keenly than James did nor made more heroic efforts to solve the problem. Always he wished to play his small handfuls of value for everything they were worth, and always he was oppressively aware of the infinitely expansive possibilities any possible subject might present, for they all manifested such a fatal tendency to spread that there was nothing save an insidious grease spot to which they might aptly be compared. New developments were constantly presenting themselves, and you were forever being called upon to decide to what extent these were indispensable to the interest and the subject, working in terror meanwhile of the vast expanse of the great canvas of life, constantly luring you on.

Beyond all this lay that most difficult and necessary of all tasks, representing processes and developments. It was easy enough to state such things or to name them, but portraying them was a very different matter. There was much that could not be represented yet must somehow be implied and brought to life in the reader's imagination if the work of art was to be successful, and so the writer must confront the task of subordination, of suggesting the background which could not be drawn in full. James realized that there was such a thing as overdevelopment, and he feared it and realized that it sometimes betrayed him, but on the whole he

feared underdevelopment more. From this he shied
as from triteness, the noted "thinness" so characteristic of popular fiction. No story, he thought, was
ever well told under the law of mere elimination,
and he did not believe a novelist had the right to
ask his readers to take anything on trust. In 1904 he
described his way of working to his agent, J. B.
Pinker:

But I can work only in my own way—a deucedly good
one, by the same token!—and am producing the best
book, I seem to conceive, that I have ever done. I have
really done it fast, for what it is, and for the way I do it—
*the* way I seem condemned to; which is to *overtreat* my
subject by developments and amplifications that have, in
large part, eventually to be greatly compressed, but to the
prior operation of which the thing afterwards owes what
is most durable in its quality. . . . It is not, assuredly, an
economical way to work in the short run, but it is for me
in the long; and at any rate one can proceed but in one's
own manner.[2]

This menace of overdevelopment became serious for James only when it threatened that other
sacred peacock in his garden: form. For with all his
tendency to exhaust his subject, he still believed in
economy, and he knew that development and symmetry could be reconciled only through very careful
planning and foreshortening. As he once put it to
Howells:

It is always the fault of my things that the head and trunk
are too big and the legs too short. I spread myself, always,
at first, from a nervous fear that I shall not have enough
of my peculiar tap to "go round." But I always (or generally) have and therefore, at the end have to fill one of
the cups to overflowing. My tendency to this dispropor-
tion is incorrigible. I begin short tales as if they were to
be long novels.[3]

Most of all James was interested in his characters, and how to make them real and interesting was the primary problem to which he addressed himself. This does not mean that he did not love a story for its own sake, for he tells us that this was a passion which had possessed him from the beginning. But when Walter Besant remarked that fiction without adventure was impossible, James inquired testily, "Why, without adventure, more than without matrimony, or celibacy, or parturition, or cholera, or hydropathy, or Jansenism?"[4] To his way of thinking, the significance of incident lay wholly in its mystic conversion into drama through the sense of it which the characters entertained. "The maximum of intensity with the minimum of strain is the ideal." And this brings us directly to the long and significant passage in the preface to *The Portrait of a Lady*, here quoted only in part, in which James cites Turgenev as having taught him to begin with his people rather than with the things they do.

I have always fondly remembered a remark I heard fall years ago from the lips of Ivan Turgenieff in regard to his own experience of the usual origin of the fictive picture. It began for him almost always with the vision of some person or persons, who hovered before him, soliciting him, as the active or passive figure, interesting him and appealing to him just as they were and by what they were. He saw them, in that fashion, as *disponibles*, saw them subject to the chances and complications of existence, and saw them vividly, but then had to find for them the right relations, those that would most bring them out; to imagine, to invent and select and piece together the situations most useful and favourable to the sense of the creatures themselves, the complications they would be most likely to produce and to feel.

From this beginning James goes on to tell how "the spacious house" of *The Portrait of a Lady* was constructed around Isabel Archer.

Both the difficulty and the importance of developments in fiction were increased by the fact that "a character is interesting as it comes out, and by the process and duration of that emergence." An interesting character must have "high lucidity" and a certain quality of intelligence. Although they are well in their place (indeed, no story is possible without them), "fools" cannot be central in a work of art. Yet, with his sympathetic insight, James often found worthy of attention characters who, even after they had been glorified by his art, seemed insignificant to many of his readers. There was, for example, the Daisy Miller type, the "mere young thing," who interested him as she had interested Shakespeare. As he looked at the world, "the Isabel Archers, and even much smaller female fry" insisted "absolutely" and "inordinately" upon "mattering." Moreover, he could not see it as "an attestation of a value, or even of our imperfect sense of one," that it should be represented badly.

Intensity and reality were among the qualities he valued most in a work of fiction. You picked your subject from the garden of life; a penciled jotting of another's experience might serve for an anecdote, but for a really developed piece you could use only phenomena at which you had in some sense "assisted." In many of its aspects, reality sickened James. "How can one consent to make a picture of the preponderant futilities and vulgarities and miseries of life without the impulse to exhibit as well from time to time, in its place, some fine example of the reaction, the opposition or the escape?" So he felt the charm of the fairy tale, that genre in which we roam over "an annexed and independent world in which nothing is right save as we rightly imagine it," and of the ghost story, of which he himself produced such distinguished examples. Yet it is in discussing the latter that he betrays most nakedly his own concentration on character, for he felt himself as showing ghosts best "by showing almost exclusively the way they are felt, by recognizing as their main interest some impression strongly made by them and intensely received."

James appreciated fine work, like Stevenson's, even when it had been done under a different inspiration from his own. Himself, he is neither realist nor romanticist as commonly conceived, and he doubts that any writer ever committed himself to either the realistic or the romantic ideal "with as little mitigation as we are sometimes able to find for him," for, in the last analysis, the real simply consists of the things we cannot possibly not know sooner or later, while the romantic consists of what we never can know directly.

He pondered these distinctions in many connections. In 1890 he wrote Howells, "The novelist is a particular *window*, absolutely—and of worth in so far as he is one, and it's because you open so well and are hung so close over the street that I could hang out of it all day long."[5] Again he writes:

The air of reality (solidity of specification) seems to me to be the supreme virtue of a novel—the merit on which all its other merits . . . hopelessly and submissively depend. If it is not there they are all as nothing, and if it be there, they owe their effect to the success with which the author has produced the illusion of life. . . . It is here in very truth that he competes with life.[6]

But for James that was only part of it and probably not the most significant part. He was never satisfied to stop with reproducing what already existed. Indispensable as observation is, he believed that if you try to write under a too immediate impression, there will be no perception. Late in life he even advised his brother William to stop reading his books, since he seemed unable to enjoy them, assuming as he did that life, "the elements forming its subject-matter, deviate from felicity in not having an impossible analogy with the life of Cambridge."[7] In the last analysis, then, the interpenetrating power of the creative imagination was even more important than intimate knowledge, and it was less deadly to be false to material fact than to one's own vision.

The power to guess the unseen from the seen, to trace the implication of things, to judge the whole piece by the pattern, the condition of feeling life in general so completely that you are well on your way to knowing any particular corner of it—this cluster of gifts may almost be said to constitute experience.[8]

If a writer's material does not go through this transforming process, it merely ceases to be matter of fact without becoming matter of truth, for "the affair of the painter is not the immediate, it is the reflected field of life, the realm not of application, but of *appreciation*—a truth that makes our measure of effect altogether different." All this reflected James's idealism as well as his understanding of the creative process. If the futilities, vulgarities, and miseries of life predominated in the human scene, he did not on that account refuse to grow up or fly away to the Never-Never-Land, but if you drove him to it, he could always shelter himself behind as romantic a plea as Stevenson or Cabell or de la Mare might have entered ("if the life about us for the last thirty years refuses warrant for these examples, then so much the worse for that life"), and if you find Daisy Miller unreal, he is quite capable of retorting that his "supposedly typical little figure was of course pure poetry." But if realism admitted of qualification, intensity did not, for it was "the grace to which the enlightened story-teller will at any time, for his interest, sacrifice if need be all other graces whatever." And for intensity, clarity was prerequisite, for "a work of art that one has to *explain*, fails in so far, I suppose, of its mission."[9] Indeed, James even objected to illustrations in a novel on the ground that they tended to take over part of the function of the text.

It is as incorrect to assume that James was primarily interested in the novel as form as it would be to believe that his interest in human beings was mainly in their manners. In 1884 he wrote that

Only a short time ago, it might have been supposed that the English novel was not what the French call *discutable*. It had no air of having a theory, a conviction, a consciousness of itself behind it—of being the expression of an artistic faith, the result of choice and comparison. I do not say that it was necessarily the worse for that: it would take more courage than I possess to intimate that the form of the novel as Dickens and Thackeray (for instance) saw it had any taint of incompleteness.[10]

Nevertheless it was not the Dickensian or Thackerayean novel that James wished to write. The closest he came to that was in the three long novels which followed *The Portrait of a Lady*: *The Bostonians, The Princess Casamassima*, and *The Tragic Muse*.

Even as late as 1896 he could appreciate work like Kipling's which did not conform to his standards: "I am laid low by the absolutely uncanny talent—the prodigious special faculty of it. It's all *violent*, without a dream of a *nuance* or a hint of 'distinction'; all prose castanets and such—with never a touch of the fiddle-string or a note of the nightingale. But it's magnificent and masterly in its way, and full of the most insidious art."[11] But in other moods he could be querulous or condemnatory. There may be life, he says, in *The Newcomes*, *The Three Musketeers*, and *War and Peace*, but "what do such loose baggy monsters, with their queer elements of the accidental and the arbitrary, artistically mean?" And in 1912, when Hugh Walpole asked him about Dostoevsky, he met the issue head on:

At least when you ask me if I don't feel Dostoieffsky's "mad jumble, that flings things down in a heap," nearer truth and beauty than the picking and composing that you instance in Stevenson, I reply with emphasis that I feel nothing of the sort, and that the older I grow and the more I *go* the more sacred to me do picking and composing become. . . . Don't let any one persuade you . . . that strenuous selection and comparison are not the very essence of art, and that Form *is* [not] substance to that degree that there is absolutely no substance without it. Form alone *takes* and holds and preserves substance—saves it from the welter of helpless verbiage that we swim in as in a sea of tasteless tepid pudding and that makes one ashamed of an art capable of such degredations. Tolstoi and D. are fluid puddings, though not tasteless, because the amount of their own minds and souls in solution in the broth gives it savour and flavour, thanks to the strong, rank quality of their genius and their experience. But there are all sorts of things to be said of them, and in particular that we see how great a vice is their lack of composition, their defiance of economy and architecture, directly they are emulated and imitated; *then*, as subjects of emulation, models, they quite give themselves away. There is nothing so deplorable as a work of art with a *leak* in its interest; and there is no such leak of interest as through commonness of form.[12]

In the same vein, to H. G. Wells, who had so mercilessly revealed his own gamin aspect by caricaturing James in *Boon*, he went so far as to cry, "it is art that *makes* life, makes interest, makes importance,"[13] or, in other words, as he puts it elsewhere, "the content and the 'importance' of a work of art are in fine wholly dependent upon its *being* one; outside of which all prate of its representative character, its meaning and its bearing, its morality and humanity, are an impudent thing." One must aim at "absolute singleness, clearness and roundness," concentrating upon a single target. He speaks from the heart when he says that "a story is a story, a picture a picture, and I had a mortal horror of two stories, two pictures, in one." And again, "I delight in deep breathing economy and an organic form."

Obviously, if one is to strive for symmetry, very careful planning becomes necessary, and to James any plan was defensible, provided only that it *was* a plan. "If the art of the drama, as a great French master of it has said, is above all the art of preparation, this is true only to a less extent of the art of the novel, and true exactly in the degree to which the art of the particular novel comes near that of the drama." There is, for instance, the danger of unequal proportions. There is the danger of creating extraneous characters, and James thought that Henrietta Stackpole was such a character in *The Portrait of a Lady*. There is, too, the danger of being overwhelmed by detail. "*I* like a rope (the rope of the *direction and march of the subject*, the action) pulled, like a taut cable between a steamer and a tug, from beginning to end."[14]

The most important of James's special devices for securing unity was his use of "point of view." The definitive statement is in the preface to *The Golden Bowl*:

I have already betrayed, as an accepted habit, and even to extravagance commented on, my preference for dealing with my subject-matter, for "seeing my story," through the opportunity and the sensibility of some more or less detached, some not strictly involved, though thoroughly interested and intelligent witness or reporter, some person who contributes to the case merely a certain amount of criticism and interpretation of it. Again and again, on review, the shorter things in especial that I have gathered into this Series have ranged themselves not as my own impersonal account of the affair in hand, but as my account of somebody's impression of it—the terms of this person's access to it and estimate of it contributing thus by some fine little law to intensification of interest. The somebody is often, among my shorter tales I recognise, but an unnamed, unintroduced and (save by right of an intrinsic wit) unwarranted participant, the impersonal author's concrete deputy or delegate, a convenient substitute or apologist for the creative power otherwise so veiled or disembodied. My instinct appears repeatedly to have been that to arrive at the facts retailed and the figures introduced by the given help of some other conscious and confessed agent is essentially to find the whole business—that is, as I say, its effective interest—enriched *by the way.* I have in other words constantly inclined to the idea of the particular attaching case *plus* some individual view of it; that measure having thus to become an imagined observer's, a projected charmed painter's or poet's— however avowed the "minor" quality in the latter—close and sensitive contact with it. Anything, in short, I now reflect, must always have seemed to me better—better for the process and the effect of representation, my irrepressible ideal—than the mere muffled majesty of irresponsible "authorship." Beset constantly with the sense that the painter of the picture or the chanter of the ballad (whatever we may call him) can never be responsible *enough,* and for every inch of his surface and note of his song, I track my uncontrollable footsteps, right and left, after the fact, while they take their quick turn, even on stealthiest tiptoe, toward the point of view that, within the compass, will give me most instead of least to answer for.

James began experimenting with point of view early. Compare Rowland Mallett in *Roderick Hudson* and Christopher Newman in *The American.* As time went on, he became increasingly convinced that the mirroring consciousness must belong to a superior character; while coarser threads were useful in subordinate positions, the leading interest of any human hazard could be seen only in a consciousness subject to fine intensification and wide enlargement. Sometimes he used a leading character, not a "thoroughly interested and intelligent witness or reporter," and sometimes he presented two or more points of views successively. We shall also see that, even in his later works, his practice tended to be much less rigid than his theory.

In his comments on his art, James often refers to himself as a dramatist. Defining the drama simply as "a catastrophe determined in spite of oppositions," he explains his preference for it as for "a small straight *action*, and so placed . . . in that blest drama-light which really makes for intelligibility as nothing else does, orders and regulates, even when but faintly turned on; squares things and keeps them in happy relation to each other." This indeed was a method he delighted to employ increasingly as time went on and he gained fuller and fuller possession of his craft.

The play consents to the logic of but one way, mathematically right, and with the loose end as gross an impertinence on its surface, and as grave a dishonour, as the dangle of a snippet of silk or wool on the right side of a tapestry. We are shut up wholly to cross-relations, relations all within the action itself; no part of which is related to anything but some other part—save of course by the relation of the total to life.

"The relation of the total of life." That of course was the ultimate test. James ridiculed those to whom "art means rose-colored window-panes, and selection means picking a bouquet for Mrs. Grundy" and who stick up prohibitions all over the place like keep-off-the-grass signs. "To what degree a purpose in a work of art is a source of corruption I shall not attempt to inquire; the one that seems to me least dangerous is the purpose of making a perfect work."[15] Yet if he thinks a subject silly or unclean, he will wash his hands of it altogether, and in the final analysis he was sure that the morality of a work of art was hopelessly dependent on the amount of felt life which had been involved in producing it. These questions must be asked of every such work: Is it valid? Is it genuine? Is it sincere? Is it the result of a genuine perception of life? It was the enveloping air of the artist's own humanity which must be depended on at last to give "the last touch to the worth of the work," making it either rich and magnificent or poor and ungenerous. "Tell me what the artist is, and I will tell you of what he has been conscious."

# 3

# Beginning: *Watch and Ward; Roderick Hudson*

Henry James's first novel, *Watch and Ward*, was written in Cambridge, Massachusetts, in 1870, serialized in the *Atlantic Monthly* between August and December 1871 (the editor, William Dean Howells, had opened the serial course of his own first novel, *Their Wedding Journey*, in July), and published in a revised form, largely to protect the copyright, by Houghton, Osgood and Company in 1878.[1] In the early days its author spoke of it both vauntingly and disparagingly; later he repudiated it altogether, not only excluding it from the New York Edition but calling *Roderick Hudson* his first novel without qualification.

A critic who wished to be frivolous might call *Watch and Ward* James's *Daddy Long-Legs*, but it would be more illuminating to view it in relationship to that subdivision of the long line of educational novels running clear back to the eighteenth century in which a man adopts a girl with a view to forming for himself a perfect wife. *Wilhelm Meister* and the novels of George Sand and Oliver Wendell Holmes have been cited as possible influences, with side glances toward Balzac, Dickens, and

Thackeray, to which William Veeder has recently added a once very popular novel, *The Initials*, by Jemima Montgomery (1807–1893), later the Baroness Tautphoeus.[2]

The sexual overtones implicit in the theme (though of course absent from *Daddy Long-Legs*) are more or less prominent in these various works; their presence in *Watch and Ward* has occasioned some discussion. The alleged sexuality of the famous passage in Chapter 5, in which Nora, partly undressed, fumbles first with Roger's watch key and then with Hubert's, must have been much less obvious to James and his contemporaries than it seems to the Freud-oriented readers of today; certainly the editors and publishers can never have been conscious of what now seem its implications or they would no more have accepted it than D. W. Griffith and the critics and movie fans of 1915 could have tolerated the heroine's business with the bedpost in *The Birth of a Nation*, which often rouses unseemly mirth in modern audiences. This passage does not stand alone, however. At one point, Roger "caught himself wondering whether, at the worst, a little precursory love-making would do any harm. The ground might be gently tickled to receive his own sowing; the petals of the young girl's nature, playfully forced apart, would leave the golden heart of the flower but the more accessible to his own vertical rays." This seems as sexual as the "Veil" chapter in *Jurgen*, and however uncomprehending the readers of the 1870s may have been, to suppose James himself to have been innocently inadvertent here would be to impute a higher degree of naiveté to him than he can reasonably be supposed to have been capable of at any age. Nor must we forget that William James had been shocked by some passages in the manuscript.[3]

The melodrama for which James had a strong taste in his youth that he never entirely threw off is in evidence in *Watch and Ward*. Having been rejected, finally and irrevocably, by Isabel Morton, the comfortable, cultured, leisured Roger Lawrence, age twenty-nine, informally adopts Nora Lambert, twelve, after her distracted and irresponsible father has blown his brains out in a hotel room adjacent to Roger's own. Since Nora is not an attractive child,[4] this act is triggered by pity and a somewhat characteristically quixotic Jamesian sense of responsibility, but the idea of molding the girl into a prospective wife is early aborning. The plan is menaced by the intrusion of two worthless young men by whom the inexperienced Nora is temporarily attracted: George Fenton, of St. Louis, who claims to be her cousin and whose motives are wholly mercenary (James's handling of him shows a suspicion of Western "vulgarity" which was widely entertained on the Eastern seaboard at the time and has even yet not wholly died out), and Roger's own cousin, the Reverend Hubert Lawrence, who, if not exactly a hypocrite, is a good deal of a fribble, "one of the light-armed troops of the army of the Lord" who "loved doubtless, in this world, the heavenward face of things, but . . . loved, as regards heaven, the earthward." The climax comes when, shocked upon discovering Roger's previously unsuspected plans for her, Nora flees to New York, seeking shelter first from one of these admirers and then the other, only to be cruelly disillusioned in both. In the last chapter, Roger, having followed her, functions in almost *deus ex machina* terms, and she tumbles conveniently into his arms.[5]

It is the technical naiveté of *Watch and Ward* that must first strike those accustomed to the importance of "method" in James's later work. "I undertake, however, to tell no secrets." "It is sufficient to explain. . . ." "For, as you will have guessed. . . ." "I shall have told my story ill if these things seem to lack logic." Yet James's fastidious mind is also operative. The long opening description of Roger, though prentice work compared to the introduction of Isabel in *The Portrait of a Lady*, is still carefully wrought, and there is a reasonable amount of figurative language. "She unsheathed one of her own steely beams, and for one tenth of a second there was a dainty crossing of blades." We are told of one minor character that "she was a kindly woman enough, but so thoroughly the mistress of a public house that she seemed to deal out her very pity over a bar." Excepting only the melodrama into which not only George but even Hubert's fiancée Amy finally decline, the low-life scenes in New York at the end are among the best in the book, which stands in sharp contrast to our being obliged to read the first half of the volume nearly through before we learn that we are in Boston. Much of the figurative language fits ill, however, those to who it has been assigned; there are unbelievable encounters, and Nora, despite and besides her naiveté, is given both insights and the ability to voice them that we cannot quite accept.

In spite of the limitations of James's art, however, Nora remains a figure of considerable charm, at her best representing his discovery of the young girl growing into life of whom he never wearied, and interesting, even when she is least convincing, as his first fumbling effort to handle a moving theme. Nanda Brookenham of *The Awkward Age* is the later heroine who comes to mind first of all in this connection, and though the difference between Nora and Nanda is that between an artist learning his craft and one who has wholly mastered it, there will al-

ways be readers who see Nora more clearly, at least
at moments, and feel her more poignantly than they
ever make contact with Nanda through all her creator's folds of "method."

Nora's greatest limitation as a heroine is that her
development is told rather than shown. At the outset
she is physically unattractive, and

the heterogeneous nature of her own culture testified to
some familiarity with the scenery of Bohemia. The common relations of things seemed quite reversed in her brief
experience, and immaturity and precocity shared her
young mind in the freest fellowship. She was ignorant of
the plainest truths and credulous of the quaintest falsities;
unversed in the commonest learning and instructed in the
rarest. She barely knew that the earth is round, but she
knew that Leonora is the heroine of *Il Trovatore*. She
could neither write nor spell, but she could perform the
most surprising tricks with cards. She confessed to a passion for strong green tea, and an interest in the romances
of the Sunday newspapers. Evidently she had sprung from
a horribly vulgar soil; she was a brand snatched from the
burning. She uttered various impolite words with the
most guileless accent and glance, and was as yet unsus-
picious of the grammar and the Catechism.

Yet when we leave her, she is not only a dazzling beauty of the late bloomer variety but in every
respect a highly cultivated young lady. James un-
characteristically chose the easiest way with her
transformation by having Isabel Morton, now the
happily widowed Mrs. Keith, take her out of the
book and "form" her, and in none of the popular
romances in which a gutter girl is turned into a great
actress or singer has the job been more thoroughly
done.

There has been wide diversity of critical opinion concerning *Roderick Hudson*; an unsophisti-
cated reader who should turn from William Veeder's

*Henry James—The Lessons of the Master* to Kenneth Graham's *Henry James: The Drama of Fulfilment* might surely be excused if he supposed himself to be reading about two different books. The novel was begun in Florence in 1874, continued in the Black Forest and in Boston, finished in New York, run through its serial course in the *Atlantic* in 1875, and published by James R. Osgood and Company in 1876, thus beating *Watch and Ward* into independent covers by two years. James himself thought it vilely written in its first state. It was slightly revised for the London (Macmillan) printing of 1879 and, much more thoroughly, for the New York Edition in 1907.

James himself is partly responsible for what unfavorable critics have said of it, for though he gave it Volume I in his definitive edition, his preface is nothing if not disparaging. It was a mistake, he thought, to name Roderick's town Northampton, Massachusetts; he ought not to have followed Balzac's example to the extent of such specificity unless he wished to "do" the place much more thoroughly than he did or could have done in this book. Roderick's engagement to Mary Garland, on the eve of his departure for Europe, is not believable, and the novel's time scheme is wrong, making Roderick's deterioration far too rapid. About all he will give himself credit for is having centered his narrative in the reflecting consciousness of Rowland Mallet and creating in Christina Light a character of sufficient vitality so that he had enough of her potential left at the end to feel it necessary to revive her in *The Princess Casamassima*.

About Northampton it is hardly worthwhile to dogmatize. About Mary Garland, James was probably right; Roderick himself afterward says that "I felt extraordinary desire to spill over to some woman, and I suppose I took the nearest." Indeed, James might well have added that if the reader finds it hard to believe that Roderick could have loved Mary (or thought he did), it is even harder to accept Rowland's falling in love with her almost simultaneously.

James exaggerates when he declares that "the center of interest through 'Roderick' is in Rowland Mallet's consciousness, and the drama is the very drama of that consciousness." Roderick, not Rowland, is the (unheroic) hero of the book, and there are passages in which the author intrudes himself into the narrative, quite as Thackeray and Trollope used to do.[6] As for James's first great character, Christina, although she is unquestionably the triumph of the book, he is unjust both to her and to himself when he calls her the "well-nigh sole agent" of Roderick's catastrophe. She accentuates and—in a sense, but only in a sense—triggers his problem, but the seeds of disintegration were there from the beginning, and James prepares for his hero's doom more carefully than he gives himself credit for.

The sources of *Roderick Hudson* have been discussed almost as eagerly as those of a play by Shakespeare. Viola Dunbar's view that the direct source of the fable was a play by Dumas *fils*, *L'Affaire de Clemeceau*, has been widely accepted, but this is of interest mainly as showing how James could take the materials of popular melodrama and transform them into something else. Veeder has pointed out resemblances between Christina and both Hildegarde in *The Initials* and Emmeline de Mirveil in *Le Roman d'une honnête femme* by Victor Cherbuliez, but here again we are dealing with material that was of no use to James until after he had recharactered it. It is no wonder, then, that Cornelia

Kelley, Oscar Cargill, and others should have conjectured the influence of Dickens, Turgenev,
George Eliot, George Sand, and even Nathaniel Parker Willis nor that real-life originals should have
been suggested for both Roderick and Christina.
Certainly James could not have written a novel in-
volving art life in Italy without thinking of and
being, in some measure, influenced by Hawthorne's
*Marble Faun*, but he assimilated the objets d'art into
his story more successfully than either Hawthorne
or George Eliot in *Romola*. I have nowhere seen
any mention of the possible influence on Christina
of either the fictional Beatrix Esmond or the real
Marie Bashkirtseff, but there are resemblances in
both cases, and Christina's passion for analyzing
herself comes very close to that of Beatrix.[7]

The plot of the novel is simple. Rowland Mallet,
a wealthy New Englander of Puritan background
but cultivated tastes, a lover of art but himself without artistic capacity, discovers a young sculptor,
Roderick Hudson, whose gifts might well, he believes, amount to genius, and takes him to Rome as
his protegé. The young man's initial attempts are
brilliant and warmly received, but he soon gives
indications that his staying power is weak and develops a taste for the dissipation he had wholly
avoided in America. His problem is complicated by
his infatuation for a fantastically beautiful, half Italian and half American, tortured, and sophisticated
girl, Christina Light, whose bust he sculpts and who
seems for a time to be weighing his appeal against
that of the wealthy, completely decent but dull
Prince Casamassima, whom her mother wishes her
to marry. When Christina breaks her engagement to
the prince, Roderick's interest in life, though not his
art, revives, but after she yields to pressure and mar-

ries his rival, there is little hope left for him. The coming of his mother and his fiancée to Italy is no help; whatever affection he may ever have felt for the girl is dead, and although he creates an excellent bust of his mother, he regards her only as a subject. After a tense scene in which Rowland not only admits his own love for Mary Garland but forces upon Roderick his moment of truth, the latter wanders off into the mountains and, in the midst of a storm, either jumps or falls to his death.

It has been said that Roderick Hudson and Rowland Mallet represent different sides of James's own character; this is true only to the extent that James was, on the one hand, an artist and that, on the other hand, he conspicuously possessed that "sympathy . . . as an active faculty" with which Rowland credits himself. But Mallet's role in the novel is not simple. He is not *merely* the observer; neither is he wholly disinterested. Nor is this only because he is himself in love with Roderick's fiancée (he keeps that to himself until the end). It was not for nothing that his cousin Cecila accused him of officious meddling when he placed himself in charge of Roderick's destiny. Rowland *needs* Roderick to do for him what he cannot do for himself, making him a creator, as it were, at one remove; and the echo of *Othello* at the end ("his occupation was gone") is quite in order. Finally, it must not be forgotten that if he took a chance when he pulled Roderick out of Northampton, he took a far more dangerous one at the end when he forced him to face up to his delinquencies. In a sense, he may even be said to have failed Christina, who, despite her declaration that she does not like him, clearly trusted him more than any other man she knew. But those of James's readers who find themselves inclined to

blame him must, in all fairness, ask themselves
whether they would have done any better in dealing
with two such phenomenally difficult people.[8]

Of the minor characters, Mary Garland, "a good,
plain, honest girl" of "extreme personal force" but
lacking in "pliancy," "the daughter of a minister,
the granddaughter of a minister, the sister of a minister" but "not a person to represent sport for the
artistic temperament or to minister to the joy of life,"
is the most important. Christina's antithesis, she suf-
fers inevitably in contrast to that showy personage,
nor does she gain through the instantaneous dislike
she takes to her rival, in contrast to the latter's generous, almost envious, appreciation of her. As for the
two mothers in the novel, Mrs. Light, as Rowland
instantly perceives, is as shallow as her daughter is
deep—surely one of the worst mothers in fiction.
She neglected Christina shamefully until she realized that the girl was going to be a spectacular
beauty, after which she proceeded to wrong her
even more by spoiling her outrageously and system-
atically grooming her for a great marriage, turning
her into what Madame Grandoni rightly calls a better "draw" than the two-headed calf or the learned
pig. When Mrs. Light hesitates about the bust Roderick wishes to make of her daughter, Christina is
as accurate as outrageous when she says, "Mamma
hesitates because she doesn't know whether you
mean she shall pay you for the bust or you'll pay me
for the sitting." And she adds, "You can always get
something for it. You always get something for
everything. I dare say that with patience you'll get
something even for me." But though she sees her
mother as clearly as do the author and his readers.
Christina never recovers from what Mrs. Light has
done to her. Mrs. Hudson, of course, is no such
monster, but we are told at the outset that her whole

notion of art is that it consists in painting or sculpting people who have no clothes on, and except that we sympathize with her later over Roderick's careless treatment of her and her subsequent grief at his death, there is really not much more to say about her. Mrs. Light's hanger-on, slave, and former lover, the Cavaliere Giacosa, is a rather absurd, pathetic, endearing little man; one wonders a bit why Christina, who has lived all her life with the knowledge that Mrs. Light is her mother, should be so distressed when she learns that he is her father. Madame Grandoni is primarily an expository device, but there is life in her nevertheless.

Effective contrasts are provided by the artists who surround Roderick. The sculptor Gloriani— clever, intelligent, cynical—who can do whatever an artist can achieve without a spark of idealism, represents the corruption or prostitution of art in the interest of worldly advantage. (James would revive him, with modifications, in both *The Ambassadors* and "The Velvet Glove.") Sam Singleton is the perfect embodiment of a rather simple man of small talent who, because he is also a man of character, makes the very best that could have been made of it, and Augusta Blanchard paints flowers "with the dew-drops very highly finished, or else a wayside shrine and a peasant woman, with her back turned, kneeling before it. She did backs very well, but was a little weak on faces."

Roderick Hudson himself is the classical Romantic hero, tormented by a demon of unrest, handicapped by "an excessive want of breadth." Even at the beginning he reminds Rowland of "some beautiful, supple, restless, bright-eyed animal, whose motions should have no deeper warrant than the tremendous delicacy of its structure and seem graceful to many persons even when they should be least convenient," and Cecilia is quite as much concerned for his moral and sentimental security in Europe as for the development of his talent. When he gets there, he gives the impression that, like the naked boy in his statue *Thirst*, he will eat his cake all at once and have none left for tomorrow. Even when he is at the height of his social success in Rome, his "childish unmodulated voice" is noted, and what some call his "delightful freshness" impresses others as his "damned impertinence." He thinks of himself as Hellenist rather than Hebraist, doing Adam and Eve brilliantly but never reaching the "ripping Christ" he contemplated, who was to be idealistically rather than rationalistically conceived, "to symbolize the perfection of spirit." In the traditional Byronic pattern, he demands complete freedom for the artist as the condition of his development, but when he hits his first snag, he rushes off to the distractions of Baden-Baden, where, instead of refreshing him, his holiday produces only sterility. Like Poe, he is enthralled by supernal beauty, and the suggestion that his given name may have been derived from Roderick Usher is not fanciful. On the score of their shared romanticism at least, he and Christina ought to have been able to understand each other, but even if she had broken away from her mother and married him, it seems doubtful that he could have loved her as she needed to be loved to solve her problem. He "never saw himself as part of a whole; only as the clear-cut, sharp-edged, isolated individual, rejoicing or raging, as the case might be, but needing in any case absolutely to affirm himself."

He describes himself as "damnably susceptible, by nature, to the grace and the beauty and the mystery of women, to their power to turn themselves 'on' as creatures of subtlety and perversity."

We may grant freely that it was the worst possible luck for such a man to encounter a Christina Light, but it is selfishness and weakness of will and lack of staying power, not lust, that creates his basic problem; he would have ended badly even if she had never crossed his path. Her beauty is of the radiant, not the sensual, variety, and whatever may be her condition in *The Princess Casamassima*, only one critic seems ever to have doubted that to the end of *Roderick Hudson* she is wholly chaste; even when she is most interested in Roderick and comes closest to seeing him as the answer to her need to admire something better than herself, she is capable of wishing that he were not her lover but her brother.

Roderick never faces the truth about himself until the end. If his death is a suicide, he dies in despair; if it is an accident, it constitutes a kind of Gordian knot cutting by James or a choice of the easiest way. Yet the reader does not feel this as a defect, for he knows that Roderick's life was suicidal even if his death was perhaps a fortunate accident. Indeed, an accidental death would seem to suit him best (perhaps that is why James refused to commit himself); since he had never exerted his will to live, why should his death be an act of will? "I believe," he had said, "there is a certain group of circumstances possible for every man, in which his power to choose is destined to snap like a twig." This is the very sign of the surrender which marks his doom, and if Rowland is ever a chorus character, he is just that when he replies that "the power to choose *is* destiny" and that if a man can desire, he can also reason and judge. Roderick never effectively makes that assumption, and even at the end his revulsion is aesthetic, not moral. What distresses him is only that he has been stupid and lacking in the kind of perception an artist should have. "It was egotism always—the shock of taste, the humiliation of a proved blunder, the sense, above all, of a flagrant want of grace; but never a hint of simple sorrow for pain inflicted."

James gives Christina Light an even more impressive entrance into *Roderick Hudson* than Thackeray had accorded Beatrix into *Henry Esmond*; she passes silently across the scene, like "beauty's self" or "a phantasm, a vapour, an illusion," with her remarkable poodle, Stenterello, whom she regards as "a great Florentine personage" and much more of a gentleman than many of the men she has seen, "combed and decked like a ram for sacrifice."[9] She has the "troublous faculty of seeing everything in different lights," and her complexity, which extends even to her name,[10] divides both the critics and the other characters in the novel, who are generally to be found discussing her when she is not discussing herself. Provided only that you have allowed for her incorrigible faculty for self-dramatization, what she says of herself always rings true, and she has insight, too, for she understands Roderick, Rowland, and Mary Garland. As for the others, Miss Blanchard glances keenly at her paradox when she says that she looks like a cross between a Madonna and a ballerina, but much of what the others say of her, even when sound, seems too expository in its presentation, and Mrs. Light is quite unconvincing in her confidences to Rowland; even if she were capable of seeing herself thus clearly, such frankness would surely be beyond her.

If Christina is neither mad nor bad, she is certainly dangerous to know. The key to her character is the disappointed romantic idealism which has been frustrated by her corrupt, mercenary, and self-seeking mother, who has built a prison about her from which she never escapes. Her contempt for her mother is boundless, and in some moods her self-distrust matches it, while in others she knows that there must have been some good in her, for otherwise her spirit could not have survived at all. "I'm not young; I've never been young! My mother took care of that. I was a little wrinkled old woman at ten." And again: "I don't know what I'm saying! I'm weary and dreary; I'm more lonely than ever; I wish I were dead!" She needs desperately to be respected and, like others in the book, to be understood, and she begs Rowland to prove to her that she may be better than she thinks. If she cannot have the luxury of respecting herself, the next best thing would be to find a man to whom she could look up as something better. For a little while she half thinks she has found him in Roderick, and if she had been less intelligent, she might have continued to think so. Gloriani, then, reveals nothing but his own cynical lack of insight when he compares her to Salome in the Bible; James shows this clearly in Chapter 13, where he uses but reverses the traditional situation of the girl who tests her lover by setting him a task he cannot perform without risking his neck, which he does perform successfully and then repudiates her. Roderick idiotically embraces his risk to fetch the blue flower (that perfect Romantic symbol!) for Christina from a desperately perilous height in the Colosseum *against* her will, and she is nearly prostrated by the strain. Whatever may be said of her elsewhere, there can be no question of her sincerity here.

Nevertheless, she is profoundly histrionic, partly because she has never found out quite what kind of a person she is. There are actors like Coquelin who remain outside their characterizations and are consequently always completely in control

of the illusion they create to enthrall others, and
there are actors who are part of their own audience
to such an extent that they fail to distinguish between actor and character and end by enthralling
themselves. Such, in a measure at least, is Christina
Light. But dangerous as this is, for herself and for
others, it would be a serious mistake to try to save
her by curing her histrionism, for she could not
possibly survive without it. Her "real" life, however
that word be read, is so disappointing that her only
possible refuge is to try to create another self and
possess it imaginatively.

Her tragedy of course is that she can never quite
get free. As Madame Grandoni says,

"She's certain to do every now and then something disinterested and sincere, something for somebody other
than herself. She needs to think well of herself; she knows
a fine character when she sees one; she hates to suffer by
comparisons, even though the comparison be made by
herself alone. . . . Her attitudes and pretences may sometimes worry one, but I think we have most to pray to be
guarded from her sincerities."

And her unacknowledged father is quite in line with
this when he says that Christina might act sincerely
and go very far but that in the end she would always
go back.

She is therefore quite in character when she
sends the prince packing because, after meeting
Mary Garland, she feels sure that that is what a girl
like Mary would do ("I've done it," she writes Rowland. "Begin to respect me"), but she is in character
too when she yields to pressure from her mother
and marries the prince. Mrs. Light's weapon is the
threatened revelation of her daughter's bastardy,
and it has often been pointed out that, like the skeleton in the Bellegardes' closet in *The American*, this
is melodrama. But perhaps James was wise in not

attempting to explain just how such a threat could secure the desired end; where an improbability must be embraced in a work of art, it is better not to explore it too minutely but simply force the reader to swallow it and digest it as best he can, as we are obliged to deal with such things in life. Perhaps even it was appropriate that so theatrical a personage as Christina should be defeated by a theatrical device. When she meets Mallet again after her marriage, she insists that she had been sincere and adds, "You remember I told you that I was in part the world's and the devil's. Now they've taken me all. It was their choice; may they never repent!"[11] When she beckons Roderick to her at Interlaken just before the end, she behaves as if this were true, and although she will not be consistently so bad as this in *The Princess Casamassima*, we shall still be conscious of what she has lost.

In a sense, then, Christina, like Roderick, fails through the pressure of circumstances and insufficient strength of will, and a romantic temperament is not all they have in common. The most important difference between them seems to be that while Roderick's defect was apparently inborn, hers was induced, or at least fostered, by her unfortunate rearing. Evelyn Nesbit once remarked of her association with Stanford White, "Stanny was the lucky one. He died. I lived." So it may have been with Roderick and Christina.

# 4

## Continuing: *The American;*
## *The Europeans; Confidence;*
## *Washington Square*

It has been said that *The American* is a favorite novel with readers who do not especially like Henry James. It is at least a very good novel with which to begin reading him, for it presents fewer difficulties than almost any other major work. Although it makes no concession to the gentle reader in the way of a happy ending, it is romantic and melodramatic, and it has considerable charm. As James's preface in the New York Edition makes clear, it was written in a happy mood, and he was quite aware of both its attractions and its limitations. It was, too, his first "international novel," which is to say that it was the first in which the contrast between two different cultures was an important part of the action.[1]

The book began with James's vision of an American wronged in an aristocratic society who should forego the revenge which lay within his grasp, but he dropped the idea into "the deep well of unconscious cerebration" before trying to work it out on paper. Writing began in Paris in December 1875 and continued at Etretat, Bayonne, etc.; he could not remember whether he had finished it before crossing the Channel in autumn 1876. The story was serialized in the *Atlantic Monthly* between June 1876 and May 1877, published in book form by James R. Osgood and Company on April 30, 1877, and slightly revised for Macmillan's London edition in 1879. Turgenev's novel *A Nest of Gentlefolk* (1858) may well have contributed to the plot (Cornelia P. Kelley called it a hybrid of Turgenev and George Sand), and there were certainly influences from such contemporary French dramatists as Émile Augier and Alexandre Dumas *fils*; in the latter's *L'Etrangère*, which came out while James was working on *The American* and in which Sarah Bernhardt appeared, Mrs. Clarkson's given name is Noémie.[2]

Christopher Newman, an American who has made his pile, is in Europe in search of culture and a wife, "a great woman" and "the best article on the market." He finds her, as he supposes, in Claire de Cintré, the daughter of the Marquise de Bellegarde and the late marquis, Legitimists and aristocrats of the Faubourg Saint-Germain. Claire has been widowed after a desperately unhappy marriage which had been forced upon her by her family. Because of his wealth, the cold, overbearing marquise and her like-minded son, Henri-Urbain, the present marquis, allow Newman to pay court to Claire, and to their surprise she accepts him. But after having unwillingly given a fete to announce the engagement, they decide they cannot go through with an alliance to "a commercial person." Claire, now broken in spirit, yields to her mother's commands, but instead of agreeing to the family's alternative plans for her future, cannot be moved from her determination to become a cloistered (Carmelite) nun. Meanwhile, her younger brother, Comte Valentin, who has made a friend of Newman, has been fatally wounded in a duel over an utterly worthless girl, Noémie Nioche. Before he dies, he tells Newman that there is a skeleton in the Bellegarde family closet and that Mrs. Bread, his and Claire's old nurse, who still lives in the family, can tell him about it. Mrs. Bread gives Newman the note which the dying marquis had entrusted to her, in which he accused his wife of having killed him by refusing him the medication on which his life depended. Newman confronts the Bellegardes with his evidence, but, though obviously shaken, they are still defiant. Having first planned to expose them, he finally decides it would not be worthwhile and burns the accusing paper.

Christopher Newman is the "lighted figure" through whose eyes we essentially, but not rigidly, see the others. He is the new man, what we have now learned to call the American Adam, and he is making Christopher Columbus's voyage in reverse.[3] Except that he made his fortune in California, his provenance, like his military and business background, is but vaguely indicated, and there are few localisms in his speech. Not a frontiersman, he is abstemious by nature rather than principle, and although he emerged from the Civil War a brigadier general, he hated the whole business.

A culture seeker, he is at once humble and arrogant. He is naive about art and music, and he has never read a romance in his life. His attitude toward women is idealistic, and he decides to marry Claire, quite unaware of the dangers involved in such an unequal mating, without even knowing her, quite as if she were the Princess Faraway in a medieval romance. He wouldn't "like to resemble anyone," and he tells Claire that her people "don't think I'm as good as themselves. I do, you see." To him the whole complex Parisian world seems "a very simple affair"; in a sense, he expects to be able to buy what he wants.

James does not scant Newman's gaucherie. He telegraphs the news of his engagement to America before it has even been announced, and he plans to give a fete without waiting for the Bellegardes to do it. But while the reader is expected to be aware of these things, he must not judge Newman harshly because of them nor view him in anything like a basically satirical way; no "hundred per cent" American "patriot" could be clearer than James is about that. Newman is so good a man that we must find it quite in character that he should find the treachery of the Bellegardes, "like all great strokes of evil, unnatural and monstrous." Like James himself, the reader is expected to view his gaffes with something like the indulgence he would accord those of a charming, well-meaning, but uncultivated child.[4]

Over against him stand the Bellegardes. Cargill calls James's characterization of them "passably accurate in a static way," and Richard Poirier, who shows us convincing reason to believe that James's treatment of them reflects his own attitude toward French civilization, based upon both extensive reading and much less extensive personal contact,[5] calls them "fixed" characters, opposed almost allegorically against Newman as "free." It is clear almost from the beginning that there is something about this family worse than their hidebound formality or inordinate pride. When Newman tells the old marquise that he is rich, she asks bluntly, "How rich?" thus leaving herself in a poor position to gag at "a commercial person" as a husband for her daughter. In later years, James did not believe that the Bellegardes would have broken off the engagement; rather, they would have jumped at Newman's money, and in the novel itself, Mrs. Tristram, an American who knows both them and him, tells him that they were inconsistent when they accepted him, not when they gave him up. "They wanted your money, but they've given you up for an idea." This may be true, but if the reader has accepted the initial inconsistency, it will be all the harder to make the shift. There is no one thing we can point to as having triggered their decision except Newman's having caused Madame de Bellegarde to parade about the ballroom on his arm at the fete ("I succumbed to the scene that took place the other night in these rooms"), and even with a lady whose religion is form and who has none other, this seems hardly adequate. At the very least, one is tempted to say that if she had had any imagination at all, she must have known that this was just the way he would behave, but perhaps the answer to this objection would be that she had none. Just how deep the chasm was between French aristocratic dignity and American freedom is never better shown than by the way Valentin is shocked by Newman's suggestion that Claire might go to see Madame Dandelard, a woman without social standing, who seems in danger of going astray.

His companion stared. "Go and see Madame Dandelard—my sister?"

"She might talk to her to very good purpose." Valentin shook his head with sudden gravity. "My sister doesn't have relations with that sort of person. Madame Dandelard's nothing at all; they'd never meet."

"I should think," Newman returned, "that Madame de Cintré might see whom she pleased." And he privately resolved that, after he should know her a little better, he would ask her to go and pick up, for such "pressing" as might be possible, the little spotted brown leaf in the dusty Parisian alley.

To get the full force of this we must remember that Valentin and Claire are the Bellegarde rebels;

...wman sees them as temper-
... But Claire resembles Irene in
...a in that we never see her except
...s' eyes; consequently, we cannot be
...that she would have accepted Newman
...e would have forsaken him. It is only phys-
...that her image is quite clear. Her beauty was
...of the dazzling variety, and vulgarians like Tom
Tristram could see nothing in her.

She was tall and moulded in long lines; she had thick fair hair and features uneven and harmonious. Her wide grey eyes were like a brace of deputed and garlanded maidens waiting with a compliment at the gate of a city, but they failed of that lamplike quality and those many-colored fires that light up, as in a constant celebration of anniversaries, the fair front of the conquering type. Madame de Cintré was of attenuated substance and might pass for younger than she probably was. There was something still young and still passive, still uncertain and that seemed still to expect to depend, and which yet made, in its dignity, a presence withal, and almost represented, in its serenity, an assurance.

In his preface, James told why he had "obscured" her. It was not only because Newman was to be "the lighted figure" but also because

Since Madame de Cintré was after all to "back out" every touch in the picture of her apparent loyalty would add to her eventual shame. She had acted in clear good faith, but how could I give the *detail* of an attitude, on her part, of which the foundation was yet so weak? I preferred, as the minor evil, to shirk the attempt—at the cost evidently of a signal loss of "charm"; and with this lady, altogether, I recognise, a light plank, too light a plank, is laid for the reader over a dark "psychological" abyss. The delicate clue to her conduct is never definitely placed in his hand.

James told his friend Lizzie Boott that Claire did not really love Newman, but her farewell to

him—"Do you suppose I'll go on living in
world, still beside you, and yet not *with* you?
would certainly seem to indicate that she did.[6] B
whether or not her motives for breaking off ar
either adequate or adequately explained (if she
could stand up to her mother on the convent issue,
why not on the marriage?), one cannot say that what
happens has not been adequately prepared for.[7]
Mrs. Tristram enlarges on Claire's subservience to
her mother and brother as early as Chapter 6, and
she herself warns Newman that she is not a heroine
and has little courage. We learn too that she is distressed over the lack of sympathy between her be-
trothed and her family, and Mrs. Bread says that the
sooner the marriage is celebrated, the better it will
be for everybody concerned. When the crisis comes,
Claire says, "My mother addressed to me her command," and adds that she is afraid of her mother,
and that is about all we get except for one statement
which may carry deeper implications: "It's like a
religion. There's a curse upon the house: I don't
know what—I don't know why—don't ask me. We
must all bear it." She cannot escape from either her
heritage or her destiny. Perhaps, although she does
not say so, she even felt that what she was doing
took on something of the character of an atonement.

The other Bellegarde rebel, Valentin, is charming and good-hearted but has nothing of Claire's
sanctity about him. His attachment to Newman from
the beginning may or may not be entirely convincing, but he himself tells us that he was suspected
of low tastes in his youth, and his interest in Noémie
shows that he has not outgrown them—"God
knows," he says, "I've been vicious enough!"—yet
his fatal flaw is that his rebellion did not go far
enough. Still in bondage to an outworn, technical,
amoral conception of "honor," which, if it ever had

any meaning, has utterly lost it in the world he lives in, he throws his life away in a duel with a boor over a tart and dies like a fool to soft music. James tells us that "the exposure, the possible sacrifice of so charming a life on the altar of a stupid tradition" struck Newman as "intolerably wrong," and there can be no question that the novelist agreed with him.

The most important of the minor characters are the Nioches. The old man, contemptible yet pitiful, is completely under the thumb of his pretty, ruthless daughter, Noémie, the copyist on her way to be a courtesan, who, as she herself admits, paints like a cat and who, at the beginning, helps us grasp Newman's ignorance of art by impressing him with her daubs. As her social triumphs and her moral degradation increase, her father professes to be so shocked by her way of life that he even thinks of killing her, but all he does is live whiningly on the fruits of her trade. Their story seems at first a loosely connected subplot, but it is successfully fused with the main action when Valentin, ironically introduced to Noémie by Newman, becomes involved with her. In the Nioches the cynical conscience-lessness of the noble Bellegardes is paralleled in a lower-class family: the marquise has killed her husband, and Noémie occasions, quite without remorse, the death of his son.

The Tristrams and Mrs. Bread are utility characters. James bluntly calls Tom Tristram a fool, and though his wife is better, she strains reader sympathy when she admits that a cold curiosity was part of her motive in bringing Newman and Claire together. As for Mrs. Bread, although she need be no more than a piece of machinery to serve her function in the novel, James brings her alive through a number of wryly amusing touches. She hates Madame de Bellegarde for having impugned her precious respectability by accusing her of an intrigue with the marquis, but she hates her also for declaring that if Mrs. Bread sat in the children's schoolroom, she might be good for a pen wiper, and what a perfect lower-class touch is her reflection upon what might be the consequences for her of the fall of the family: "And me at my age out of a place, sir!" Only Babcock, the priggish young Unitarian minister from Dorchester, Massachusetts, shows a tendency to dangle. Although he serves a purpose in showing that it *is* possible for an American to be even more naive and uncomprehending about Europe than Newman, he is quite unconnected with the plot and soon drops out of the book. It is amusing that William James thought he saw himself in the character.

The unhappy ending of *The American* caused controversy from the beginning, and James's friends were divided about it. As an editor, Howells would have preferred the romance to be consummated, and James wrote him a long letter explaining why this could not be.[8] To Lizzie Boott he defended the unhappy ending on the ground that he was a realist, thus ignoring the fact that a realistic ending perhaps carried more weight than a romantic novel could bear.

When James dramatized *The American* for Edward Compton (1890), he realized that if his play was to be successful, it must be good in a bad way—simple, bald, and rudimentary, with the emphasis upon situation—and took Scribe, Sardou, and Dennery as his models;[9] in the dramatic version, therefore, Newman wins Claire by giving up her father's letter. Inferior as the drama is, it makes some motivations clearer. There is no question here that Claire loves Newman, and the Bellegardes are franker and more brash than in the novel about their economic motive. They pretend to throw Newman over because they suspect impropriety between him and Noémie, but their real motive is that they believe Lord Deepmere to be a better catch. Deepmere plays a much larger role in the play than in the novel, and Valentin duels with him instead of with the German brewer. More significantly, however, the late M. de Cintré was Madame de Bellegarde's lover. This is why she forced him upon her daughter, and it was because she wished to continue her affair with him that she killed her husband. James seems to have felt that this at least was an improvement in the dramatic version, for in the revised novel such a connection is hinted at, though not openly stated, by both Mrs. Bread and the old marquis in his farewell note.

Newman passes an important milestone in his development as an ethically mature person when he decides to forego vengeance upon the Bellegardes. This is a decision of comparable significance to Silas Lapham's risking financial ruin because of ethical considerations and Huckleberry Finn's decision to "go to hell" rather than surrender Nigger Jim to the slave catchers. It is interesting that all three of the outstanding American fictionists of their time should have saved their heroes from priggish self-righteousness by the complications introduced into these situations. Silas is denied the self-satisfaction that was his due by his regret over having unintentionally but inevitably injured his partner, Rogers, who was no party to his decision; Huck actually feels that he has done wrong because he has grown up in a slaveholding society and intellectually has never questioned its code; and forgiveness in the ordinary sense of the term never enters Newman's mind. It would be much closer to the facts of the case to say that he has at last developed the capacity to submit to the inexorable logic of life, accepting the inevitable limitations it imposes upon the human will, even, in a sense, making terms with the unconquerable element of evil or perversity in the nature of things.

Like everything else in *The American*, Newman's decision has been carefully prepared for. Creedless in the ordinary sense, he is far from insensitive to the realities of religious experience. He was still in his money-grubbing days when he achieved "his most vivid conception of a supernatural element in the world's affairs" so that "there seemed to him something stronger in life than his personal, intimate will." The chance came to crush a rival to whom he owed a grudge, and he was on his way to do it when, in a dirty hack, he suddenly "realized I had turned against myself worse than the man I wanted to smash," and so he dropped his advantage, along with the half million it would have netted him. "You may depend upon it," he says, "that there are things going on inside of us that we understand mighty little about." After that, even nature was changed: "I spent the morning looking at the first green leaves on Long Island." In a completely untheological way, he had undergone a classical conversion experience, such as Masefield described in *The Everlasting Mercy* and William James in *The Varieties of Religious Experience*.[10]

In the preface to the New York Edition, James defines Newman's action as simply turning "at the supreme moment, away, the bitterness of his personal loss yielding to the very force of his aversion." Claire is lost to him, whatever he does. He has learned that, as Sarah Bernhardt used to say, hatred is "too fatiguing"; while he entertained the thought of it, even Mrs. Bread had noticed that he did not look like himself. He no longer wishes to hurt the

Bellegardes; he has almost forgotten them; all he wants is "to banish them from his mind and never think of them again." His aversion now embraces even the insignificant and marginally connected Noémie: "She seemed an odious blot on the face of nature; he wanted to put her out of his sight." Dismissing "the most unpleasant thing that had ever happened to him," he turns to the "very various hospitality" of Notre Dame and uses it as George Stransom would use his "altar of the dead" in the great story of that title.[11] The Bellegardes are nothing. Evil has been disarmed. Because he has ceased to resist it, it can no longer touch him. To use a great phrase of Woodrow Wilson's, unfortunately soon abandoned by himself, he is "too proud to fight." In the sense that his primary concern is now not with others but with his own soul, it might even be said that he had achieved a sublime, sacred egotism. But it is the kind of egotism in which the distinction between self and others has been blotted out so that he finds himself at home in the universe and at peace.[12]

Between *The American* and the next work he included in the New York Edition, *The Portrait of a Lady*, James wrote three short novels—*The Europeans*, *Confidence*, and *Washington Square*—which were serialized profitably and were sufficiently successful to set him free for the sustained labor and concentration required to produce the masterpiece of his first period. *The Europeans* is, in a sense, a pendant to *The American*; this time, instead of taking an American to Europe, James brings a pair of Europeans to America, to New England, but it is not only because of its comparative slightness that it cannot really be called a companion study. Although transatlantic contrasts are important in both books, *The Europeans* is social comedy

rather than romantic melodrama, and there is so
much less at stake here that there is less need for
either author or reader to take sides.

The book began in March 1877, when James
arranged with Howells to fill a hundred *Atlantic*
pages with a four-part story. It ran from July through
October 1878, after which Macmillan published it in
London and Houghton, Osgood in Boston. James
called it "A Sketch"; later he told William that it
was, like *Daisy Miller*, "A Study" and ought not to
be called a novel. He laid the scene about seven
and a half miles out of Boston "upwards of thirty
years ago." In a rather mean, nitpicking review,[13]
Thomas Wentworth Higginson fell foul of his an-
achronisms and found the picture of American society more like what might have been expected from
Alexandre Dumas *fils* than from a native American.
"The truth is that Mr. James's cosmopolitanism is
after all limited; to be really cosmopolitan a man
must be at home even in his own country." Higginson to the contrary notwithstanding, there is considerable local color in the book, and James seems
to know quite as much about New England character as he needs for his story.

Although Turgenev's *A Month in the Country*
has been suggested as a source for the plot, critics
have in general been more concerned with the tone
of *The Europeans* than the story. Jane Austen and
Restoration comedy have been invoked, but perhaps the closest resemblances are to modern French
comedy. "Method" is, this time, of no importance,
and the story is told from no particular point of view.
William James thought the book trifling, and Henry,
as always, responded angelically, at the same time
showing clearly that he knew exactly what he was
doing and that he was well aware that William did
not. The book was a kind of preliminary exercise,

he said, looking forward to more important things to come. "I think you take these things too rigidly and unimaginatively—too much as if an artistic experiment were a piece of conduct, to which one's life were somehow committed." To Lizzie Boott he admitted that Mr. Wentworth's "frosty personality" derived from a mutual acquaintance, Frank Loring, and, rather oddly in view of the way he treats her, that he did not like Gertrude; he also confided that both the length of the story and the wholesale marrying at the end had been prescribed by the conditions of serial publication.[14]

Eugenia Camilla Dolores, the Baroness Münster of Silberstadt-Schreckenstein,[15] and her brother, Felix Young, are the children of Mr. Wentworth's deceased half sister, who went to Europe, married a European there to the disapproval of her New England family, and thereafter had no further contact with them. Eugenia is the morganatic wife of the younger brother of a German princeling who, for dynastic reasons, now wishes to dissolve the marriage, and she and her brother have come to New England to visit their American relatives and look over opportunities there before Eugenia makes a decision about her marriage. Felix falls in love with Gertrude, the younger Wentworth daughter, and at the end of the book is to be married to her, but the baroness fails to bag Robert Acton, a wealthy, traveled, and comparatively sophisticated relative of the Wentworths. The other marriages indicated at the end unite Gertrude's sister Charlotte to the Unitarian minister Brand, who had long supposed himself in love with Gertrude, who would have none of him, and the young and slightly but not dangerously wayward Clifford Wentworth, who had been rusticated from Harvard, to Acton's sister, Lizzie.

Leon Edel finds the characters in *The Europeans* "without development, almost stock personages," and Kenneth Graham calls its "balanced encounters and crises" choreographic.[16] Perhaps the key passage for the understanding of the New Englanders is Mr. Wentworth's reply to Felix's observation that they do nothing to amuse themselves: "Amuse ourselves? We are not children." He is a kindly and respectworthy man, and James handles his shortcomings as tenderly as he had treated Newman's in *The American*, but he receives his relatives and places a house at their disposal as he does everything else, because he believes it the right thing to do; there is no spontaneity about it because there is none in his way of life. As Felix says, "he looks as if he were undergoing martyrdom, not by fire, but by freezing." Europe and art are alike suspect; when Felix, who dabbles in art, suggests "doing" his head, which he thinks "interesting" and "mediaeval," the old man replies, "The Lord made it. I don't think it is for man to make it over again." To him, "sitting for one's portrait is only one of the various forms of idleness," and when Felix adds that he would like to paint him "as an old prelate, an old cardinal, or the prior of an order," Mr. Wentworth is really alarmed: "Do you refer to the Roman Catholic priesthood?" The Wentworths look at life as discipline rather than opportunity; as Gertrude says, they employ every form of dreariness, and nothing makes them happy.

Charlotte Wentworth, who takes everything literally, is quite at home in this atmosphere. It would be wholly beneath her to "try to look pretty," and though she is in love with Mr. Brand, it never occurs to her to let either him or Gertrude know it. Instead, she believes that Gertrude should marry him because he has done so much for her in the way of helping her "struggle" with her "peculiarities" and learn to govern her temper. Gertrude is the rebel of the family; if, in *The American*, Claire and Valentin are Americans temperamentally, as Newman believes, she is at least an embryonic European. Alone among the Wentworths, she prays W. H. Auden's prayer to be delivered from the "prepared response." She does not "care for the great questions of life," at least in the sense in which they appeal to Mr. Brand, not at all because she is morally inferior to her sister but because she understands that if she is to live at all, she must be herself, developing her own potentialities and realizing that not all questions are closed questions and that the fact that a thing always has been done in a certain way is not alone sufficient reason for going on doing it thus.

Felix Young, "a better favored person" than his sister, is just the fairy prince Gertrude needs to deliver her, for his bohemian cosmopolitanism is as innocent as her rebellion. Besides painting, he has "traveled through foreign lands giving provincial concerts" and "been a momentary ornament of a troupe of strolling actors, engaged in the arduous task of interpreting Shakespeare to French and German, Polish and Hungarian audiences." Having "lived in every city in Europe," he "can't tell" about his country, religion, or profession. He has never made a plan, and he is sure he will never "settle" anywhere. Nevertheless, he is at bottom "a terrible Philistine," in other words, "a plain, God-fearing man." There is no harm in him, and Mr. Wentworth could nowhere have found anyone to whom it would have been safer to trust his daughter's future.

Richard Poirier's is one of the most penetrating studies of *The Europeans*, but he is very hard on Robert Acton and lets Eugenia off much too lightly; although he admits that James "is far from being entirely committed to the virtues of Eugenia," he tends to leave the impression that *he* is. It is true that "by letting the one person in this society who might have accepted Eugenia be the agent for rejecting her, James gives a most complex definition in this novel to European-American relationships."[17] Poirier is certainly correct also in discerning a certain frigidity in Acton, and it is surely not accidental that the last sentence in the book should read: "Robert Acton, after his mother's death, married a particularly nice young girl." Acton himself feels that if he is in love with Eugenia, love has "been overrated." She fascinates him like a mathematical problem, and James adds slyly that "this is saying a good deal; for Acton was extremely fond of mathematics." On the other hand, he does not reject her merely because she tells social lies framed to spare people's feelings. Though technically chaste, Eugenia is incurably devious, with much of the spirit of the adventuress, and she weighs her American against her European opportunities with cool calculation. To her brother, who knows that charming though she is when she wishes to be, she can also be "hard and perverse," she says bluntly, "Do you suppose that if I had not known they were rich I would ever have come?" In a sense, to be sure, Felix, too, is a fortune hunter, but Felix is sincerely in love with Gertrude, and he plays the game fairly, laying all his cards on the table and staking all he has on his chance, while Eugenia admits that she does not particularly like Acton. All in all, she is certainly the most complex character in *The Europeans* and consequently, in a sense, the most interesting, but she is far from being the most admirable.

*Confidence*, too, is set back in time some "five and twenty years ago." The subject matter is mating, and again the tone is comparatively light, but it is a much less finished work than its predecessor. As James first conceived it and described it in his note-book, Blanche was to be actually, not merely po-tentially, unfaithful to Gordon (I use the names fi-nally employed in the novel), after which "it is left to be supposed—it is not made definitely clear" that he kills her, which so shocks Angela that she breaks her engagement to Bernard "and flings herself back into retirement—into a religious life."[18] Fortu-nately, none of this was used, although Gordon seems quite crazy enough for it not long before the end, but what was substituted for it to produce an ending more in harmony with the tone of the book as a whole is not altogether convincing.

*Confidence* ran in the old *Scribner's Monthly* from August 1879 to January 1880, and Chatto and Windus brought it out between covers in London in December 1879 and Houghton, Osgood and Company in Boston in February 1880.[19] It has re-minded critics of Marivaux, Augier, Sardou, Cher-buliez, Feuillet, and other French writers, and it has been suggested that some of Bernard's traits were derived from Henry Adams or John La Farge. The book's method is loose, but if there is a central con-sciousness, it is Bernard's.[20] While James was work-ing on the book he thought it much better than *The Europeans*, but although he included it in the Col-lective Edition of 1883, he excluded it from the New York Edition.

Posterity has generally regarded it as one of his weakest novels. It has been objected that the title has virtually nothing to do with the story, that though all the characters except Blanche's vaguely moronic hanger-on, the English captain Augustus Lovelock, are Americans, they have no distinctively American traits, and that though the locale shifts from Siena to Baden-Baden, Paris, New York, California, Le Havre, Blanquais-les-Galais, etc., it might just as well have remained stationary since none of these places are realized. The first two charges are true, but the last is not. Certainly nothing is made of California, where Bernard tarries but a moment, but there is a good deal of local color at Baden-Baden, and New York, where "the broad sidewalk of the Fifth Avenue was scattered over with dry leaves—crimson and orange and amber," is "the freshest, the youngest, the easiest and most good-natured of great capitals." Best of all, however, in this connection, is the scene on the beach at Blanquais, just after Bernard has reencountered Angela:

When his friends went away Bernard walked home with them. He bade them good-night at the door of their chalet, and then slowly strolled back to the Casino. The terrace was nearly empty; every one had gone to listen to the operetta, the sound of whose contemporary gayety came through the open, hot-looking windows in little thin quavers and catches. The ocean was rumbling just beneath; it made a ruder but richer music. Bernard stood looking at it a moment; then he went down the steps to the beach. The tide was rather low; he walked slowly down to the line of the breaking waves. The sea looked huge and black and simple; everything was vague in the unassisted darkness. Bernard stood there some time; there was nothing but the sound and the sharp, fresh smell. Suddenly he put his hand to his heart; it was beating very fast. An immense conviction had come over him—abruptly, then and there—and for a moment he held his breath. It was like a word spoken in the darkness—he held his breath to listen. He was in love with Angela Vivian, and his love was a throbbing passion! He sat down on the stones where he stood—it filled him with a kind of awe.

Like the last chapters of *Roderick Hudson* and the storm in *The Wings of the Dove*, such a passage reminds us that James was perfectly capable of making effective use of an appropriate nature background when he needed it.

Bernard Longueville, a leisured young man "of a contemplative and speculative turn" with an interest in sketching, is summoned by his friend Gordon Wright, an amateur scientist who has much more money than Bernard but with it "a firmly-treading, rather than a winged intellect," to meet Angela Vivian. Gordon is in love with Angela or thinks he is, yet he does not wholly trust her and is vaguely afraid of her, "afraid she's cleverer than I—that she would be a difficult wife; that she might do strange things." As it turns out, Bernard has already encountered Angela for some five minutes at Siena, where she accidentally intruded herself into a scene he was sketching; when she moved to leave, he begged her to remain for a few minutes until he had finished, which she rather ungraciously did. For some reason he cannot fathom, she does not choose to remember this encounter and even commands him not to speak of it.

Gordon leaves Baden briefly, and during his absence Bernard is thrown into considerable intimacy with both Angela and her mother. He gains the impression that the mysterious girl is a coquette, and when Gordon returns, he makes his report: "I think she would marry you—but I don't think she cares for you." Gordon thereupon departs, leaving Bernard conscience-stricken over having spoiled Angela's chances and possibly done her an injustice.

Thereafter Gordon marries the featherbrained Blanche Evers, who had been in Mrs. Vivian's charge at Baden, and Bernard, reencountering Angela some two years later at Blanquais, realizes that he has been in love with her all along without realizing it, and they become engaged. Angela relieves her lover's conscience by telling him that despite his unfavorable report concerning her, Gordon did propose to her again before he left Baden and that she rejected him.

Gordon, now convinced that his marriage to Blanche was a mistake, takes the engagement of Bernard and Angela very badly, accuses Bernard of having betrayed him, and plans to divorce Blanche and renew his addresses to Angela, who, however, convinced that Blanche and Gordon really do love each other, takes it upon herself to make them realize it and succeeds brilliantly.

If *Confidence* has a theme, it is the study of the extraordinary misunderstandings of self and others of which human beings are capable and the futility of trying to regulate human conduct from an exclusively intellectual or scientific point of view. And if there is a moral, it must be that love affairs should be conducted to please the two persons concerned and not regulated by reference to advice from onlookers. Bernard is startled when he realizes that "a great many things had been taking place in his clever mind without his clever mind suspecting them." No gambler, he "lays down a couple of pieces at roulette" one evening at the casino and leaves the table with ten thousand francs in his pocket, but when it is over he is disgusted not because "he had given countenance to the reprehensible practice of gaming" but because "he had passed out of his own control—that he had obeyed a force which he was unable to measure at the time." Some critics have found him a priggish hero, but he is certainly no such ass as Gordon, who, even more than Robert Acton, goes at a love affair as if it were an experiment in the laboratory ("I want to marry with my eyes open. I want to *know* my wife. You don't know people when you are in love with them. Your impressions are colored"). His foolishness is no flaw in the novel, however, for James is fully aware of it. Subjecting people to experiments in love and other relationships is part of the subject matter of all the novels James had written so far, and the people in *Confidence* are under the same need to discover what they are as was Gertrude Wentworth. If James was strongly impressed with anything, it was not only the danger but the positive immorality of attempting to control another human being, even for his own good.

Angela Vivian has obviously been created by the same writer who created Christina Light and the Baroness Münster. Although neither of the others can compare in interest and complexity with Christina, one reader at least finds Angela more sympathetic than the baroness, but she is less successfully handled in the book as a whole. Fascinating at first because we lack the key to understand her apparently rude and capricious behavior, she is convincing up to the point, two-thirds of the way through the book, where she and Bernard reach an understanding and we realize that she had loved him from the beginning and had never had any idea of permitting herself to be sold to Gordon and also that she had deliberately behaved as unlike herself as possible at Baden because she was sore and resentful, "knowing that I had been handed over to you to be put under the microscope—like an insect with a pin struck through it!" Thereafter, unfortunately, she becomes quite too much of a good thing. How did she know that Gordon and Blanche really loved each other when they did not even know it themselves? and what had there been in James's portrayal of Blanche up to this point to enable the reader to believe that she had any capacity for love or that there were any depths in her to be sounded? It is all very well for a novelist to permit the reader to begin with misapprehensions concerning a character; Jane Austen did that very successfully in *Pride and Prejudice*. But Mr. Darcy, always an honorable man, is merely changed from an overbearing snob to a true lover, and the reader is permitted to assist at the stages of his transformation, while Angela Vivian becomes at one fell swoop a kind of combination of All-Wise Mother, skilled psychiatrist, and *deus ex machina* combined, and this is just too much to credit.[21]

To what extent the popularity of *Washington Square* has been bolstered by the great success of Jed Harris's 1947 production of *The Heiress*, its dramatization by Ruth and Augustus Goetz, which was filmed two years later by William Wyler, is speculative, but it has certainly attracted more favorable attention during the years that have passed since than it ever did before. James got the idea from an anecdote related to him by the veteran actress Fanny Kemble about her own brother Henry, who had jilted a girl under similar circumstances to those which prevail in the story, and though he created a new transatlantic locale for the abortive romance, he followed the outline very closely. Early in 1880 he described *Washington Square* to Howells as "a poorish story in three numbers," but it turned out to need six, in *The Cornhill Magazine* from June through November and in *Harper's Magazine* from July through December, with both periodicals using very poor illustrations by the famous George du Maurier. Harper and Brothers published the American edition of the book in December; in London Macmillan brought it out in a volume with two other stories in January 1881. To Grace Norton, James described it as "a slender tale of rather too narrow interest. I don't honestly take much stock in it." To William James he denied that Morris Townsend was a portrait of anybody and added that Catherine was the only good thing in the book.[22]

Cornelia Kelley long ago suggested Balzac's *Eugénie Grandet* as a source. Edel seems to accept this as a possibility, to which he adds Edmond de Goncourt's *Chérie*, and then proceeds to one of the wildest of the many reckless speculations, often presented as less conjecture than fact, by which he has unfortunately permitted what might have been a definitive biography to be disfigured; this time Catherine is James himself "as victim of his brother's—and America's—failure to understand either his feelings or his career" while both her father and her lover derive from William James![23] The only comment that needs to be made on this is Bernard Shaw's reported reply to a passerby who had hailed him with "Mr. Kipling, I presume?" "If you can presume that," said Shaw, "you can presume anything," and strode on.

The method of development in the book is scenic, and the story is told, in an uncommonly comfortable and companionable way for James, by the omniscient author: "On the Sunday after the conversation I have just narrated. . . ." "I hardly know how to tell it." "Our story has hitherto moved with very short steps."

Dr. Austin Sloper lives in Washington Square with his only daughter, a plain, quiet, unattractive girl of sterling character who has, in her own right, an income of $10,000 a year from the bequest of her mother, with the prospect of a great deal more upon her father's death. Catherine attracts a fortune hunter, Morris Townsend, with whom she falls passionately in love. Her father opposes the match, making it clear that if she marries Morris, he will cut her out of his will. The lovers persist for a time (Dr. Sloper takes Catherine to Europe for a year), but when Morris finally gets it through his head that the doctor will stand firm, he takes off. Years later Dr. Sloper dies; still later, Morris returns—fat, bald, and unsuccessful—in search of a reconciliation, but Catherine declines any further contact with him.

Grace Norton apparently complained to James about the absence of local color in *Washington Square*, and James agreed with her, but recent opinion appears to be veering away from this judgment. William Veeder insists that "James did not call his novel *Catherine* or even *Fathers and Daughters* because he wants us to see in Catherine's domestic struggle the operation of her entire milieu," a view ably supported by Mary Doyle Springer.[24]

There are no complexities in either Morris Townsend or the doctor's sister, Lavinia Penniman, a widow who has lived with him since Catherine was ten years old. Morris is merely a beautiful parasite (he tells the doctor that he cannot leave New York because his sister depends on him, but the truth is that he is living off her). Although he obviously has a taste for vintages and cigars and has run through a modest inheritance, he is not cruel or vicious; he merely has no interest in anything except getting through the world without doing anything except amusing himself. Aunt Penniman, Catherine's only confidante and a complete fool, is, in her own opinion, "a woman of powerful imagination," which she devotes entirely to matchmaking, and it might have been said of her, as Mephistopheles says of Dame Martha Schwertlein in the opera, that she would have married (or married her niece to) the devil:

Mrs. Penniman's real hope was that the girl would make a secret marriage, at which she should officiate as bride's woman or duenna. She had a vision of this ceremony being performed in some subterranean chapel; subter-

ranean chapels in New York were not frequent, but Mrs.
Penniman's imagination was not chilled by trifles; and
the guilty couple—she liked to think of poor Catherine
and her suitor as the guilty couple—being shuffled away
in a fast-whirling vehicle to some obscure lodging in the
suburbs, where she would pay them (in a thick veil) clan-
destine visits; where they would endure a period of romantic privation; and when ultimately, after she should
have been their earthly providence, their intercessor,
their advocate, and their medium of communication with
the world, they would be reconciled to her brother in an
artistic tableau, in which she herself should be somehow
the central figure.

The best thing about James's characterization
of Dr. Sloper is that, cruel as Sloper is to Catherine,
the author has carefully refrained from making him
the conventional "heavy father" of melodrama. Except for his late wife, Dr. Sloper did not entertain
an exalted opinion of "the more complicated sex."
He felt that women lacked reason, the quality by
which he believed all conduct should be governed.
He would have liked to be proud of Catherine, but
since he found this impossible, he was convinced
that no suitor could possibly be attracted to her by
anything except her money. It even gave him some
satisfaction that her beautiful mother "had not lived
to find her out." But "for fear of being unjust to her,
he did his duty with exemplary zeal, and recognized
that she was a faithful and affectionate child."

Although he fails to take Catherine's full measure, he is completely right about Townsend. When
Catherine first meets the young man, Sloper receives him at his table, admits his attractiveness,
and makes a careful investigation before setting his
face against him. He allows his daughter complete
freedom of action, insisting only that she must take
the consequences of displeasing him. Sometimes he

"almost" pities her (once he feels so sorry for her "that he turned away, to spare her the sense of being watched"), but he does not love her. He almost never addresses her "save in the ironical form," he is pleased when Morris jilts her ("since it's a great pleasure to be in the right"), and after he has stopped looking at her or speaking to her, he finds that "on the whole, he rather enjoyed having to be disagreeable." When his sensible sister, Mrs. Almond, asks him whether he will ever relent, he replies, "Shall a geometrical proposition relent?" Actually, he treats both his daughter and her suitor as types, not individuals: "I say simply that you belong to the wrong category," he tells Morris. It is no wonder that he has reminded critics of Dr. Rappaccini, Roger Chillingworth, and Ethan Brand.[25]

The novelist's problem with Catherine was how to make a young woman so lacking in glamour sufficiently attractive to the reader and emotionally important so that he will care what becomes of her. Catherine "was not ugly; she had simply a plain, dull, gentle countenance." She "was not quick with her book, nor, indeed, with anything else." People called her stolid, and she was "uncomfortably, painfully shy." James dares to allow her to be addicted to elaborate, not always suitable clothing in order to boost her ego and even to tell the reader that in her younger days she had been "a good deal of a romp" and "something of a glutton." Her great virtue is that she alone among the characters in this novel is capable of growth. Her development starts at the beginning of her association with Townsend and at first takes the form of merely evading her father's questions or replying to them with dissimulation. Later, after Morris has departed, and her birdbrained aunt is sure that she has a secret, she replies, "If I have, I shall keep it." Years later, she allows her father to cut her out of his will because she will not promise him never to marry Morris, although by this time she knows perfectly well that she will do nothing of the kind.

Her victory, to be sure, is not complete. During her later years, she mingles "freely in the usual gayeties of the town," becomes "an inevitable figure at all respectable entertainments," and acts as "a sort of kindly maiden aunt to the younger portion of society." As James W. Gargano remarks, "her change . . . has taken place in the innermost part of her being, where, in Emily Dickinson's words, 'the meanings are.' "[26] But she never recovers from what her father and Morris Townsend have done to her. She has missed the love experience, both in the home into which she was born and in the home which she might, through her own rich sensibility and capacity for tenderness, have established. That is why she not only sends Townsend away when he reappears (she is not cherishing resentment but simply recognizing that what she had loved is not there and never was there, except in her own heart) but also refuses other opportunities to marry, one of which at least held considerable promise. Here again James echoes Hawthorne, who tells us in *The House of the Seven Gables* that "it is a truth . . . that no great mistake, whether acted or endured, is ever really made right." It was a great pity. But Catherine had saved what she could, best of all her own integrity.

Are we to suppose, then, that it was James's idea that Dr. Sloper should have allowed Catherine to marry Townsend, unwise as this would have been? It is almost as difficult in fiction as in life to tell what would have happened if something else had not happened. But lightweight though he is, there is no reason to suppose that Townsend would have mistreated Catherine. If she had continued to love him, she might even have been reasonably happy with him; many good women have loved unworthy men. Even if the scales had sooner or later fallen from her eyes, she could hardly have been hurt worse than she was when he jilted her. But this was not for James the primary consideration, nor should it be for us. Dr. Sloper chose to make for his daughter a decision which no one has a right to make for another. To achieve moral maturity a human being must be allowed freedom of choice, and freedom of choice necessarily involves the possibility of choosing wrongly, facing the consequences of such choice, and, if possible, rising above them.

There are two chapters in *Washington Square* that at least one reader finds incredible. The first is Chapter 14, in which Dr. Sloper consults Townsend's sister, Mrs. Montgomery, about his and Catherine's problem. I am doubtful, to begin with, that a man so confident of his own judgment would ask advice from such a woman, and even if I could get over this, I could not believe that she would say, "Don't let her marry him!" The other is Chapter 24, the scene in the Alps, so hopelessly out of accord, in tone as in setting, with the rest of the book, where Sloper, for the first time since they had left home, goes at Catherine again about Morris: "I am very angry." "I am not a very good man. Though I am very smooth externally, at bottom I am very passionate; and I assure you I can be very hard." "I have been raging inwardly for the last six months." "Should you like to be left in such a place as this to starve?" To Catherine, "the strangest part was that he had said he was not a good man," and the reader shares her reaction. Surely such spiritual nakedness is completely out of character for a man like Sloper, and such utterances, in such a setting, can

only be described as melodrama. Even if it should
be replied that the scene was not meant to be taken
literally but rather symbolically or expressionisti-
cally, this would not help, for such an interpretation
would leave it wholly out of tune with all the rest
of a literal and realistic book. Henry James was not
Iris Murdoch.[27]

# 5

# Achievement: *The Portrait of a Lady*

*The Portrait of a Lady* was the "big" novel James
had had in mind for some time, and with its publication there was no longer any doubt that he was
a front-ranking novelist. He began writing it Florence in the spring of 1880 (not 1879, as he misre-
membered it in the preface to the New York Edition), returning at this time to "an old beginning,
made long before,"[1] and continued working on it in
England until February 1881, when he went to Venice, where his notebooks suggest without actually
saying that he finished it. It was serialized in *Macmillan's Magazine* in England (October 1880
through November 1881) and in the *Atlantic
Monthly* in Boston (November 1880 through December 1881); he received £250 for the English serial rights and $2,500 for the American. Late in 1881
Macmillan published the book in London and
Houghton, Mifflin and Company in America. James
revised the text between magazine and book publication and again, much more thoroughly, for the
New York Edition.[2]

After her father's death, Isabel Archer is discovered in the family home at Albany, New York,

by her aunt, Lydia Touchett, and taken first to England and then to France and Italy. At the Touchett country house in England, she receives and rejects an offer of marriage from a radical English peer, Lord Warburton, and another, for neither the first nor the last time, from her persistent American admirer, the industrialist Caspar Goodwood. Before Mr. Touchett's death, his invalid son Ralph persuades him to leave her £70,000 so that she may have all the resources she could reasonably need to develop what both regard as her extraordinary potentialities.

Isabel meets and makes a friend of Mrs. Touchett's friend Serena Merle, and after they have proceeded to Italy, where Mrs. Touchett spends most of her time, Madame Merle introduces Isabel to another expatriate American, Gilbert Osmond, a cultivated dilettante with a fifteen-year-old convent-bred daughter, Pansy. Isabel falls in love with Osmond and marries him in defiance of all advices.

She is soon disillusioned by Osmond's complete lack of heart, and ultimately she learns that he married her for her money and that Madame Merle is a discarded mistress, whose interest in the matter has been to ensure the welfare of her unacknowledged child, to whom Isabel has become much attached. When Isabel receives word that Ralph Touchett is dying in England, she goes to him in defiance of her husband's wishes, but having received and rejected there a final appeal from Caspar, she returns to Osmond in Rome.

James tells us that his novel began with "the mere shade of an intelligent and presumptuous girl" "affronting her destiny." Among his predecessors in recognizing the importance of such "frail vessels," he cites George Eliot and Shakespeare and especially Portia in *The Merchant of Venice* as "the

very type and model of the young person intelligent
and presumptuous," but he clearly feels that he has
gone beyond his predecessors in making Isabel his
central figure.

The George Eliot influence has been explored
intensively,[3] and the case for her and the other
sources suggested up to 1961 has been well sum-
marized in Cargill's *The Novels of Henry James*;
these include Hardy (*Far From the Madding
Crowd*), George Sand (*Indiana*), Edmond About
(*Germaine*), and even a general influence from
Sainte-Beuve. Blair Gates Kenney would add Trollope (*The Duke's Children*),[4] and William Veeder
has done a masterly job in exploring the literary tra-
ditions which lie behind Osmond, Madame Merle,
and others.[5] There are significant quotations in the
*Portrait* from *The Tempest* and *Paradise Lost* and
less significant ones from Pope and Cowper. Richard Chase[6] and other writers have called attention
to American influences upon the novel, but most of
these are fairly general. One does not need to be a
literary detective to perceive that Isabel, who has a
book on German philosophy by her side when Mrs.
Touchett first encounters her, is a good disciple of
Emerson and Thoreau in her emphasis upon self-
reliance and independence nor yet to realize that
Osmond would have been quite at home with those
of Hawthorne's villains who have committed the unpardonable sin by cutting themselves off from
human kinship.[7]

No other source that has been cited, however,
comes so close to the *Portrait* as Victor Cherbuliez's
*Le Roman d' une Honnête Femme* (1866),[8] and we
have other evidence which shows that James did
know and enjoy Cherbuliez's writings. In *Honnête
Femme* a girl named Isabel, much concerned with
her freedom and her destiny, is removed from her

secluded life by the Baroness de Ferjeux, who plans to marry her to a nephew, the Marquis de Lestang, who like Osmond is a dilettante. She soon learns both that he has chosen her as a work of art and that there is an ex-mistress, Madame de Merveil. She decides to remain her husband's wife in "the eyes of the world," to which he is agreeable because of his respect for forms, but from here Cherbuliez proceeds to "a series of melodramatic incidents" and violence which James did not use. There is even a likely original for the scene in which Isabel Archer finds Osmond and Madame Merle in intimate conference. But Cherbuliez's heroine nearly runs off with a lover, after which there is a reconciliation and a conventional happy ending. "James," says Joseph L. Tribble, "took the ingredients of a minor novel and used them to fashion a major work of art."

But the novel has likely sources in life as well as literature. It has been less conclusively established that James's cousin, Mary (Minny) Temple (1845–1870), suggested Isabel Archer than that she was the original of Milly Theale in *The Wings of the Dove*, but she was enough like Isabel and James was sufficiently attached to her that it is hard to believe he could have created Isabel without thinking of her. In the *Dove* she dies, but it would have been a graceful act of piety to keep her alive in the *Portrait* for the wider experience she craved but never had. Isabel's house in Albany is clearly the home of James's grandmother, Catherine Barber James. His friend Lizzie Boott, later Mrs. Frank Duveneck, is widely believed to have influenced the portrait of Pansy, with her father, Frank Boott, contributing his appearance, though not his character, to Osmond. Katherine (?) Hillard, who was a kind of protegée of William James but whom Henry seems not to have liked, may be reflected in Henrietta Stackpole, and Sara Stambaugh has pretty well established that there are some uncomplimentary references to the fin-de-siècle aesthetes and that Oscar Wilde's mother is caricatured as the "American Corinne."[9] But Leon Edel's notion that Isabel and Osmond represent different sides of James's own personality holds good only to the extent that every writer necessarily derives much of his knowledge of human nature, and therefore of his characters, from himself. James was an artist as Isabel was not, and the attempt to find him in Osmond is about as reasonable as the attempts that have been made by other writers to find Milton in Satan. Evil was potential in Milton and in James and in all of us as it is potential in human nature, and that is all. Because James was sick at the time he knew Minny Temple best, some have attempted to find him in Ralph Touchett, but if the description of Ralph's appearance suggests anybody, it is Robert Louis Stevenson rather than James. Did Stevenson notice this, and did it contribute to his savage dislike of this novel, in spite of his admiration for James's other work, or was he repelled by the ending? Mrs. Stevenson had divorced her first husband to marry him, and he was neurotically touchy on the subject. When in Chapter 38 Lord Warburton asks Isabel whether she is happy, she replies, "Do you suppose if I were not I would tell you?" It is interesting to note that this is exactly what Isabella Stewart Gardner, whom James knew from at least 1897, once replied to an impertinent reporter.

James centered the *Portrait*, as he planned, in "the young woman's consciousness"; she was conceived first and the satellites later (it seemed to him that he woke up one morning in possession of them in response to his query, "Well, what will she *do*?"). He aimed for "the maximum of interest with the minimum of strain," and as late as the time of the New York Edition, he thought that except for *The Ambassadors*, the "structure reared with an 'architectural' competence" around her was "the most proportioned" of his works. But although the other characters interest us mainly in their relationship to Isabel, James does not limit himself to her point of view. His method is loose and leisurely, especially in the first half, and he enters pretty freely into the minds of all his characters whenever it seems convenient to do so, thrusting himself, or his persona, into the narrative at will, sometimes naively or coyly, as in "I may not attempt to report in its fulness our young woman's response to the deep appeal of Rome" or "it is our privilege to look over her shoulder, and if we exercise it we may read the brief query." Once he even tells us that "for the convenience of the reader," he has combined disconnected remarks of Madame Merle's into a connected discourse.[10]

The first main division of the novel embraces the first twenty-one chapters. In the first fourteen (which include expository flashbacks), we see Isabel at Gardencourt, getting acquainted with it and its inhabitants and receiving and rejecting Lord Warburton's proposal. In Chapters 15 through 17, Isabel is in London with Ralph and Henrietta (where Caspar Goodwood proposes again), and they are drawn from there back to Gardencourt by Mr. Touchett's illness. There Isabel meets her evil genius in her aunt's friend Madame Merle, Ralph persuades his father to leave Isabel a fortune, and Mr. Touchett dies. After Isabel has gone with Mrs. Touchett first to Paris and then to Italy, there is a six-month interval.

In Chapters 22 through 30, Madame Merle and Osmond plan his marriage to Isabel for her fortune.

Osmond visits Isabel repeatedly at Mrs. Touchett's palazzo in Florence, and she visits him and his daughter in Rome. After Chapter 30 there is another interval of a year, during which Isabel has traveled, including three months in the Near East with Madame Merle, and has also accepted Osmond against the advice of everybody around her.

Chapters 31 through 35 are largely taken up with these remonstrances and with another proposal from Caspar, who has come from America in response to Isabel's announcement of her engagement. This section is followed by the longest interval in the book, at least three and a half years.

The fourth section comprises Chapters 36 through 50. It is now the autumn of 1876,[11] and Pansy is nineteen. Osmond and Isabel have lost a child and do not get on well. Pansy is being wooed by Ned Rosier, whom she loves but whom her father rejects for his lack of means, and by Lord Warburton, whom Osmond desperately wishes to capture. Isabel fears that Warburton's attraction to Pansy may be motivated by a desire to be near her, and Osmond's feeling that his wife has not done her best to further this match deepens the rift between them. Isabel's suspicions are aroused when she comes upon Osmond and Madame Merle in confidential interchange, but even Madame Merle is now estranged from Osmond, feeling that he has made her as vile as himself and that she has gained nothing. After Warburton withdraws without making an offer for Pansy, Osmond sends the now-grown girl back to convent school.

Chapters 51 through 55 make up the final section. When Mrs. Touchett sends word from England that Ralph is dying, Isabel defies Osmond to go to him. Before she leaves, Osmond's sister, the Countess Gemini, enlightens her as to the relations between Osmond, Madame Merle, and Pansy, and Merle herself tells her that Ralph was the real architect of her fortune. Isabel remains at Gardencourt until Ralph dies, and Chapter 54, in which these two people at last achieve complete understanding and acknowledge the depth of their affection for each other, is the most moving in the book. But after Caspar has appeared at Gardencourt to make his final appeal and give Isabel the only passionate kiss in the novel,[12] she returns to Rome.

Other divisions of the material of the novel are no doubt possible;[13] the important thing to remember is that Isabel's "portrait" is not an impression gained on a single occasion or at a single sitting but a moving picture and that the book is the study of a young woman's development and a record of the changes she undergoes through the experiences life brings her.

Isabel Archer is "undeniably spare, and ponderably light, and proverbially tall; when people wished to distinguish her from the other two Miss Archers, they called her the willowy one." Her eyes are light gray, but her hair is almost black. She is a "limited" heroine; you cannot record developments unless there is something to develop out of and into. She cannot see the Gardencourt ghost until she has suffered, and she does see it at the end when Ralph dies. But we must not allow James's frankness about her shortcomings and limitations to mislead us into supposing that he did not love her and expect his readers to do so. He planned her marital disappointment from the beginning as "the open opposition of a noble character and a narrow one,"[14] he prepares for her disillusionment very carefully,[15] and he twice thrusts his head boldly through the curtains to guide our response: "she would be an easy victim of scientific criticism if she were not intended to awaken on the reader's part an impulse more tender and more purely expectant" and "if there was a great deal of folly in her wisdom those who judge her severely may have the satisfaction of finding that, later, she became consistently wise only at the cost of an amount of folly which will constitute almost a direct appeal to charity."

Isabel is Emersonian in her independence and self-reliance and Goethean in her passion for growth and knowledge. She tells Caspar that she insists on judging for herself and is not conventional, and even after Mrs. Touchett has rescued her from Albany, she declares that she is fond of her liberty and is not a candidate for adoption. She does not take suggestion easily, and when she comes to Europe, she wishes to know what she should not do, not so that she may do it but so that she can choose. She will allow things to be settled for her only if they are settled the way she likes them. There is "something pure and proud" about her, but there is also "something cold and dry," and she is "always planning out her development, desiring her perfection, observing her progress." Her cousin Ralph warns her to save her conscience for important issues and occasions, and she admits that she has a tendency to look at life too much as if it were a doctor's prescription. "She had an infinite hope that she would never do anything wrong," but she obviously thought people were justified in regarding her as a superior being; when Osmond hypocritically told her that for him she would always be the most important woman in the world, "she looked at herself in this character—looked intently, thinking she filled it with a certain grace."

She was hungry for experience; when she traveled, it was "rapidly and recklessly; she was like a thirsty person draining cup after cup." She liked places where things had happened, even if they were sad things, and she wished to be heroic, yet she was afraid of suffering; people suffered too easily, she thought; we were not made to suffer. Passionately as she desired freedom, part of her was afraid of it, too, and her relations with Caspar indicate that she was afraid of sex. These contradictions were partly the result of youth and ignorance. She had been brought up by a rackety father whom she adored, but her curiosity and imagination had been nursed more directly by Gounod, Browning, and George Eliot than by life. She had been absurdly romantic about the Civil War, and she had seen too little evil to be expected to recognize it when it approached her in the person of Madame Merle.

James has been accused of evading an important part of his problem by passing over the happy beginning of Isabel's married life. Although we are told that Osmond behaved charmingly during their courtship, none of the other characters seem to have felt his charm, and James has warned readers too carefully for them to be able to feel it. We do not see Isabel as a married woman until after her baby has died, by which time "the flower of her youth had not faded, it only hung quietly on its stem" and "she had more the air of being able to wait." She had changed, and not, as yet, for the better, being more disposed than before to live on the surface of life. Her humor, too, "had lately turned a good deal to sarcasm," and "covert observation had become a habit with her." She had had a certain will to power from the beginning; we are told as early as Chapter 17 that she enjoyed exercising it on Caspar, and when she came into her inheritance, she "made up her mind that to be rich was a virtue because it was to be able to *do*, and that to do could only be sweet."

She *does* when she enriches Osmond, does with splendid generosity, but it is still *she* who is *doing* with *her* money. When she realizes that her now-estranged husband is not going to capture Lord Warburton for his daughter, she cannot repress "a momentary exultation" and "a horrible delight in having wounded him," and although she is not without pity for Madame Merle in her final defeat, James can still write that her "only revenge was to be silent still" when for the last time they confront each other, with Merle knowing that Isabel at last knows everything and neither speaking of it. Whether we agree with Isabel's decision to return to Osmond in the last chapter or regard her as a masochist, it is quite clear that she is not a broken woman. She knew "that life would be her business for a long time to come" and that "she should some day be happy again." She "was still young, after all, and a great many things might happen to her yet."

As for the other characters in the *Portrait*, the Touchetts are her relatives and questionable benefactors, Henrietta Stackpole her amusing, loyal, but unavailing friend, and Caspar Goodwood and Lord Warburton her unsuccessful lovers. Her enemies are her husband and Madame Merle, but she loves and tries to serve their child.[16] By blood, Osmond's sister, Countess Gemini, belongs in the enemy's camp, but though far from being a blameless woman, she is not unlikable; she differs from her brother in that she has a heart, and before the end she is on Isabel's side.

Daniel Touchett, a wealthy retired American banker resident in England, dies early in the story. Although his relations with his niece by marriage are very pleasant, his principal effect upon her destiny is through the legacy he leaves her. His wife, Lydia, is an amusing, though in no sense comic, eccentric. When she is not traveling, Mrs. Touchett spends most of her time in Florence, communicating with her family only through cryptic, obscure telegrams. When she comes back to Gardencourt, having found Isabel in Albany, she goes straight to her room without greeting her family, appointing the hour at which her son is to come to her and embracing him when he arrives with gloved hands. Mrs. Touchett is not an evil character; she is completely honest and reliable, but though she "might do a great deal of good, she never pleased." It has often been said that Dobbin is the hero of *Vanity Fair*, "A Novel Without a Hero." If *The Portrait of a Lady* has a hero, it is Isabel's cousin Ralph, who loves her with complete unselfishness (his invalidism has put him out of the running for matrimonial stakes). It is at his instigation that his father leaves Isabel a fortune, and the deepest irony of the book is that this is what attracts Osmond to her and comes close to ruining her life.

Caspar, the honorable but rigid American businessman who vainly woos Isabel throughout the book, is rejected by her as representing everything she was trying to get away from by coming to Europe, yet "she had never felt equally moved . . . by any other person." To Henrietta, his partisan, she admits that she had encouraged him; until her marriage she feels that she has an account to settle with him, and she does not dismiss him out of hand, as she does Lord Warburton, until the end. Her rejection of the dazzling offer she receives from this radical, admirable, yet somehow lightweight peer has puzzled others besides Mrs. Touchett. When she first meets him, she likes him immensely and even comes close to seeing him as a hero of romance. Nor does his passion frighten her, as Caspar's does. But she simply does not love him, and at the time she receives his proposal she has not yet got sufficiently tired of trying her wings so that she wishes to be swallowed up in what she sees as the establishment to which he belongs. Her inclination is all for subsuming, not being subsumed.

Some writers have found Gilbert Osmond unsatisfactorily portrayed. Such is Leo B. Marx, who calls him "a figure of unrelieved malignity, but scarcely a believable human being" and accuses James of having displayed an inhumanity toward him comparable to Osmond's toward Isabel, in contrast to the author's treatment of the villains in his later novels, where, "in a gesture of nearly religious love," he seems to have forgiven all their sins.[17] Although I do not claim that we ever see Osmond as clearly as Isabel, this seems to me an exaggeration. Osmond is a monster of a very special sort. He is simply a man in whom aestheticism has replaced all other passions and desires so that he takes "the plastic view" of even his own child's innocence and sends her to the convent as a school of good form. Mrs. Touchett, who sees through him from the beginning, although she is taken in by Madame Merle until she perceives that the latter is "using" her, sums him up with complete adequacy when she declares, "There's nothing *of* him," but she also realizes that there is no reason why Isabel would not marry him if she looked at him in a certain way. He is an uprooted, unattached American whose fastidiousness has been so shocked by vulgarity that he has become more vulgar than those he despises. Without means or talents, he has abdicated from life in a passion of disgust. "He had a fine, narrow, extremely modeled and composed face, of which the only fault was just this effect of running too much to points," and James was never more wise or subtle than in making him incapable of physical cruelty.

When Madame Merle first tells him about Isabel, he asks, "Is she beautiful, clever, rich, splendid, universally intelligent and unprecendentally virtuous? It's only on these conditions that I care to make her acquaintance." Isabel's having refused a peer commends her to him. Although he would never have married her without her money, he genuinely likes her at first, insofar as he is capable of liking anybody, but what he really wants is a wife who would behave like his daughter, who says, "I'll do anything" and "If you like I won't listen." He wishes to "tap her imagination with his knuckles and make it ring"; if she had submitted to that, then indeed they might have been as closely united, to use his own horrible simile, as the candlestick and the snuffers. It was Isabel's misfortune that she mistook the polished surface for the reality and interpreted as a noble detachment and disinterestedness what was merely emptiness, and it was her weakness that she was too much concerned with appearances and that on one side of her nature she preferred art to life and theory to experience. Gilbert was a collector of beautiful things, and for the time being she was content to be collected. Soon, however, it was as if he had the evil eye, withering everything in her life that he touched, almost malignantly putting the lights out one by one. If beauty is one of the attributes of God and devotion to beauty a virtue in human beings, Osmond proves the truth of what Bunyan knew in another area of experience, that there is a road to hell even from the very gates of the Heavenly City.[18]

Madame Merle is deeply involved in Osmond's guilt. She betrays Mrs. Touchett, and she betrays Isabel; if it is easier to forgive her than him, it is only because she is less inhuman. The welfare of her unacknowledged child is her main interest in the conspiracy, and the pathos of her position at the end, when, having lost all the stakes she had played for, she exiles herself to America, is deepened by the fact that Pansy, who does not know that she is her mother, dislikes her. As Osmond is not convention but conventionality itself, so Madame Merle is not worldly but the great round world, and nothing could be more illuminative of the differences between her and Isabel than their conversation in Chapter 19 about the relationship between the individual and the environment. I am by no means sure that I agree with those who find her lamentations at the end that Osmond has made her as vile as himself and that, after all, she has been vile for nothing among the most moving in Victorian fiction; there seems to me a strong intermixture of melodrama here. Yet it is no more sentimental to be affected by the pathos of her position at the end than by the even more wicked Lady Macbeth in the sleepwalking scene, and if she had won her game, we should certainly feel more hostile toward her than we do.

Isabel's return to Osmond at the end of the *Portrait* has occasioned more difference of opinion than anything else in the book, and James knew perfectly well that it would. As he told his notebook:

The obvious criticism of course will be that it is not finished—that I have not seen the heroine to the end of her situation—that I have left her *en l'air*.—This is both true and false. The *whole* of anything is never told, you can only take what groups together. What I have done has that unity—it groups together. It is not complete in itself—and the rest may be taken up or not, later.[19]

This is what is known as an "open" ending, and the opening was wider as the novel originally appeared than it is in the New York revision. In 1881 the last words spoken were Henrietta's to Caspar, "Look here, Mr. Goodwood, just you wait!" to which James added only, "On which he looked up at her." In the New York Edition the author weakened this by continuing as follows:

but only to guess, from her face, with a revulsion, that she simply meant he was young. She stood shining at him with that cheap comfort, and it added, on the spot, thirty years to his life. She walked him away with her, however, as if she had given him now the key to patience.

But surely even this does not quite slam the door. Henrietta, though not the most perspicacious character in the book, had been right about Isabel's marriage from the beginning, and if James intended her "cheap comfort" to be dismissed without any consideration, he surely erred by giving it the most emphatic position in the novel. If the ending is "open," we cannot be quite sure that Isabel returns to Osmond to stay; if we are sure of this, the ending is not "open"; we cannot have it both ways. This has frequently been ignored by commentators who attempt to ride two horses going in opposite directions at the same time and who also insist upon discussing Isabel's last recorded decision in terms of what they believe about marriage and divorce or what they assume James or his father to have believed, ignoring how it fits in with Isabel's situation and character and the design of the book.

Isabel's motivation is not, except in a very general way, religious. That Osmond is nominally a Catholic we might infer from his choice of the convent for Pansy and his preference for all the "old" forms, but we are not told whether he is a practicing Catholic, and he is obviously quite incapable of possessing the spirit of any reputable religion. For him the convent is a finishing school, and he would like to be pope for the power the office wields! In his mouth, the sermon he preaches Isabel on the indissolubility of marriage just before she leaves for England ("I think we should accept the consequences of our actions, and what I value most in life is the honour of a thing!") makes the reader gag, but it is quite in harmony with both his conventionalism and his concern for his own interests. Isabel, on the other hand, though a very "gentle" heretic, is, we are told, specifically Protestant in her religious orientation.

We may believe with Marion Montgomery that Isabel commits spiritual suicide by returning to Osmond or with writers like Sheldon W. Liebman and William J. Krier that she is opening up to herself the possibility of spiritual growth through a life of contemplation. But whichever side we take, we ought not to be surprised by what she does. She could not repudiate "the most serious act—the single serious act—of her life." She tells Henrietta that "one must accept one's deeds. I married him before all the world. I was perfectly free; it was impossible to do anything more deliberate." To her way of thinking, "marriage meant that a woman should cleave to the man with whom, uttering tremendous vows, she had stood at the altar" and "certain obligations were involved in the very fact of marriage, and were quite independent of the quantity of enjoyment extracted from it." As Buitenhuis has observed, George Eliot had let Dorothea Brooke off the hook by kindly killing off Grandcourt (in pre-divorce age fiction, unworthy husbands and wives are generally very nice about dying), but James was not so kind.

Yet Isabel's weakness as well as her strength is involved in her decision. She has promised Pansy to come back to her (although it is not clear that she will be permitted to do much for her), and she sets great store by her word. But a woman can hardly cleave to a husband who has no cleaving in him. Isabel did *not* marry Osmond "before all the world." The world neither knew nor cared anything about her marriage, and what the world thinks about a moral issue has no significance anyway. Nor did she choose Osmond freely; she was tricked into marriage by him and Madame Merle, and there is an element of either monstrous quixotism or monstrous pride in her refusal to face this fact and recognize the way it modifies her situation. Moreover, as has already been observed, Isabel is afraid of sex and consequently, in a way, of life. In her heart she cared more for Caspar Goodwood than for any other man except Ralph, whom, even at the end, when they come closest together, she calls her brother. James has accented sex through the very language he uses to describe the various encounters between Isabel and Caspar, and his account of their final meeting makes it as clear as any modern novelist could make it by using all the four-letter words in the dictionary that she has been roused as never before in her life, roused in the true sense perhaps for the first time in her life, for though she had given Osmond a child, his appeal to her had been from the beginning, in her sweet, stupid innocence, almost wholly aesthetic.

But there is another element in the situation which many commentators have ignored. The novel in which Isabel figures is not only the portrait of a lady but the portrait of a Victorian lady. Isabel's choices were limited by the mores and standards of her time, and it is not fair to judge them or her from our point of view a hundred years later. Obviously this does not mean that we must believe she chose wisely: we may even see her as a slave to the prejudices of her society and to her own limitations. But we can and should stop applying irrelevant and anachronistic considerations to her.[20]

As *The Portrait of a Lady* enters its second century, it is clear that its fame has been honestly earned but equally clear that it is not a flawless work. James himself feared that the action was too psychological with not enough incident (when Lawrence Barrett wanted him to turn it into a play, he replied that he did not think it could be done), that Isabel was too much analyzed in the first half, that too much was made of Lord Warburton's radicalism in the beginning and nothing afterward, and that although Henrietta Stackpole's was not really an exaggerated characterization, most readers would find it so.

The Luces, whom James does not mention, seem to me almost wholly irrelevant, but I would defend Henrietta, whose blatant Americanism, contrasting effectively with Isabel's sensitiveness and receptivity, makes her an amusing foil, and when, toward the end, she and the Englishman Bantling make what seems to be the only successful marriage in the book, a wryly effective note of irony is sounded. James had a right to be proud of Chapter 42, in which Isabel, brooding over the midnight fire, takes stock of her position; static and completely "inward" though it is, it marks an important turning point, although its method is almost straight exposition.

The *Portrait* is not "difficult" like the masterpieces of the final period, yet it would seem to have provoked more contradictory interpretations. Some of these we owe, no doubt, to the obtuseness of readers, but others may well be due to James's sending out contradictory signals.

The scene at Gardencourt in Chapter 1 has the

charm of a long summer afternoon, but except for the amusing discussion of Mrs. Touchett's telegram, the talk is not particularly good, and while Chapter 22, which brings Merle's plan to Osmond, is useful as exposition, it lacks the style and subtlety of the later James. Pansy is generally convincing enough in what she does and in what the narrator says about her, but the insight and maturity James packs into her long discourse in Chapter 30, like her talk when she learns of Isabel's engagement to her father in Chapter 35 and her penetration concerning Warburton in Chapter 45, are frankly incredible.

Even making full allowance for Isabel's youth and inexperience, she seems made to speak more rudely in many passages than would be necessary to establish either her complexity or her independence. "You must be our crazy Aunt Lydia" is her first greeting to Mrs. Touchett. When Ned Rosier seeks to enlist her aid in wooing Pansy, she quite unnecessarily tells him that if he had proposed to her, she would have refused him on the spot, and even Ralph is told on one occasion that she does not wish to dine with him because she would be tired of his company in an hour. It is hard to believe that she would call her rejected suitor "Poor Lord Warburton!" to his face; that she would ask Ralph, who is protesting against her engagement to Osmond, "Are you thinking of proposing to me?"; or that she would remind Osmond of his poverty by saying, "It wouldn't be remarkable if you did think it ridiculous that I should have the means to travel when you've not," even though she adds, "you know everything, and I know nothing." Moreover, this kind of gaucherie is not confined to Isabel. Caspar tells her he would rather see her dead than married to another man, and when the dying Ralph thanks him for his kindness in offering to escort him back to England, he replies, bluntly and amazingly, that he is doing it for Isabel's sake and not for him. It is hard to believe also that such a smooth customer as Osmond would ask Isabel what she thinks of his sister, with whom he is not on good terms, when she has just met her, and when the Countess herself tells Merle that she and Osmond together are like a dangerous chemical combination, the information seems designed only for the convenience of the reader.[21]

*The Portrait of a Lady* not only marked an important stage in James's development as an artist; it is a book of permanent value. But it was a way station, not a goal. When, in 1898, A. C. Benson asked the author for a sequel, he declined on the ground that he could now do better than that. He could, and he did. The supreme masterpieces were yet to come.[22]

# 6

# Explorations: *The Bostonians; The Princess Casamassima; The Tragic Muse; The Reverberator*

After *The Portrait of a Lady*, James wrote, in rapid succession, three other very long novels—*The Bostonians, The Princess Casamassima*, and *The Tragic Muse*—which would be the last long novels he would write until his three supreme masterpieces—*The Ambassadors, The Wings of the Dove*, and *The Golden Bowl*—appeared early in the new century. With the novels of our present concern, all of them somewhat less "forward" technically than *The Portrait of a Lady*, James came closer than he ever did elsewhere to the Victorian "three-decker." They are not at all alike in their subject matter; what they have in common are a certain panoramic quality; a wide range of characters, including some Dickens-like eccentrics, representative of various social strata; much attention to backgrounds; a vast amount of detail, physical and otherwise; and a decided tendency toward structural sprawl. The characters, too, are much more involved in extrapersonal interests and in various aspects of the life of their time than in the later books, and James himself pointed out that he went "'behind' right and left."[1]

In *The Bostonians*, Olive Chancellor, a pas-

sionate, neurotic Boston feminist with means, intelligence, and devotion but no capacity for public
relations encounters Varena Tarrant, a young girl of
personal purity but sleazy background, with a pre-
ternatural gift as a speaker, and conceives the idea
of "adopting" her, with a view to making the girl
her own voice or other self, the public projection
and propagandist of her ideas. The plan is frustrated
because Verena falls in love with Olive's own cousin, a reactionary Mississippian Confederate war
veteran, Basil Ransom, whose antifeminism is as fa-
natical as Olive's diametrically opposed ideas and
whose articles all magazine editors have so far rejected as better suited to the sixteenth century than
the nineteenth. Shorn of its many divagations and
secondary developments, *The Bostonians* is essentially the record of the long duel between Olive and
Ransom for Verena, who is almost as much the object of contention between them as the soul of a man
between God and the devil in the morality plays.

Set in "187–," *The Bostonians* is by all means
James's most elaborate American fiction, and it is
not surprising that it should have begun with the
desire "to write a very *American* tale, a tale very
characteristic of our social conditions." James asked
himself "what was the most salient and peculiar
point in our social life" and found his answer in "the
situation of women, the decline of the sentiment of
sex, the agitation in their behalf." Verena was the
character he thought of first, and the title gave him
much trouble. Should it be "The Newness," "The
Reformers," "The Precursors," "The Revealer," or
maybe even "Verena"? The final choice was made,
one gathers, in desperation, and James later explained that he had intended it to cover only Olive
and Verena "as they appeared to the mind of Ransom."

The novel ran in the *Century* from February 1885 through February 1886, and the book was published by Macmillan on both sides of the Atlantic in the latter year.[2] The editor of the *Century*, Richard Watson Gilden, said that nothing ever published in the magazine had roused so little interest. The reviews were bad (Mark Twain said he would rather be damned to John Bunyan's heaven than have to read the book), and in 1888 James would write Howells that the failure of *The Bostonians* and its successor had reduced the demand for his work to zero. When the author finished the novel, he judged it his best to date; later he thought the middle part "too diffuse and insistent—far too describing and explaining and expatiating" and the whole thing "too long and dawdling." This was apparently not his final judgment, however, for much later he would have liked to include it in the New York Edition if only there had been opportunity to undertake the extensive revision he deemed necessary.

James himself said that Daudet's *L'Evangéliste* had given him "the idea of this thing," and the resemblance to certain aspects of *The Blithedale Romance* is evident, although James thought the necessary psychological motivation for what he was trying to write was lacking in both works. Among other possible sources, Cargill mentions *Adam Bede*, Howells's *Dr. Breen's Practice* (to which he might have added *The Undiscovered Country*), and, interestingly though inconclusively, the *Antigone* of Sophocles. More recently, Balzac's *La Fille aux veux d'or* has been suggested, Howard Kerr has directed attention to the writings of Orestes Brownson and Bayard Taylor (especially the latter's *Hannah Thurston*), and two writers have plausibly invoked the pastoral tradition.[3]

But the influences from life may well have been

more important than those from literature. There
was the whole vast background of contemporary
American feminism, spiritualism, radicalism, and
reformism,[4] and there were such strong resemblances between some of the characters and actual
people that the novel sometimes approaches the
roman à clef. In the beginning, about the only evidence James received that his book had not fallen
dead from the press came in the form of protests
from Lowell, his own brother William, and his aunt
Kate Walsh, who felt that in the book's sole survivor
from the heroic golden age of New England aboli-
tionism, Miss Birdseye, James had caricatured Hawthorne's sister-in-law, Elizabeth Peabody. James
denied it, as novelists always deny such charges,
and professed himself deeply distressed. Miss Birdseye, he averred, like all his characters, had been
evolved from his own consciousness, and the most
he could have been indebted to Miss Peabody for
was her displaced spectacles, but he rather gave
himself away by going on to admit that he had feared
this accusation might be made. Howard Kerr has
pointed out that contemporaries might have been
expected to connect "Mrs. Ada T. P. Foat" with the
prominent spiritualist lecturer Ada Hoyt Foye, and
the sexless but not unkindly Dr. Mary Prance, the
complete professional woman, must surely have reminded the book's first readers of the pioneer American woman doctor Mary Walker. Leon Edel has not
presented any evidence to support his conjecture
that in describing the relationship between Olive
and Verena, James may have been thinking of Ka-
tharine Loring and his own sister, Alice, and in any
case there are more likely originals. Although Verena is a much more attractive girl than either Anna
Dickinson, the famous girl orator of Civil War times,
or the journalist Kate Field who so enthralled Anthony Trollope, it is hard to believe that James could

have created her without at least thinking of Anna.
Sara deSassure Davis sees Susan B. Anthony and
Whitelaw Reid (who wished to marry Anna and
who, not succeeding, became her bitter enemy as
editor of the New York *Tribune*) playing Olive and
Ransom to Miss Dickinson's Verena and mentions
that Miss Anthony's biographer also saw her subject
as competing with Wendell Phillips for control over
the girl. Although Ransom may have been made a
Southerner because of the *Century*'s interest in
Southern themes and postwar North–South reconciliation, it is interesting that although Reid hailed
from Ohio, he had both Alabama and Mississippi
connections. Kerr also suggests another possible influence upon Verena by his reference to another
prominent spiritualist of the time, Cora L. V. Hatch,
later Tappan and still later Richmond, whom James
is known to have heard.[5]

James apologizes for his backgrounds on the
ground that he did not know Boston well enough,
but it is hard to see how we could have done with
more of that city, of Cambridge (especially Harvard
and Memorial Hall, the scene of one of the most
moving episodes in the story), and of Marion, Massachusetts, where James had visited Gilder's summer home and which he renamed Marmion.[6] One
is surprised to find him writing thus of the New York
neighborhood where Ransom lived:

I mention it not on account of any particular influence it
may have had on the life or the thoughts of Basil Ransom,
but for old acquaintance sake and that of local colour;
besides which, a figure is nothing without a setting, and
our young man came and went every day, with rather an
indifferent, unperceiving step, it is true, among the objects I have briefly described.

If we must have greater methodological naiveté
than this, the author stands ready to oblige. As we

have seen, he admits going behind his people
freely, but this does not prevent him from professing
ignorance whenever, for no apparent reason, it suits
him to do so. He gives us elaborate formal descrip-
tions of his characters à la Walter Scott, and he permits "I" to comment, sometimes coyly, sometimes
apologetically, in obedience to his own whim, all of
which forms a startling contrast to the wit and graceful stylistic balance he often achieves and his ability
to use even the physical surroundings of his characters to symbolize both them and the civilization
of which they are both the product and a part.

The tense, morbid Olive Chancellor, with her
devotion to female emancipation, her hatred for
men as a class, her perverse hunger for martyrdom,
and her desire to monopolize Verena's affection, is
the most interesting, though not the most attractive,
character in the novel. Verena herself seems as
vague and undefined as Mélisande when she first
appears; later she becomes, as William James called
her, *liebenswürdig*, but even in the great scene at
the Music Hall, where Ransom prevents her from
speaking and carries her off for himself, her role is
comparatively passive. Her father is a "mesmeric
healer" and "a moralist without moral sense," with
a more than questionable background, her mother
the not disinterested daughter of an old abolitionist
of standing, now somewhat coarsened by her association with her husband and not averse to using
her daughter or anything else at her disposal to regain a position in society. The girl "had sat on the
knees of somnambulists, and had been passed from
hand to hand by trance-speakers; she was familiar
with every kind of 'cure,' and had grown up among
lady-editors of newspapers advocating new reli-
gions, and people who disapproved of the marriage-
tie." Clearly, she is one of those curious people,

incomprehensible to others and probably even more to themselves, whose innocence is so irrefrangible that they can apparently respond to all influences and live in any environment without corruption; if, at this late date, anybody still thinks James needs defending against the stupid charge of snobbery, it can be found certainly in his handling of her. Verena is not exactly a trance speaker, nor does she go in for glossolalia, but there is something mediumistic in her personality nevertheless; in her first phase, she is called an *improvisatrice*, who cannot function until her father turns her on ("it's not me, mother"). Later all this is modified. Olive's control over her is less mystical; the two work together quite rationally and self-consciously on the speech that is to launch Verena on her great career at the Music Hall; she even rehearses. Perhaps the transition between the two phases might be more carefully prepared for. We see Verena most clearly, I think, at the end of Book II, but even here her charm does not make it easier for us to understand her. As "the most good-natured girl in the world . . . she had always done everything that people asked" and was always able to "expose herself, give herself away, turn herself inside out, for the satisfaction of a person who made demands of her." Consequently, she passes from her father's control to Olive's and from Olive's to Ransom's without undergoing any essential change in her inner being. Her beauty, her flaming red hair, and her gift for publicity make her a vivid figure, yet her function in the book remains essentially catalytic, and we see her most clearly in her effect upon others; to her innermost depths, if there are any, we are never admitted.[7]

The chapters describing the decline and death of Miss Birdseye are, by all means, the most touching in the book, and the closing scene at the Music Hall is superbly managed melodrama, but the greatest chapter by far is 39, which describes Olive's anguish as her world crashes around her; if there is anything in *The Bostonians* worthy to rank with the picture of Isabel Archer before the fire in Chapter 42 of *The Portrait of a Lady*, it is this. "These hours of backward clearness come to all men and women, once at least, when they read the past in the light of the present, with the reasons of things, like unobserved finger-posts, protruding where they never saw them before." Certainly it is a tribute to James's art that he should have been able to win such a triumph with a character with whom neither the author nor his readers can greatly sympathize.

The one thing we must not do, however, when Ransom carries Verena off at the end, is interpret the scene in terms of the brave young prince delivering the enchanted princess from the castle of the wicked witch.[8] It is true that Verena's gift is essentially the gift of gab and that her giving up her career for domesticity is not analogous to what a similar choice would be on the part of Miriam Rooth. What is too bad is that she should not have made her commitment to normal human activities through a less selfish and pigheaded man. For Ransom is wholly amiable only in his kindly treatment of Miss Birdseye, and when Verena casts her lot with him, she is not delivered but simply exchanges one captivity for another. James had already committed himself by speaking of Ransom's "narrow notions," calling Olive "distinguished and discriminating," and making her reactionary sister Adeline Luna, who shares Ransom's views, makes a play for him, and turns into a vulgar virago when he fails to respond, "the dupe of confusions in which the worse was apt to be mistaken for the better," and he makes his position even clearer through the last words in the book, where he tells us of the weeping girl Ransom carries off that "it is to be feared that with the union, so far from brilliant, into which she was about to enter, these were not the last [tears] she was destined to shed." If there is a choice to be made between the contending fanaticisms which swirl about poor Verena's flaming head, all the advantages are with Olive, who wishes to liberate women, while Ransom desires only to keep them down, seeing no use in the world for a "a truly amiable woman" save "to make some honest man happy," in Verena's case, himself.[9]

The only reservation that needs to be entered here is that the captivity into which Ransom dragoons Verena is somewhat more "normal" than that from which he delivers her. Of late years there has been much talk about the alleged lesbianism in *The Bostonians*. All James says on this subject is that he proposed to study "one of those friendships between women which are so common in New England," but although he permits Ransom to wonder what Olive's sex was ("great heaven"), he also vouches for her complete celibacy: "She was a spinster as Shelley was a lyric poet, or as the month of August is sultry." There can then be no possible question about a physical relationship between the two women. We can be sure that such a possibility never entered Verena's mind; whether it entered Olive's or James's is another question and one that cannot be answered with complete certainty. All we can be sure of is that Olive's intense attraction to Verena did have an element of infatuation in it and that what she hoped to accomplish for the world and for her sex through their association was robbed of complete disinterestedness by the fact that their relationship did satisfy a deep emotional need for her.

yield an "image," they could not supply "a progression, an action . . . a drama." The standard view is that for this he turned to Turgenev's *Virgin Soil*, whose hero, Nezhdanov, he had described in *Transatlantic Sketches* as

the natural son of a nobleman, not recognized by his father's family . . . who, drifting through irritation and smothered rage and vague aspiration into the stress of occult radicalism, finds himself fatally fastidious and sceptical and "aesthetic"—more essentially an aristocrat, in a word, than any of the aristocrats he has conspired against.

There were other literary influences, of course. David Seed has nominated the second adventure in *The Dynamiter* by Robert Louis Stevenson and his wife, and Marcia Jacobson has, more importantly, called attention to a whole school of English working-class novels by George Gissing, Walter Besant, Grant Allen, and others, finding Hyacinth Robinson more like Arthur Golding in Gissing's *Workers in the Dawn* than like Nezhdanov. Edel speaks of Balzac and Zola as standing by James's elbow alongside Turgenev, and Zola's influence seems indisputable upon the deterministic aspects of the *Princess*.

Besides all these, there was Dickens. The visit to Millbank Prison at the beginning is Dickens shadowed by Gissing and other late-nineteenth-century influences, and Mrs. Bowerbank, "the big square-faced, deep-voiced lady who took up, as it were, all that side of the room," who, once she has seen Hyacinth, feels a little easier about taking him to his dying mother because she is sure that "in her position, I should go off easier if I had seen them curls," has Dickens written all over her. Rosy Muniment, too, inevitably suggests Jenny Wren, and there are touches in a number of minor characters which show to what good purpose James had read the great Victorian.

Item: the "little besmirched slavey" who wore "shoes that didn't match, though of an equal antiquity and intimately emulous in the facility with which they dropped off." Item: the upper-class girl "with a straight back and long arms, whose neck was encircled so tightly with a fur boa that, to look a little to one side, she was obliged to move her whole body," whom Hyacinth meets through the princess and who cannot think of anything better to ask him than "with what pack he hunted and whether he went in much for tennis." Item: Mrs. Crookenden, her head decorated with "the plumage of a cockatoo mingled with a structure of glass beads," who "looked at him with an almost awful fixedness of charity and asked him three distinct times if he would have a glass of negus" and who inspired the foreman's wife to close her eyes "as if in the presence of a blinding splendour" whenever she spoke to her.[11]

Hyacinth Robinson, the son of a Frenchwoman, Florentine Vivier, whose father had died on the barricades in Paris, by Lord Frederick Purvis, whom she later murdered, is brought up in London by the dressmaker Amanda Pynsent. A sensitive, aesthetically oriented young man, he becomes a bookbinder who does beautiful work and aspires to authorship, but he also falls in with a group of radicals and revolutionaries and is taken up by the Princess Casamassima. Through Paul Muniment, he meets the great German anarchist leader Diedrich Hoffendahl, to whom he binds himself to carry out any commission that may be entrusted to him; it is tacitly understood that this will take the form of the assassination of a great personage, for which he will pay with his life. Through a trip to the Continent which the small legacy Miss Pynsent leaves him enables him to make and his penetration into the world of culture through his friendship with Christina, Hyacinth becomes a hopelessly divided personality. Still bound, as he sees it, by his "sacred vow" and still committed to the cause of the dispossessed, he is increasingly seduced by the charms and values which, with all its sins and injustices, the civilization which the anarchists wish to destroy has produced and increasingly doubtful that terrorist tactics can achieve the desired end, and when at last his call comes, he can find no "out" save to lodge the bullet that had been intended for the duke in his own heart.

Critics have argued that James did not know enough about anarchism to write about it, but the truth is that he knew quite as much as he could use. He played into the hands of the enemy when he ended his preface by declaring "that if you haven't for fiction, the root of the matter in you, haven't the sense of life and the penetrating imagination, you are a fool in the very presence of the revealed and assured; but that if you are so armed you are not really helpless, not without your resource, even before mysteries abysmal." But this, surely, is the only way fiction of quality *can* be written; without this, one can only produce blue books, and many a potentially good novel has been spoiled because the writer knew too much and felt obliged to get it all in. Henry James, Sr., was not exactly a conservative, and James grew up in a radical, though not a revolutionary, atmosphere. The scene of his novel is laid in 1881, when the anarchist agitation and the fears engendered by it were both riding high, and James was much better informed about all this and more sensitive to its causes than many of his critics have realized.[12]

A contemporary reviewer rejoiced that in the *Princess* James had for once written of "conspirators, and harlots, and stabbings, and jails, and low-lived men and women who drop their h's, and real incidents, and strong emotions, and everything 'in a concatenation accordingly,'" upon which the only adequate comment would seem to be Sam Weller's "Everyone to his own taste, as the old lady said when she kissed the cow." But the reader of this book must by now be quite sufficiently aware that James was never afraid of either melodrama or the fairy tale and also that he never used either more effectively than when he disguised it so ingeniously that most readers failed to recognize it. As Lionel Trilling has expressed it, he here

asks us to accept a poor young man whose birth is darkly secret, his father being a dissipated and authentic English lord, his mother a French courtesan seamstress who murders the father; a beautiful American-Italian princess who descends in the social scale to help "the people"; a general mingling of the very poor with persons of exalted birth; and then a dim mysterious leader of revolution, never seen by the reader, the machinations of an underground group of conspirators, an oath taken to carry out an assassination at some unspecified future day, the day arriving, the hour of the killing set, the instructions and the pistol given. . . . .

upon which he comments by reference to Rebecca West's finding it

one of the big jokes in literature that it was James, who so prided himself on his lack of naivety, who should have brought back to fiction the high implausibility of the old novels which relied for their effects on dark and stormy nights, Hindu servants, mysterious strangers, and bloody swords cleansed on richly embroidered handkerchiefs.

Surely, after the tension achieved all through Book VI, James had no need to take off his hat to his friend Stevenson or any other master of romance.

It has often been remarked that since, for once,

James was dealing with working people and not with the leisure class, he was driven to the somewhat desperate expedient of having much of his action take place on Sundays. Nevertheless, although there are a number of time lapses and a good deal happens at which the reader does not "assist" but of which he learns only in retrospect (most importantly, Hyacinth's interview with Hoffendahl takes place between Books II and III), the narrative line is considerably more direct and tightly pulled than in *The Bostonians*. Moreover, although one cannot say that either here or in *The Tragic Muse* James wholly abandons authorial commentary, he certainly indulges himself considerably less freely than in the earlier book.[13]

The unfortunate hero of *The Princess Casamassima* is "a youth on whom nothing was lost." There was "something jaunty and romantic, almost theatrical, in his whole little person," and even his shabby work clothes had a suggestion of "arrangement" about them. He was "exotic," too, and there was "a certain conscious cockneyism" about him.

As a child he preferred "a ballad with a vivid woodcut at the top" to a sweet and was always sure he would never see enough of "the wonderful world illuminated by . . . playhouse lamps." Vice repelled him; good literature and art attracted him. When he finally reached Paris, he saw the city in terms of what he had read and dreamed about it, and he held its bloodstained shame and glory in his mind with a sense of almost mystical awareness. In his milieu he could earn a living only through being apprenticed to a trade, and it was quite in character that he should choose one of the most elegant among them, the binding of fine books, and become a master craftsman.[14]

James works Zolaesque determinism pretty

hard in stressing the two sides of Hyacinth's ancestry by way of explaining the conflict in his sympathies that finally undoes him, but however unscien-
tific the explanation may be that there could be no
peace "between the two currents that flowed in his
nature, the blood of his passionate plebeian mother
and that of his long-descended supercivilised sire,"
his creator no more relies on this alone to bring
about the hero's doom than he lays the full responsibility at Christina's door; Miss Pynsent's poverty-
stricken gentility, the encouragement she gives the
boy to think himself superior, the trip to the Continent, and the stay at Medley which gives him an
insight into aristocratic ways and privileges are all
important influences. After he has rashly bound
himself to the anarchist leader to commit an act of
violence, the shift in his sympathies is carefully
traced until "the sense of the wonderful precious
things" the society about him has produced and the
"fabric of beauty and power it has raised" threaten
to crowd out his sympathies for the toiling oppressed masses. Unlike Christina, who now believes that there will be time enough for beauty after
the economic problem has been solved, he thinks
that "there can't be too many pictures and statues
and works of art. The more the better, whether people are hungry or not," until at last he cries, "I don't
know what I believe, God help me!"

His suicide has been spoken of as the solution
of his problem. It is not, but merely an evasion, an
admission on his part that he could find no solution,
perhaps that there is none. He has been described
as a sacrificial lamb. He is not that, either, for he
sees the civilization which now claims his allegiance as encrusted with guilt and himself as shar-
ing the taint.[15] At the end, he recalls Isabel Archer
upon returning to Osmond; his change of sympa-

thies could not invalidate his "sacred vow." There are some things "which one can't change. I didn't promise to believe; I promised to obey." Once you have committed yourself, there is "an indelicacy in not being ready to pay for it," and even when you can no longer give your sympathy to "the beastly cause," you can still give your life.

This seems a tragic situation, yet Hyacinth does not, for many readers, quite achieve tragic stature, nor does what happens to him seem quite inevitable. Is it James's frequent application of the adjective "little" to him which leaves one feeling that he is more pathetic than tragic? And if David Seed exaggerates when he calls him a prig and a egotist, does he not have a point in seeing him as one who failed quite to achieve maturity, and do not both Christina and Millicent Henning feel this? But pathos has its place in art as well as tragedy, and although Hyacinth Robinson may not move us so deeply as the heroes of Shakespeare to whom James, in the preface, so audaciously compares him, he is still completely credible and of a piece.

It seems an odd thing to say of so glamorous a creature as the Princess Casamassima that so far as the plot is concerned, she exercises a function only ancillary to that of a "little bastard book-binder."[16] How does she differ from the Christina of *Roderick Hudson*? She is older, more disillusioned, and "world-weary" (like all romantic idealists, she has been disappointed in everything), and she has become a revolutionary, up to her neck, as Paul Muniment tells her, in the anarchist movement. She has gained in savoir faire also, being somewhat less frank and considerably less blunt than she was in the old days, but she has lost and gained in beauty and charm only as the appeal of a mature woman differs from that of a girl. Mystery still envelops her, and this is due both to the complications of her personality and to the fact that James never goes behind her. We see what she does (except when he chooses to keep it from us), and we watch her effect upon others, but there is nothing like Chapter 42 in *The Portrait of a Lady*.

Her beauty is still of the radiant rather than the voluptuous variety. It "had an air of perfection, it astonished and lifted one up, the sight of it seemed a privilege." To Madame Grandoni, who knew and recognized all her faults and who felt obliged to desert her at last, Christina looked like "an angel who came down from heaven yesterday and has been rather disappointed in her first day on earth!" When she visits the Muniments in their working-class flat, Lady Aurora finds her "divine and a revelation of beauty and benignity"; she is "gentler, fairer, wiser than even a chemical expert could have guessed in advance." Even at the end, "her gentleness, when she turned it on, was quite divine—it had always the irresistible charm that was the humility of a high spirit" and had "worked itself free of all earthly grossness."

Their common romanticism is the bond that attaches her to Hyacinth. In spite of the splendor with which she carries herself, she is sensitive and afraid ("she never engaged in a fresh encounter nor formed a new relation . . . without a fit of nervousness, a fear that she might herself be wanting"). Painfully aware of her own shortcomings, she is still searching for somebody better than herself to look up to, yet she has keen insight into the weaknesses of others.

Despite one or two ambiguous statements, it seems as nearly certain as anything of the kind can be with a writer so capable of evasiveness as James that although Hyacinth stayed for a period in her house, they had no sexual contacts, but the same statement could not be made with confidence concerning her relations with Paul Muniment, whom James evidently intended to endow with the coarse animal magnetism proverbially irresistible to women, since he makes even the simon-pure Lady Aurora fall hopelessly in love with him.

Is Christina's revolutionary ardor sincere? I do not see how this can be doubted. It is true that she is seeking self-expression in her work as a revolutionist, but this is true of all effective workers in all lines of endeavor, since without it no good work can be done. "Her disgust with a thousand social arrangements, her rebellion against the selfishness, the corruption, the iniquity, the cruelty, the imbecility of the people who all over Europe had the upper hand" seems quite genuine, and, on its own terms, her statement of the case for revolution is unanswerable: "There's less and less work in the world, and there are more and more people to do the little there is. The old ferocious selfishnesses must come down. They won't come down gracefully, so they must just be assisted." Even the conservative Madame Grandoni tells the prince, when he calls his radical wife the devil, that "she's not the Devil, because she wishes to do good."[17]

For all that, she is volatile, unpredictable, sincere but not single-minded, and those who know her best realize that they can never count on her to see anything through. She is (in the bad sense) theatrical also, as is shown by the way she receives Hyacinth at Medley, not seeing him at all the day he arrives and then admitting him to her presence while she plays the piano and keeping him waiting for some time to admire her art before they can talk together. Nor is this the only occasion when he waits for her with "much the same feeling with which, at the theatre, he had sometimes awaited the entrance of a celebrated actress." There is arrogance here too, commanding as it were the extension of his visit to Medley, regardless of the claims of his work, and telling him that he ceases to be insignificant from the moment she has anything to do with him. She does not achieve selflessness even when she gives up the palatial estate where she has been living and goes to dwell amid the squalors of Madeira Crescent, for although she has relinquished much, she pretends to have given up still more.

We cannot be sure that Muniment is right when he tells Christina at the end that she will ultimately give up revolution and return to her husband, and although he *is* correct in telling her that the conspirators have valued her only for her (actually her husband's) money and that they do not really trust her, this is somewhat undercut when we learn that they do not trust him, either! That they would be right in entering such a judgment of her is indicated, however, by her frantic though futile attempt to save Hyacinth from his fate, which proceeds even to the length of offering to do the deed herself if only he can get off. Startling as this is, there are no indications that we are not supposed to believe what she says. That she would actually have done it is far from clear, however; if she had, it would have been the first time she ever carried anything through.

Ironically enough, it is Christina's general failure to go to extremes or make a full commitment that makes her sympathetic at the end, in contrast to Muniment, the career revolutionist, to whom people are nothing and the work in hand everything, even if one has no emotional involvement with it. If Christina did not have it in her to be the perfect saint in revolution or in anything else, by the same token she could never be the perfect devil either, and she nowhere shows her insight into character more clearly than when she asks Muniment why, if the deed needs to be done, he does not do it himself. Unfortunately, we are never told to what extent, if at all, she realizes, as she bends over Hyacinth's bloodstained body at the end, that her having finally "chucked" him for Muniment, if, as he believed, that is what she did, contributed toward bringing him to his doom.

If Christina serves as a foil to Hyacinth, the other characters are arranged around these two. They are brilliantly handled on the whole, and they deserve much more analysis than they can be accorded here. Muniment is a monster; judge his cause good or bad, he has still been completely dehumanized by it, and his cruelty contrasts not only with Christina's womanly sympathy but also with the attitude of the Poupins, for James's radicals in this book are by no means all of a piece.[18] Another effective foil to Christina is furnished by the eccentric, absurd, untidy, unglamorous, but admirable Lady Aurora, whose work among the poor is motivated by sheer goodness of heart, with no ideological foundation.

Prince Casamassima is touching in his continued affection for the wife who hates him because she despises herself for the weakness she showed when she yielded to maternal pressure in marrying him and rather pathetically amusing in his fear of the scandal she may bring upon his precious name. Madame Grandoni is as sensible and devoted as she was in *Roderick Hudson*,[19] and if the reader is likely to remember Miss Pynsent's devotion to Hyacinth less than that of Anastasius Vetch, the fiddler in the theater orchestra who got him his job as a bookbinder and whose own radicalism has been tempered by helplessness with advancing age and in-

creasing conviction of the futility of efforts for amel-
ioration, it is only because Miss Pynsent dies comparatively early in the book and escapes the agony of
the denouement. Paul Muniment's crippled sister
Rosy is a small, acerbic masterpiece, admirable in
her courage but repellent in her ability to exploit
her disability for everything she can get out of it.

The most puzzling character is Captain Sholto,
and Millicent Henning is, in some ways, the most
completely realized. Dupee sticks his neck out and
then draws it partway back in again when he calls
Sholto "a police spy (apparently)"; nothing is certain about Sholto except that he is sinister and
worthless. Of the vulgar, good-hearted Millicent,
whom under other circumstances Hyacinth might
have married (even at the end he wonders whether
he had not liked her better than anybody else) and
who would have bullied him and babied him and
taken the best possible care of him, Edel says rightly
that "she is as cockney as Shaw's Eliza, and rings
as true in everything she does and says." There are
plenty of vulgar characters in James who are successfully realized on their own terms, but none
other is portrayed so triumphantly at such length.
Chapter 41, which describes the Sunday she spent
with Hyacinth, is not the most characteristic chapter
in James, but it is completely successful, winning,
and delightful. And certainly he could have found
nothing else so wryly or bitterly appropriate than to
have the straw that breaks the proverbial camel's
back derive at last from Hyacinth's suspicion that
Millicent had at last turned from him to, of all people, Sholto.

The Tragic Muse in the novel which bears that
title is the actress Miriam Rooth, the only character
who, in the course of the action, completely commits
herself on the side of "art" in its conflict with the

"world," the struggle which, in his preface, James defines as the theme of the book.[20] As the only completely creative person among his heroines, she is to some readers the most fascinating among them, and, unlike the Princess Casamassima, she *is* the principal character in her novel, for although James chooses not to go behind her but instead to show her to us through what she says and does and the effects she creates, the others are grouped around her and developed in their relationship to her. Yet since the novel is Nick Dormer's story as well as hers, *The Tragic Muse*, too, falls short of being an all-embracing title. Moreover, although Madame Carré sees Miriam as "pure tragedy" and the book ends with her triumph as Juliet, she aspires to be not a tragedienne merely but the best all-round actress in London.

In the summer of 1887 James wrote Grace Norton that he was "just beginning" a novel which would probably be called *The Tragic Muse* and that it would be half as long as the *Princess* and would not be serialized. But in March 1888 he agreed to supply Thomas Bailey Aldrich with a serial to run through the twelve 1889 numbers of the *Atlantic*; the story, he said, would be about an actress and a great deal besides but would not be improper! It began in the January number but did not end until May 1890, after which Houghton, Mifflin brought out the book in the United States and Macmillan in London. The author did not "stay put" during his labors; neither did he hew to the line. He began serializing before he had finished writing, and on February 2, 1889, he confided to his notebook that he had not labored seriously on the *Muse* since the previous autumn, having foolishly taken time out to do four articles. This time William James was ecstatic, calling the novel original, wonderful, delightful, and admirable and rejoicing because everybody in it was so human and good and because it left such a good taste in the reader's mouth.

Structurally, *The Tragic Muse* is less sprawling than *The Bostonians*, but its double plot makes it less compact than *The Princess Casamassima*, and it has more charm than either of the other books. Gabriel Nash and Peter Sherringham (the brother of Julia Dallow, whom Nick is apparently finally intended to marry) links up Miriam's world with Nick's; the most direct confrontation between the two occurs in Chapter 26, when Julia, who hates art and has her heart set upon a political career for her prospective husband, finds him painting Miriam in his studio and draws unwarranted conclusions about their relationship. We learn only incidentally that Miriam is playing successfully in London, and the important news that Nick plans to give up his seat in Parliament reaches us at second hand through his sister, Biddy. At the end, James engages in the pretence that he is writing history, which is as old in English fiction as Defoe and Mrs. Behn; he will not, he says, describe in detail so famous an occasion as Miriam's first appearance as Juliet, and he must refrain from coming too close to "contemporary history." Technically *The Tragic Muse* is not innovative or experimental. There are again a number of Dickensian touches, as with "the little drama" of Mrs. Rooth's "lost and recovered shawl perpetually going on," and although the author refrains from frequent intrusive personal commentary, he obviously has no feeling against it.

In the preface, James fails to recover any sources beyond having always wished to "do something about art" and also to write about a young man who should abandon public life. A notebook entry of June 19, 1884, makes it clear, however, that the

germ of the Miriam–Peter story lay in a suggestion
made to James by Mrs. Humphry Ward, and he must
also have been influenced by that writer's first
novel, *Miss Bretherton* (1884), which was based on
the early London career of the American actress
Mary Anderson and which James read with care and
commented on in detail. Cargill has suggested other
possible influences from the Goncourts. Miriam's
Jewishness may have come from this source, although it would be at least as reasonable to derive
it from Rachel, upon whom the actress models herself, from Sarah Bernhardt, in whose career James
had considerable interest and whom he clearly had
in mind while writing this novel, although he never
mentions her name, or even from that other Miriam
in Hawthorne's *Marble Faun.*[21] What he was quite
clear about was that Miriam Rooth was not going to
resemble the "vivid monsters" of Anatole France.
That is why, like Marie Bashkirtseff, she rather tire-
somely insists that she is a "good girl," and it is also
why he does not permit her to have the "affair" with
Nick to whose possibility he apparently gave some
consideration. Even though she must be set apart
from the other characters, he was not going to place
the "bad" actress over against the "good" suitor;
such obviousness was not for him. As for the rest,
nobody is going to be much interested at this date
in seeing one Cyril Flowers as the possible original
of Nick Dormer nor the French actress Jeanne Bar-
tet as having suggested Mlle Voisin, although, as we
shall see, several still well known persons have
been invoked as having possibly fathered Gabriel
Nash.

Nick Dormer's family, the wealthy Julia Dallow
(who is passionately in love with him), and the aged
Mr. Carteret, who proposes to leave him a large for-

tune, provided that he steers his life into what his benefactor regards as the proper channel, combine to pressure him to pursue the political career of his late father. When a parliamentary seat controlled by Mrs. Dallow becomes vacant, Nick yields to the extent of standing for it despite his basic desire to become a portrait painter, but strain develops between him and his fiancée; he resigns and is disinherited. Julia's brother, Peter Sherringham, who is in the public service, becomes the patron of the aspiring actress Miriam Rooth, a girl of rackety but respectable background. Madame Carré, the great actress to whom Peter takes Miriam, at first finds her hopelessly crude, but the girl will not be shoved aside, and ultimately her slavish devotion, enormous capacity for work, and ability to face the truth about herself, no matter now painful it may be, carry the day ("You've learned all I've taught, but where the devil have you learned what I haven't?").

Peter, meanwhile, has fallen in love with Miriam against his will. Unable to see himself as the husband of an actress, he begs her to give up her career to become the wife of a potential ambassador, but she turns him down, and he consoles himself with Nick's sister, Biddy, herself a very minor artist, than whom there could have been no nicer consolation prize, while Miriam turns to an actor named Basil Dashwood, whose career will never clash disastrously with hers but who seems devotion and efficiency itself in managing her business affairs. It is, one feels, a good match; Miriam *needs* Basil, and there is no room in one woman's life for the kind of devotion she brings to her art and a grand passion besides. At the end of the book, Julia and Nick are friends again, and Julia has at last indicated her desire to be painted. We are left feeling that they will

probably marry and that some kind of accommo-
dation between their divergent tastes and interests
will emerge.

James thought he had failed with Nick. He
seems to me, on the contrary, to have been wholly
successful in creating a believable character, but not
of the heroic stamp. "I don't know what I am—
heaven help me," he tells Gabriel Nash early in the
book. "I'm a freak of nature and a sport of the mocking gods," and though this is an overstatement, there
is truth in it. We are obviously intended to take
Nash's estimate of Nick's abilities at face value, and
Miriam too feels that what he produces will live long
after her "screeching" has been forgotten. But she
has more confidence in him than he has in himself,
and it is nowhere established that he is capable of
a single-minded devotion to his work at all comparable to hers.[22]

One might get up a good debate on the subject
of whether Nick or Miriam has the more vulgar or
objectionable mother, but Lady Agnes would win
my vote, for Mrs. Rooth is at least amusing, and
gauche and "tacky" though she may be, she has
more heart (here again James shows his clear-sight-
edness with regard to the upper classes). Lady
Agnes is ignorant, selfish, and materialistic, and an
author does not often give a character a better
chance to damn herself than James gives her. She
tries to create the impression that by refusing to give
her what she wants Nick has destroyed her, but her
creator interpolates, "I hasten to add, [she] was not
destroyed." Her devotion to politics and the memory of her dead husband is no doubt sincere so far
as her understanding can reach, but what primarily
interests her is the benefits she and her family can
gain from Nick's denying himself everything life
could mean to him; perhaps her insensitivity ap-

pears most nakedly in her attempt to hang on to Broadwood, which Julia had given her and her daughters as a residence, even when she believed that the engagement to Nick had been broken off.

Mr. Carteret, who could not see the pencil and the brush as "the weapons of a gentleman," is quite as pigheaded, but he is too innocent to know any better, "singularly pure," as Nick perceives, and "a part of what was cleanest and sanest and dullest in humanity." As a character presented so briefly, he is singularly vivid; as one cast in so unsympathetic a role, he is surprisingly winning. Julia Dallow is a more complicated matter. A political woman, she cannot even distinguish between the connoisseurship of her late husband and Nick's creativity, and she thinks of an artist's studio as if it were "a private gambling-house or something worse," a place where women are "lolling" about, "all their things half off." Yet although I cheerfully admit that I should be willing to walk a great distance to avoid meeting her, she is not despicable. It is interesting that James once planned to have her try to bribe Nick with a direct offer of her fortune but gave this up, and his presentation of her in the crucial Chapter 15 is not unsympathetic. Julia is very generous, and she is capable of deep and sincere love. It must be admitted too that she deserves some sympathy for the humiliation Nick puts her through before really making up his mind that he is committed to her.

The problem faced by her brother, Peter Sherringham, resembles Nick's but with significant differences. Unlike Nick, Peter has no talent, and with him choice of vocation presents no difficulties; he is on his way up in the diplomatic service and completely satisfied there. But nonprofessionally he is a devotee of the theater, and in this aspect he becomes Miriam's friend and patron, the nourisher of her talent, and in her first phase, the one who understands her best. The joker in Peter's deck is that he does not understand himself. He had supposed that "the beauty of a love of the theatre was precisely in its being a passion exercised on the easiest terms," and he had not counted on the possibility of falling in love with the girl and still finding it impossible to give himself up to the artistic life even at one remove. "Mr. Sherringham, poor man," says Miriam, "must be very uncomfortable, for one side of him is in a perpetual row with the other side. He's trying to serve God and Mammon, and I don't know how God will come off." So he comes to her on the threshold of a great career and on the very night she has made the fullest revelation of her genius thus far with a proposition as selfish, and even more outrageously unreasonable, than that with which Basil Ransom confronts Verena Tarrant at the Music Hall, that she should relinquish what now seems her reasonably assured success to devote herself to his, which is still hypothetical. Miriam is neither ungrateful to him nor personally unresponsive: "Ah, why ain't we simple?" she had cried on an earlier occasion. "Why ain't we of the people—*comme tout le monde*—just a man and a girl liking each other?" But she is now a determined young woman in sure possession of a legitimate gift and unswervingly dedicated to its development who understands him as well as herself, and the manner in which they thresh the matter out between them at the end of Book Seven ought, one feels, to satisfy the most insatiable devotee of Renaissance-Reformation disputations.

The most teasing, most amorphous character in *The Tragic Muse* is Gabriel Nash. "Poor Nash," says Miriam, "isn't worth talking about." Many critics have managed it, however, and he has been interpreted from the most diametrically opposed viewpoints; depending on what you read, you can see him as the purest of idealists, the most consummately selfish of hedonists, or nothing at all.[23]

Nick does not know where Nash came from nor where he lives and is not even sure that he did not invent him and launch him as "a deadly hoax." Nash himself will not even admit that he lives in the nineteenth century nor more in London than in Samarkand. Neither youth nor age has any meaning for him; "indestructible, immortal," he looks forward to "no collapse, no transition, no clumsy adjustment of attitude." He eschews all "doing," and although he once wrote a novel, he now repudiates it. As he sees it, it makes no difference whether Nick is successful; the only thing that matters is that he should be "disinterested and independent" and take the world "in the free brave personal way." He ignores everything except beautiful, pleasant things, wishing to save as many happy moments of consciousness as possible from the dark gulf, but he does not wish to be called an aesthete, for he seeks to repudiate all formulas and generalizations, trying merely to "feel" everything and to make it his métier to "be" and his art to "live"; evidently he fails to realize that these too are formulas and generalizations.

Not only cannot Nash paint, he cannot even be painted. When at last he disappears, Nick wonders "if he hadn't at last, balancing always on the stretched tight-rope of his wit, fallen over on the wrong side," and after he is gone, his portrait, as far as Nick had got with it, fades out, so that the painter's final thought, quite in the spirit of *The Tempest*, is that he has "melted back into the elements" and become "part of the great air of the world." In other words, Nash, like many of Hawthorne's people, trembles on the verge of allegory, and for a character functioning in a predominantly realistic novel, he is managed with remarkable skill. It was eminently suitable that, like Hilda in *The Marble Faun*, and like Miss M., who, at the close of Walter de la Mare's great novel *Memoirs of a Midget* is "called away," he should just disappear at the end, even though his personality is not in the least like that of either of the others.

As the extreme opposite of the Philistines by whom Nick Dormer is surrounded, Nash obviously has his spiritual as well as aesthetic value, but it is ridiculous to suggest that he represents James's ideal. It is all the more interesting, in view of the character's own resistance to any attempt to nail him down, that critics should have suggested so many originals for him. There seems no doubt that the basic inspiration came from one Herbert Pratt, but the notion that Nash represents Henry James, Sr., or the novelist himself, who was as ardent and canny a practicing artist as Miriam, is quite preposterous. It was inevitable, however, that the "greenery-yallery" aesthetic movement of the period and such outstanding representatives of it as Walter Pater, Oscar Wilde, James McNeill Whistler, and John La Farge should be involved in the discussion. Nash does talk a little like Wilde, but neither his physique nor his personality are at all Wildean, and Pelham Edgar may well have been right in seeing him as "less a person than a point of view, a sublimation of all the influences and impulses that went to the shaping" of the aesthetic movement.[24]

The great triumph of the book, however, is inevitably Miriam Rooth. Critics have never rated *The Tragic Muse* as highly as it deserves, and she as its heroine has inevitably suffered in consequence.

Setting aside the more fantastic and obviously wrongheaded interpretations,[25] it has been objected that she is common and unfailingly histrionic, that her intelligence and sensibility in other areas do not match her powers as an actress (James believed that the histrionic gift stood largely apart from other endowments), and that once having arrived, she manifests a capacity for both dominating her associates and manipulating the press. Since James was writing a realistic novel and not a saint's legend, there is some basis for all this; only one wonders what sort of moral, spiritual, and intellectual prodigies the critics are and what kind of women they have the privilege of associating with that they can allow these things so to outweigh her superb courage, perseverance, and devotion. If she is so good an actress that she strikes Peter as having no character but rather a hundred different characters and consequently none of her own, we might do well to remember that the same has been said of Shakespeare as a writer. A critic must either understand the dramatic temperament or fail to understand it, and if he falls into the second category, he is helpless when confronting such a character as Miriam Rooth. Actually, Peter and Nick are the divided personalities in this novel; it is Miriam whose powers are centered and directed toward a clearly defined goal. It may be worth recalling that James himself, the only artist in a somewhat neurotic family, was, except for his mother, unquestionably the sanest and most "normal" member of it.

It is a convincing testimonial to Miriam's having been made for her art that she should have known all this before being able to present convincing evidence of her gift to anybody else. She is so bad at her first audition with Madame Carré that we are embarrassed for her, but she is so desperately

in earnest and so pathetically close to the end of her
nervous resources that our embarrassment is not far
from tears. When Carré, who, as she later admits,
has for once in her life misjudged an aspirant, tries
to let her down easily, she says, "You think me actually pretty bad, don't you?" Her persistence wears
down the old woman's unwillingness to accept her
as a pupil; she is ready to do anything and accept
any abuse in order to learn. Everything she encounters becomes grist to her aesthetic mill, and it
takes her some time to learn how to separate art from
life, if indeed she ever really does achieve this. But
she never wavers in her choice or her devotion.
"The only managing I know anything about is to do
my work. If I manage that decently I shall pull
through." And when her mother asks her whether
"our work" may not be of many sorts, she replies,
"I only know one."

Surely those who think her vulgar have insuf-
ficiently considered her relationship to the theater.
When she is obliged to appear in trash, she knows
it for trash and therefore remains uncontaminated
by it. As Basil Dashwood puts it of her second vehicle, "She had to take what she could get—she
wasn't a person to cry for the moon." That is what
being an artist means: to accept the material at your
disposal and force it into the service of your ideal.
Miriam recognizes the limitations of the people she
must associate with in the theater also and allows
frankly for the low estimate of actors entertained by
"society" people; only she has no illusions about
*them* either. Moreover, she recognizes the limitations of the dramatic art itself, including the dis-
honor involved in its shameless and helpless bid for
applause and immediate recognition; never for one
moment does she see it as the highest of the arts.
But it is *her* art, and she gives herself to it. She might

have cried with de Musset: *"Mon verre est petite, mais je bois dans mon verre!"*

Miriam never thinks of herself more highly than she ought to think; she knows what she has accomplished, but she also knows how far she has to go. "I'm not so very good yet. I'm only in the right direction." And much later: "I may fizzle out and . . . my little success of to-day is perhaps a mere flash in the pan. . . . It isn't to my possible glories I cling; it's simply to my idea, even if it's destined to betray me and sink me." She is sure she ought to have had "five quiet years of hard all-round work in a perfect company, with a manager more perfect still, playing five hundred things and never being heard of at all," and she does not expect ever to make up for this loss. But her confidence and her humility, as both artist and woman, are always kept within reasonable balance. "You must think me ravenously selfish—perpetually chattering about my vulgar shop. What will you have when one's a vulgar shop-girl?" But "I'm not so taken up with myself, in the low greedy sense, as you think. I'm not such a base creature. I'm capable of gratitude. I'm capable of affection." And again, "I'm not a bad sort—really I'm not." Probably this self-praise *is* vulgar, but every word she says is true.

Her fantastic mother adores her, and understands her not at all. Like the girl, she has lived for Miriam's success as an actress, yet she could see her give it all up for a brilliant marriage without a pang. Miriam is completely aware of all this, but her treatment of Mrs. Rooth cannot be faulted at any point. Anybody, she thinks, "would be kind to her mother who knew what a dear she was. 'She doesn't know when anything's right or wrong, but she's a perfect saint.'" She understands Peter, too, as she proves both by anticipating his reaction to her Juliet and consequently trying vainly to prevent him from coming to see it and by the great scene afterward in which she refuses him. She understands Nick and, even more significantly, understands how he feels about Julia, and why Julia, who understands nothing that matters to people like Miriam, loathes and despises her. She understands it so well indeed that she has no time or energy left to resent it.

Most novels about actresses and singers devote themselves largely to what the artist does off the stage; it is the special virtue of James's portrait of Miriam Rooth that he communicates to the readers the nature of her art. He himself thought her rise to fame too sudden, feeling that he ought to have built more bridges between the raw, terrified girl at whose first audition with Madame Carré the reader assists or the "tragic muse who was strident and pert" ranting at Peter's for the mere society people of whom she was not terrified at all and the "light and bright and direct" girl ("direct without being stiff and bright without being garish") who makes her debut in London. It is true that we have not witnessed all the steps in the process of transformation; unfortunately, James could not escort his readers to one of Miriam's performances nor present them with a recording of the voice whose beauty was obviously intended to suggest Bernhardt's. Nevertheless, he has notably succeeded in suggesting her quality, and nobody who has ever responded to an exciting performance by a fascinating young actress can read what he writes about Miriam without a thrill: "She was beauty, melody, truth; she was passion and persuasion and tenderness." She "had such tones of nature, such concealments of art, such effusions of life, that the whole scene glowed with the colour she communicated, and the house, pervaded with rosy fire, glowed back at the scene."

Her performance was "a thing alive, with a power to change, to grow, to develop, to beget new forms of the same life." There was an "almost aggressive bravery" in the way it could "so triumphantly, so exquisitely render life." Beauty was "the principle of everything she did and of the way she unerringly did it—an exquisite harmony of life and motion and attitude and tone." It "connected itself with universal values," transported one "from the vulgar hour and the ugly fact," served as "a corrective to the depression, the humiliation, the bewilderment of life." And because "there was beneficence in such beauty," she commanded "a gratified, a charmed subjection" from her auditors, and "people snatched their eyes from the stage an instant to look at each other, all eager to hand on the torch" she had passed to them over the footlights. She "brightened up the world for a great many people ... brought the ideal nearer to them and held it fast for an hour with its feet on earth and its great wings trembling." Surely Henry Seidel Canby must be pardoned for any possible exaggeration in his statement that *The Tragic Muse* contains "certainly the most complete and penetrating study of acting in English fiction, perhaps in the English language,"[26] and certainly no other writer has surpassed James in indicating the nature of the service a great actress can render in our troubled lives.

The last brief novel which falls within the period of this chapter does not call for extended consideration. In his preface to the volume of the New York Edition which contains it, James speaks of *The Reverberator* as a *"jeu d'esprit,"* an "exemplary anecdote," and a "little rounded drama," after which he proceeds to devote to its discussion a quite extraordinary amount—what he himself calls a "perhaps too vertiginous explanatory flight" and "roundabout approach"—of his very densest prose. *The Reverberator* was serialized in *Macmillan's Magazine* between February and July 1888, and Macmillan published the book in both England and America that same year.[27]

James recorded the basic idea for the story in his notebook in November 1887, an incident he had heard about a "scribbling, publishing, indiscreet, newspaperized American girl" who had written an inconceivable letter to the New York *World*, babbling personalities about the Venetian aristocrats whose hospitality she had enjoyed. Having imagined the girl "engaged to a young Italian or Frenchman of seductive 'position,' and pretty and *dotée*," he had his essential story, but, as he wrote it, the female scribbler survives only in the name of George Flack's assistant, Florence Topping, whom the reader never meets. Flack, a discarded suitor of Francie Dosson's, with whom she is still on friendly terms, is the correspondent of a cheap American scandal sheet, *The Reverberator*, and it is to him that Francie foolishly confides by word of mouth what she knows about the stiff-necked family she expects to enter.

Because he did not believe that he knew French aristocrats well enough to write about them (he was no longer satisfied with what he had done with the Bellegardes in *The American*), James made the Proberts transplanted Carolinians, married into the haut monde, Legitimist, more French than the French themselves, and more Catholic than the Pope.[28] The narrative spares neither the snobbery of the Proberts nor the gaucherie of the Dossons. Because the author was ignorant of and indifferent toward all aspects of American business, Mr. Dosson became a dear soul who had accumulated a fortune almost without knowing how it had come about, and all that need be said about Francie's older sister, Delia, is that "elegance indeed had not been her natural portion." Francie's lover, Gaston, was made the younger Probert son (his older brother had died for France in 1870), apparently to make more credible in him a simplicity which should almost equal the girl's own, and the length to which he goes to enlist the good offices of the most reasonable of his sisters, Susan, in order to persuade the family to accept the proposed match is fantastic and unintentionally comic. "Gaston," says another sister, "must never, never be allowed to forget what we've done for him," and even Susan speaks of the "charming primitive instincts" of the Dossons; "we must work those!" The artist Waterlow, at whose studio Gaston first encounters Francie and who was made an impressionist to enable James to bring in references to the aesthetic controversies of the time, is a winning figure who may have been studied from Edwin Austin Abbey, and Flack is the archetypal journalist; "for the convenience of society" in identifying him, "he ought always to have worn something conspicuous — a green hat or a yellow necktie."[29]

Francie's gaffe is prepared for from the beginning; she is sure that sooner or later she will do something the Proberts will not like, but although this alerts the reader, it does not seem to put her on guard. The larger part of the narrative is taken up with Gaston's winning his family over and other preliminaries. Francie does not talk to Flack until Chapter 10 out of fourteen; this is followed by an interval; then, in Chapter 11, the storm breaks. Gaston is in America on a business trip for his father and his prospective father-in-law, an absence which serves the management of the plot but lacks verisimilitude. But Francie herself is the great weakness in the story. In his preface, James classes her with Daisy Miller and others as a typical American figure in the Europe of her time, but although she is apparently much prettier than Daisy, she lacks her helpless charm. Both her creator and his critics have, generally speaking, let her down pretty lightly. She babbled "innocently," we are told; "stupidly" would be a better word. (Incidentally, it is hardly credible that she should have been so familiar with all the secrets of the Proberts on so short an acquaintance.) About the only virtue she displays afterward is honesty; she does not try to deny her fault, but neither does she show any real repentance. She still thinks the vulgar *Reverberator* "a very fine paper," and her inability to understand how the Proberts feel is hardly the mark of a fine-grained or sensitive person. Like the heroine of the Hugo von Hofmannsthal–Richard Strauss opera *Arabella*, but with far less justification, she tells her lover, "You must take me as I am," and even after he has done so, she gives no indication of having really understood what the decision to break with his family has cost him. It is no wonder that while he is still in the process of making up his mind, he should tell her, "You act as if you were doing something for a wager, and you make it worse by your talk."

Although there is no question that her fastidious creator is on Francie's side, the ending is not merely one more fictional expression of the triumph of love's young dream. Gaston has achieved more than being true to his love; as Waterlow helps him to perceive, he has seized the occasion offered by even a bad or doubtful cause to stop wavering and learn to stand on his own feet, making his own decision and behaving like a mature human being, not the

Proberts's little boy. This alone, however, is not enough to save *The Reverberator* from being nothing more than a trifle gracefully executed but hardly worthy of the talent of the greatest of American novelists at this advanced stage in his career.

# 7

# Transition: *The Other House;*
# *The Spoils of Poynton; What*
# *Maisie Knew; The Awkward*
# *Age; The Sacred Fount*

The scenic or dramatic quality of James's later novels first manifested itself strikingly in those considered in this chapter, which represent the beginning of his commitment to his famous, much excoriated, much adored "later manner." Of these *The Other House* is much the least significant and successful; since this work is sui generis in James's oeuvre and the only novel in which he deals with violent crime, it may be well to have its outline before us at the outset.[1]

Julia Bream's childhood had been made a horror by a demonic stepmother. Dying after the birth of her first child, apparently for no reason except that she had gotten it into her head that she must die, she makes her husband swear solemnly that he will not remarry during the lifetime of their daughter. After four years have passed, Tony Bream, a banker and an amiable though imperceptive man, finds himself in love with the completely desirable and suitable Jean Martle, while his wife's old friend Rose Armiger is madly in love with him. The action passes in and between Tony's house, Bounds, and the house across the stream, Eastmead, where Tony's partner, Paul Beever, lives with his clever, not unkindly, but distinctly managing mother. Which is the "other" house depends on where the action is taking place at the time; the gardens and the area between the two houses take on a sinister quality from what happens there. The title James originally contemplated, "The Promise," was much more meaningful, but the editor, Clement Shorter, did not like it, and James seems to have settled on *The Other House* after hearing a mother ask her daughter where she had been and being told that she was at "the other house."

Knowing that Tony will never break the vow he made at his wife's deathbed and well aware that he cares more for Jean than he does for her, Rose drowns Effie Bream in the stream between the two houses on the child's fourth birthday, having first taken care to manage the matter so that Jean will be suspected of the crime.

The child is lost,[2] but all the other aspects of Rose's plan go to pieces. First, Tony accuses himself of the crime to protect Jean; then Rose's own guilt is uncovered. Through the cooperation of Dr. Ramage, the murder is covered up and Rose is sent away ("her doom will be to live") in the care of Dennis Vidal, the suitor with whom she has played a cat-and-mouse game throughout the novel and who, though he now loathes her, is still willing to do anything for her except marry her.

The principal technical reason for the comparative failure of *The Other House* is that the novel, largely in dialogue, reads like the "novelized" version of a play. We have it also in its dramatic form, which seems better in the sense that it is more natural to the material as James develops it,[3] but the difference between the two versions is minimized by James's tremendously detailed stage directions. The dialogue is often more brilliant than lifelike, and the subtlety and closeness of the analysis presented would impose a tremendous strain on the attention of an audience.

James recorded the origin of his idea for *The Other House* in his notebook on December 26, 1893, making no mention of any source, but Edel is certainly correct in calling it an Ibsen play and connecting it with James's interest in Ibsen during this period (especially *Hedda Gabler*, *The Master Builder*, and *Rosmersholm*) and his friendship with the Ibsen actress Elizabeth Robins. Because they find some elements in *The Other House* unaccounted for by the Ibsen influence (in the notebook sketch, Rose was to attempt to poison the child), Daniel Lerner and Oscar Cargill have argued further dependence upon the *Medea* of Euripides, about which the only thing that can be said is that although this is not impossible or even very improbable, the case has not been proved.[4]

There seems to be some difference of opinion as to how far beyond a scenario what James submitted to the manager who considered *The Other House* as a play may have gone. He certainly must have been Edward Compton, who had produced *The American*, and Rose may well have been designed for Elizabeth Robins. What is certain is that when Clement Shorter asked for a serial for *The Illustrated London News*, James made whatever he had on hand into a novel, thinking it sufficiently "thrilling" to please the *News* audience, which, however, it did not notably achieve. It ran from July 4 to September 26, 1896; in October Heinemann published the book in London and Macmillan in New York. Later, in 1908–1909, James turned out the dramatic version we now have in Edel's *Com-*

*plete Plays of Henry James*, but there was no production. No earlier manuscript is extant.

The problem in *The Other House* was how to
make credible the brutal murder of a four-year-old
child by a well-bred young lady, and I for one do
not believe that James achieves it. There is some
Ibsen-like self-analysis at the end, where Rose says,
"It was all that I saw—it was all that was left me.
It took hold of me, it possessed me; it was the last
gleam of a chance." Again: "It has nothing to do now
with any part of me—any other possibility of what
may be worst in me. It's a storm that's past, it's a
debt that's paid. I may literally be better." But this
is not enough, and it comes too late. We have seen
Rose scheming carefully to carry out her plan and
cover her tracks, but we have not been made conscious of any inner struggle. Perhaps we just have
not been made well enough acquainted with her.
Consequently, she is not "one of us," as Conrad
would say; we cannot be moved by her fall or consider the possibility of her redemption. Tony's attempt to protect Jean may be the supreme example
of the quixotism of which Jamesian characters are
sometimes capable, but Rose's plea that Dennis
should take her as she is is only a sinister, not a
moving, echo of what we have heard from Francie
Dosson in *The Reverberator*. As for her escaping
overt punishment at the end, the legally minded are
quite correct in maintaining that this makes all the
other characters *particeps criminis*, but it is quite
in consonance with James's art and the pattern of
his mind. He did not take vengeance on his villains,
nor did he try to play either God or devil. In his
world the best and the worst that can happen to a
human being is to be compelled to live with himself.

Leo B. Levy has rightly remarked that the "scenic succession" in *The Spoils of Poynton* "escapes

the promptbook style" of *The Other House*. James
first thought of the divisions of the action in *Poynton*
in terms of a three-act play, and in Chapters 14 and
15, in which Mrs. Brigstock walks in upon Fleda
and Owen at Fleda's father's London flat, he uses
the small biscuit on the carpet and other properties
quite as a dramatist might have used them. Laurence Bedwell Holland had a valid point when he
compared Mrs. Brigstock's intrusion here with that
of the elder Duval upon his son's mistress in *Cam-
ille*, and James himself gives the cue by having
Fleda ask the visitor whether she had come to her
"as if I were one of those bad women in a play."
But for all its masterly use of scene, nobody has ever
thought of *Poynton* except in novelistic terms.[5]

Yet the author always thought of his book as
"the poor little long thing." Horace E. Scudder
wanted a story of ten thousand words for the *Atlantic*, but it grew, first to thirty thousand, and then to
seventy thousand, which the complaisant editor
printed in seven installments between April and
October 1896. Heinemann published the book in
England and Houghton, Mifflin in America; both
first editions were dated 1897. The *Atlantic* serial
title was "The Old Things," which was as colorless
as *The Other House*, but this may trouble us less if
we remember that the novel was once in danger of
being called "The House Beautiful." Similarly,
those who find Fleda Vetch an unattractive name
may take comfort in the fact that the heroine was
originally intended to be known as Muriel Veetch.[6]

Oscar Cargill has suggested Guy de Maupassant's "En Famille" as a possible literary source,
and Adeline R. Tintner has directed attention to Balzac.[7] James himself, in his preface, gives no clue to
anything more than an oral source, in the form of a
dinner-table anecdote about "a good lady in the

north, always well looked on, [who] was at daggers
drawn with her only son, ever hitherto exemplary,
over the ownership of the valuable furniture of a
fine old house just accruing to the young man by
his father's death." From James's notebooks we
learn that he heard the story on December 23, 1893,
not on Christmas Eve, as he says in the preface, and
that the real-life situation involved nastiness of
which he made no use, for litigation ensued, and
the mother attempted to save her possessions by
branding her son a bastard and therefore not her
husband's legal heir.[8]

The basic difficulty was what James saw as the
barbarous British custom of passing on property intact to the eldest son and banishing the mother to
the dower house. In *The Spoils of Poynton* the injustice is compounded both by Mrs. Gereth's being
a fantastically gifted collector of fine furniture and
objets d'art which she has practically made her life
and the son's engagement to a girl who knows and
cares nothing for such things but will yield no jot
of what she regards as her right of possession. Mrs.
Gereth meanwhile has virtually adopted Fleda
Vetch, a girl of humble background but fine taste
who shares her attitude toward her treasures. To
complicate the situation, Fleda falls in love with
Owen Gereth and he, increasingly as Mona Brigstock's mulishness makes life difficult for him, with
her, but Fleda's sense of honor is such that she will
not be a party to his breaking his engagement. At
one point, Mrs. Gereth illegally removes the treasures from Poynton to the dower house at Ricks, and
Mona refuses to go through with the wedding until
they have been returned. By this time mother and
son are not speaking to each other, and Fleda has
become their liaison man.

Having learned that Fleda and Owen love each

other, Mrs. Gereth impulsively returns the "spoils" to Poynton, thinking that this will force Fleda's hand and put her on her honor to accept Owen. It turns out to be a miscalculation, for as soon as the things have been returned, Mona grabs him. Later Owen writes to Fleda, begging her to go to Poynton while he and his wife are traveling abroad and choose some object from the collection (he suggests the Maltese cross[9] which his mother regards as the prize treasure) as a memento of him. Fleda complies, only to find that the house with all its treasures had burned to the ground the night before her arrival.

So much nonsense has been written about *The Spoils of Poynton* during recent years that Kenneth Graham has been left wondering "whether Swift's Grand Academy of Lagado may not have had a section devoted to James studies." If this seems odd in view of the fact that between the New York preface and the notebooks, where *Poynton* gets more space than any other novel, James has spelled out his intentions very precisely, we must cease to wonder at it once we have taken the full measure of the warped creativity of one type of contemporary critic. "This interpretation of the book," writes Patrick F. Quinn of his own essay, "is not one that James would have endorsed." But this does not trouble him, for "the novel we read is not the novel James thought he wrote," and this is "so much the better" since *Poynton* is "a greater achievement than its author realized." Perhaps, as Harriet Beecher Stowe, in an off moment, remarked of *Uncle Tom's Cabin*, God wrote it, or perhaps Mr. Quinn rewrote it, yet his is not the worst of the masterpieces to which his school adheres. Nina Baym too thinks that James "wrote a better novel than he planned." Robert C. McLean does not believe that Owen loved Fleda or she him but that her aim was merely to capture the spoils. Stephen Reid thinks that she was in love with Mrs. Gereth, everything else being mere "rationalization" on her part, and Dennis J. Schneider's study leaves one gasping in astonishment that such venomous passion for denigration can have been inspired by a character of fiction.[10]

Moreover, it is not only Fleda who has been misinterpreted with fantastic ingenuity and perversity. James did not have what he himself called Balzac's "mighty passion for things" and for "material objects, furniture, upholstery, bricks and mortar." He knew that there was a difference between a sales catalogue and a novel. Consequently, he did not describe either Poynton or its contents in detail, thus leaving the way open for some critical craniums to conjecture that probably the spoils were not so fine, after all, since if Mrs. Gereth and her late husband had been true connoisseurs, surely some of their good taste must have rubbed off on their son! This line of approach can even rise to the demented heights of suggesting that Fleda's taste may well have been identical with that of her father, who collected brandy bottles, ashtrays, and pen wipers, and that the only person in the book who really appreciates the spoils is Mona! It would be just about as reasonable to argue that because in *The Ambassadors* James never identifies the article upon which the fortune of the Newsomes was based, they were probably not industrialists at all but instead kept a peanut stand and that because Homer never described Helen's beauty directly, she must have been ugly, but, as Schiller says, *"Mit der Dummheit kämpfen Götter selbst vergebens."* We *know* that James greatly admired the things he had Alvin Langdon Coburn photograph as the spoils of Poynton for the New York Edition, and this alone would sufficiently refute views not worthy of consideration.

In *The Destructive Element* Stephen Spender displays an animism worthy of primitive man when he declares that the "spoils" themselves were evil. Like "things" in general, they have of course no character, either good or evil (it is not money but the love of money that the Bible calls the root of evil). Their function is catalystic, and they nourish or destroy, save or damn, depending on how they are used. To Mrs. Gereth they are beauty and sentiment ("they're living things to me; they know me; they return the touch of my hand"). To Owen they are "furniture," and the way he says it makes Fleda think of "wash-stands and copious bedding." To Mona they are literally spoils (they are "all right," and "they go with the house"); should she accept Owen without them, she would feel that he had won her under false pretenses. Only Fleda sees them rightly; unlike Mrs. Gereth, she cannot enjoy them when they have been stolen away from Poynton and crowded into Ricks; their loveliness has been dishonored by such high-handedness. It is interesting that although she is an amateur painter, Fleda has never been able to paint at Poynton but only to achieve a "Buddhistic contemplation" and that the much less splendid effects Mrs. Gereth later achieves with much humbler materials at Ricks speak to her more directly and with a warmer homeliness.

The fire at the end of *Poynton* has been criticized as melodramatic, but it is marvelously done atmospherically; if there is anywhere an excuse for attributing feeling and will to the spoils, it is here, for it almost seems, on a deeper than rational level, as if rather than pass into Mona's possession, they preferred to die. But it is not necessary to go that far, for James makes it clear that although the wretched woman moved heaven and earth to possess herself of them, she had no interest in living with them once they were hers. Instead, she preferred to drag her husband off to wander over the earth, leaving Poynton in charge of careless servants; had Owen been living there with Fleda, surely they would have had a very different sort of care. The end of the novel indeed strikes a strongly Platonic note. The physical "spoils" are gone, but their ideal beauty lives on in Fleda's mind, where alone, in the course of the novel, they have ever had the life they deserve.

James designed Fleda as the sensitive "free spirit" of the book, "a hungry girl whose sensibility was almost as great as her opportunities to nourish it had been small. The museums had done something for her, but nature had done more." Compared to her, the others are "fools," useful to the author only as they bring her out, but she has one great strategic weakness. As Mrs. Gereth perceives, she is "intelligent," not "able," and no good for action. When she bumps into a force like Mona Brigstock, who is all will with no sensitiveness whatever, she is doomed to worldly and material defeat.

The Brigstocks themselves are the book's most extreme "fools," and James gets good fun out of describing them and their dreadful house, Waterbath, in almost Dickensian terms. The house "might have passed if they had only let it alone" and not plastered it over with gimcrack ornamentation and "acres of varnish, something advertised and smelly, with which everything was smeared; it was Fleda Vetch's conviction that the application of it, by their own hands and hilariously shoving each other, was the amusement of the Brigstocks on rainy days."

Mrs. Gereth may be a trifle severe in seeing Mrs. Brigstock as "really somehow no sort of person at all," with "a face of which it was impossible to say anything but that it was pink, and a mind it would be possible to describe only had one been able to think of it in a similar fashion," but there can be no question as to the attitude we are expected to take up toward "the awful Mona." Except for her big feet, which she plants determinedly and then in effect pulls the other way whenever anybody wishes her to do anything and which she admires in their patent-leather boots, kicking them forward a little and gazing at them as she marches unseeingly through the gardens at Poynton, she is apparently physically handsome, but her notion of courtship seems to be horseplay and "romping."

Mrs. Gereth's "extraordinary genius" was for making things "compose," and her attitude toward her treasures was never vulgar or grasping. In caring for them she was "faithful to a trust and loyal to an idea." She could give them up to Fleda without a pang; it is the idea of turning them over to the tender mercies of a Mona Brigstock that she cannot endure, and the care Mona takes of them shows how right she was.

Unhappily, however, Mrs. Gereth's moral development has not kept pace with her aestheticism; worse still, she has perverted aestheticism itself by permitting it to deprive her of her humanity. Not intelligent but only clever, she is a "false" character, "the very reverse of a free spirit," who flounders "in the dusk of a proportionate passion." Her furniture means more to her than does her son, for she "had really no perception of anybody's nature" and "no imagination of anybody's life save on the side she bumped against." That is why the "mind's eye" can see her "only in her thick, coloured air; it took all the light of her treasures to make her concrete and distinct." We never learn how she reacted to the news of the fire in the last chapter, but we may be sure that she was able to save much less of her treasures from it than did Fleda. Probably the best she was able to do was to rejoice that Mona no longer possessed what she herself had worked so hard for.[11]

Finally, for all her aestheticism, Mrs. Gereth is coarse as well as cold. In her reception of the Brigstocks when Owen brings them to see Poynton, culminating in her hilarious tossing of the cheap woman's magazine that Mrs. Brigstock had thoughtfully presented to her (the athletic Mona catches it on the fly), she sinks to their level, and when she offers Fleda to Owen before the girl's face, she disappears below it. She would not have shrunk from a public confrontation with her son, and she envies her unchaste, ugly French friend, Madame de Jaunes, because she does not have to suffer under the unjust English law; perhaps this is a survival of the mother's self-alleged unchastity in the original anecdote James heard. She chuckles over the success of her stratagem in moving the spoils out of Poynton without detection. When she offers Fleda to Owen, she treats the girl as if she were a thing; when she virtually advises Fleda to put herself in Owen's way, she becomes bawdy in her Justice Shallow-like recollection of the errors of her own youth; and when the news of Owen's marriage comes, she is sure that Mona too has "let herself go."

And Owen? Is he too one of James's fools? He certainly makes a fool's marriage, but there is no evil in him. Fleda's first impression is that he is stupid, and there can be no question that he is what Matthew Arnold called a barbarian. His room, crowded with guns and whips, tobacco pots and bootjacks, is

the only ugly thing at Poynton, and in the country
"Owen shooting is Owen lost." But James has taken
pains to prevent these things from making it seem
impossible that Fleda could care for him, and it is
a testimonial to the writer's own breadth of sympathy that he should have been able to do this. Despite his weakness and intellectual shortcomings,
Owen is a far more kindly and thoughtful person
than his mother, as he proves by the consideration
he frequently shows her when the lines are drawn
between them.

Isabel Archer thought that she could supply Osmond with the financial means he needed, and
Fleda, at the outset, hoped to place her own cleverness at Owen's disposal. She never ceases to love
him because she knows he needs her, but there can
be no question that she needs him also, that she
loves him intensely and admires and trusts him. "I
love him so that I'd die for him — I love him so that
it's horrible." And again, "I'd trust him to the last
breath."[12]

But it is never her aim to keep him dependent
upon her. She will not use him as his mother tried
to use her; neither will she make his decisions for
him. "Her problem was to help him to live as a
gentleman and carry through what he had undertaken; her problem was to reinstate him in his
rights." Leo B. Marx has well pointed out that while
in the notebook entries she urges him to wed Mona
without delay, in the novel "she simply insists that
Owen take the responsibility for his pledges." "The
great thing is to keep faith. Where's a man if he
doesn't?" If Fleda could not enjoy stolen goods, neither could she live with a man she had stolen from
another woman or build her life on the grave of another's happiness, and if Owen does not now believe that he ever "really" loved Mona, how can she

think that he "really" loves her or will continue to do so? Yet when he bluntly asks her, "Do you mean to tell me that I must marry a woman I hate?" she replies, "No. Anything's better than that." In her heart she hopes that Mona will cut the Gordian knot and release them both, and this might well have happened if the clever Mrs. Gereth had not allowed the stupid Mrs. Brigstock to maneuver her into out-smarting and outintriguing herself.

For Fleda is the confidante of both Owen and Mrs. Gereth and thus is forced inevitably into an untenable position. Her supermoral critics are very hard on her because she does not always tell Mrs. Gereth the full truth about Owen nor Owen the full truth about Mrs. Gereth. What they overlook is that she could not have done this without betraying the trust of one or the other or both and that when she lies, if that is the word to use, she lies not for her own profit or advantage but to disadvantage herself and benefit others. Mrs. Gereth is not deceived for long, and if Fleda needs justification for withhold-ing the full truth from her, Mrs. Gereth herself sup-plies it by doing what she does as soon as she finds out how Fleda feels.

Fleda has been called an ethical absolutist, but she is not that when she finally yields to Mrs. Ger-eth, opts for the best possible, and too late sends the telegram which Owen, now safely captured by Mona, never receives: "I send this to Waterbath, on the possibility of your being there, to ask you to come to me."[13] The truth is that Fleda finds herself in a position where, no matter what she does, some-body is going to be hurt. She tries to arrange matters so that nobody shall be hurt except herself, and it is the irony of the situation that along with herself, she sacrifices both Owen and his mother, to say nothing of the spoils. The only person she really succeeds in protecting is Mona, who, heaven knows, needs no protection and who is left at the end enjoying the triumph of the insensitive, if, that is, the insensitive can ever really enjoy or suffer anything.

The three novels which remain to be considered in the period covered by this chapter register increasing complexity and difficulty. The style is more figurative, more mannered than in James's earlier books, but oddly enough, it is at the same time more colloquial and concrete. Dialogue is stylized, and there is more "scene." Frequently the reader finds himself inside the mind of a character who must develop his perceptions as he proceeds, and if he is to read with enjoyment, he must be prepared to share in the process.

Compared to the three great monuments of James's "later manner"—*The Ambassadors, The Wings of the Dove,* and *The Golden Bowl* —*What Maisie Knew* is still a "short" novel (361 pages of the New York Edition against *Poynton's* 264), but although it was written not long after its predecessor, it is considerably more "advanced." It is also more difficult. Thus while there is no excuse whatever for the eccentric readings of *Poynton* with which we have been blessed of late, it is only fair to say that James must bear some share of responsibility for the less extensive mauling to which *Maisie* has been subjected, for he has left in shadow a number of matters about which he might, without injury to his story or his method, have been more explicit. As with *Hamlet,* so with *Maisie*; one may find a sentence somewhere to bolster almost any misreading, however obtuse, and James is without Shakespeare's excuse that we have three texts of his play but no authorized text.

The book opens with the divorce of Maisie's parents, Beale and Ida Farange, when the child is six. By court order, each is required to give her a home for six months of the year. They use her at first as "a ready vessel of bitterness, a deep little porcelain cup in which bitterness could be mixed" to send to each other, next increasingly to evade their responsibilities, and at last to avoid them altogether. Beale makes Miss Overman, whom Ida had employed as governess, first his mistress and then his wife, while Ida marries Sir Claude (we never learn his last name nor Miss Overman's first). Neither marriage endures, and life, for Maisie's parents, becomes a matter of one pickup after another. Sir Claude and Miss Overman (now always called Mrs. Beale) are drawn together through their interest in Maisie, who loves them both, and themselves become lovers. At the end of the book Maisie is obliged to choose between staying with her quaint old governess, Mrs. Wix, or going to live with them, but she refuses to give up Mrs. Wix unless Sir Claude will also give up his lover, which he refuses to do.

Like *Poynton*, *Maisie* originated in a dinner-table anecdote, which James recorded in his notebook on November 12, 1892, but he did not settle on centering the story in the child's mind until December 22, 1895. On September 22, 1896, he recorded having written the first four chapters. The story was serialized in Chicago in *The Chap Book*, where it ran from Jaunary 1 to May 1, 1897, and in London in *The New Review*, February through September. The editor of the *Review*, William Ernest Henley, hated it and cut it considerably, and it was the cut version that Heinemann published between covers in England in September 1897. In October, Herbert S. Stone & Company, the remarkable avant-garde publishers of *The Chap Book*, brought out the book in Chicago as James had written it.[14]

"The hideous Colin Campbell divorce case" apparently helped disillusion James about the decency of English society, but only very general literary influences upon *Maisie* can be cited. If, as has been suggested, Dickens was important, it was only in the sense that after he had written about children, nobody else would be able to do it without thinking of him. Paul Bourget's *Odile* begins with a similar situation but develops it differently, and James would seem to have had his idea before he could have read *Odile*. He was certainly interested in Edmond de Goncourt's *Chérie*, but this could only have shown him how not to do it, for he thought it "failed deplorably . . . in tracing the development of the moral consciousness of a child."[15]

In *What Maisie Knew* James attempted to paint a picture of a corrupt society as seen by a child and at the same time to trace the child's own development toward spiritual maturity. His original idea was to limit his presentation to what Maisie "might be conceived to have *understood*," but he soon realized that she was too young for that; consequently, although his "*line*" remained her "dim, sweet, sacred, wondering, clinging perception,"[16] he included also what she *saw* without understanding and employed a variety of devices to supplement and interpret her perceptions. Although there are still a few glaring instances of old-fashioned direct authorial comment ("Oh, decidedly I shall never get you to believe the number of things she saw and the number of secrets she discovered!"), such passages stand in the sharpest possible contrast to his highly sophisticated employment of "suppressed scenes and indirect discourse" to achieve "variety in his handling of scenes."[17]

One asks oneself whether all the relationships portrayed in this novel, all the minute reactions of the characters, and all their kaleidoscopic regroupings are convincing. Personally I do not believe they are, but I am not sure the question is relevant. James admits in his preface that it was in the interest of symmetry that he had *both* Maisie's parents remarry. We are, I think, never made to feel what it was in Ida that attracted so many lovers nor how she could have enthralled such decent men as Sir Claude and the unnamed Captain, and it is equally hard to believe that both she and Sir Claude and Beale and Miss Overman should begin to be estranged from each other almost as soon as they are married. If we must have literary analogues for the kind of pattern James seems to be working out, let them be sought not in the realistic novel but in Restoration comedy or French classical tragedy or, better still, in the formations and figurations of classical ballet.[18]

The attempts which F. R. Leavis and others have made to interpret *Maisie* as essentially comic[19] are hopelessly one-sided; a book which eventuates in spiritual victory for the heroine and spiritual failure for almost everybody else can amuse neither God nor the devil. Nevertheless, the author has made abundant use of subordinate comic devices, sometimes embracing broad caricature; surely it was not for nothing that Mrs. Wix should have reminded Mrs. Beale of Mrs. Micawber: "she will never, never, never desert Miss Farange." Aside from one of Ida's lovers, Mr. Perriam, whom we glimpse only in passing, the most daring caricature is that of the "brown" countess[20] whom Beale has descended to living upon at the end and who "literally struck [Maisie] more as an animal than as a 'real' lady; she might have been a clever frizzled poodle in a frill or a dreadful human monkey in a spangled petticoat. She had a nose that was far too

big and eyes that were far too small and a moustache
that was, well, not so happy a feature as Sir
Claude's." But caricature appears also in the description of Maisie's parents. "Beale Farange had
natural decorations, a kind of costume in his vast
fair beard, burnished like a gold breastplate, and in
the eternal glitter of the teeth that his long moustache had been trained not to hide and that give him
in every possible situation, the look of the joy of
life." As for Ida, she has "huge painted eyes," like
"Japanese lanterns swung under festal arches," a
"barely perceptible" mouth, and an exceptionally
long arm which has contributed notably to her one
talent, billiard playing.[21] The lower the bosom of
her dress is cut, the more sure you can be that she
is wanted somewhere. As Muriel Shine observes,
she pervades the novel as "more of an ominous presence . . . than a fully rendered character," for we
never see her except "either intensely irritable or
uncontrolledly angry."[22] Chapter 19 is about as appalling an example of nonphysical child abuse, in-
volving both Ida and Beale, as can be found in literature, and when, in Chapter 21, Ida attempts, for
her own purposes, for once to play the loving
mother, the attempt breaks down when she flies into
a rage upon Maisie's innocently mentioning one of
her lost lovers, the Captain, whereupon she rejects
the child as "a dreadful dismal deplorable little
thing." Actually it did not matter much, for Ida's rare
affection is as violent as her displeasure; when she
clasps Maisie to her bosom, the child feels "amid a
wilderness of trinkets . . . as if she had suddenly
been thrust, with a smash of glass, into a jeweller's
shop-front."

Maisie's governess, Mrs. Wix, is, however, in
this novel, James's greatest grotesque. The girl's
first impression of her was "frightening" and "ter-

rible," but soon "something in her voice" touched the child "in a spot that had never yet been reached." James uses every device Dickens would have used in describing Mrs. Wix except one; he does not invent a distinctive speech for her. She is too elaborately rendered to make it possible to quote all the relevant material, but mention must surely be made of her greasy gray hair, originally yellow, arranged in "a glossy braid, like a large diadem, on the top of her head, and behind, at the nape of her neck, [in] a dingy rosette like a large button," the spectacles she calls her "straighteners," and her "little ugly snuff-colored dress trimmed with satin bands in the form of scallops and glazed with antiquity"; the overall effect is that of the "polished shell or corslet of a horrid beetle." Mrs. Wix has her limitations as both an intellectual and a moral guide, but when the chips are down, she stands with the sheep, not the goats; it is all the more interesting, then, that James should not have refused to see the comic side of either her much-vaunted "moral sense" or her devotion to the memory of her daughter, Clara Matilda, who had been killed in traffic and for whom Maisie must in a measure act as surrogate.

There is no grotesquerie, however, in James's presentation of Maisie's second set of "parents." Miss Overman, later Mrs. Beale, is beautiful and as charming as a woman can be without virtue. Maisie loves her, and she returns the child's love, but it is not in her nature to make a sacrifice for either a person or an ideal. That her moral sensitivity is less than that of her lover is made clear at the end, where it is he, not she, who understands why it would be outrageous to attempt to make Maisie a third party in their ménage. Yet in a sense this makes the man the guiltier of the two; simply because he sees more clearly, he becomes immoral in a situation in which she is merely amoral. For all his kindness to Maisie and his affection for her, his weaknesses are indicated early in the narrative; in Chapter 10 Maisie had seen the situation "as if she must somehow take care of him," and at the end she makes the decision that he lacked the strength to make. If Mrs. Wix is a bit melodramatic in seeing him as "the slave of his passions," it is still both odd and suggestive that a man so dependent on women as he is should be so much afraid of them. He is afraid of Ida, he is afraid of Mrs. Beale, and he would be afraid even of Maisie if she were a little older. When the curtain falls, we have assisted at the moral downfall—or the failure to rise—of an amiable man of good qualities whom we know and like. And it is all very sad.

But what, then, *did* Maisie know? James plays a cat-and-mouse game with the idea, comparable to that of Henry Adams with education. And this not only makes for the difficulty of the book but determines its method. From first to last, the pages of the novel are studded with passages reflecting childish innocence. When Maisie returns to Beale's establishment from Ida's and finds Miss Overman there, she asks, "Did papa like you just the same when I was gone?" and when she is told that a lady can't stay with a gentleman without some proper reason, she asks what reason *is* proper. When Mrs. Beale speaks of Sir Claude being so "awfully delicate" about what they do, Maisie thinks that her "we" indicates Mrs. Beale and herself, and when she learns that the reference is rather to Sir Claude and Mrs. Beale, she cries, "But you don't do any harm— you don't." When she hears that her mother is abroad with two companions, she supposes them maids. When Mrs. Wix tells her that the countess "pays" Beale, she asks whether Mrs. Wix does not get paid too, and when Mrs. Beale tells her that Ida

has in effect "sold" her to Sir Claude, she is so delighted to be in charge of one she loves that she
cries, "Why that's lovely of her!"

On the other hand, she sometimes shows an insight and even prescience that reveals her as being
in unconscious possession of a wisdom as old as the
everlasting hills. The most touching example is in
the great, powerfully underplayed scene in Chapter
17 in which she has her only encounter with the
Captain, who seems to have been the most decent
and deluded of her mother's many lovers. Having
learned that he thinks Ida an angel and likes her
better than any other woman, Maisie begs him not
to love her "only for just a little," like "all the
others," but to "do it always." This wonderful hit
seems to have killed two birds with one stone, for
when Maisie innocently mentions the Captain to
Ida in Chapter 21 and Ida must make an effort to
recall him as "the biggest cad in London," the
reader understands that the girl has done both his
and her mother's business for them. It must have
been hard to top this, yet James accomplishes it. The
child's immediate reaction is a flare of anger, which
is at once succeeded by "a fear, a pain, a vision ominous, precocious, of what it might mean for her
mother's fate to have forfeited such a loyalty as that.
There was literally an instant in which Maisie fully
saw—saw madness and desolation, and ruin and
darkness and death."

No wonder that Maisie could cry "Oh, I know
more than you think!" and that having been "condemned to know more and more," she must go on
until she knew "most" on the way to knowing
"everything" or that Mrs. Wix should, on the very
last page, still have "room for wonder at what Maisie
knew." "She knew as well in short that a person
could be compromised as that a person could be

slapped with a hairbrush or left alone in the dark."
"There's nothing she hasn't heard," says Mrs.
Beale. "But it doesn't matter—it hasn't spoiled her."
But James carefully explains that "small children
have many more perceptions than they have terms
to translate them" so that actually Maisie did not
know what she knew. "Everything had something
behind it: life was like a long, long corridor with
rows of closed doors." She saw "much more than
she at first understood, but she also even at first
[understood] much more than any little girl . . . had
perhaps ever understood before." "Taken into the
confidence of passions on which she fixed just the
stare she might have had for images bounding across
the wall in the slide of a magic-lantern," she was
"introduced to life with a liberality in which the
selfishness of others found its account, and there
was nothing to avert the sacrifice to the modesty of
her youth." Consequently, she was left with "a collection of images and echoes" in her mind "to which
meanings were attachable—images and echoes kept
for her in the childish dusk, the closet, the high
drawers, like games she wasn't yet big enough to
play."

*What Maisie Knew* ends when Sir Claude asks
Maisie whether she would give up Mrs. Wix to live
with him and Mrs. Beale. Being afraid of herself,
she first asks time to consider and then declares that
she will not go with him unless he gives up Mrs.
Beale. Harris W. Wilson advanced the idea that
Maisie was here offering her virginity to Sir Claude,
but he seems to have been swallowed whole hog
only by Oscar Cargill, although, to my way of thinking, both Edward Wasiolek and John A. McCloskey
make far too many concessions to him.[23] If the corruptionists are right, James obviously did not know
what he was doing, for although when Mrs. Wix asks

the girl whether she has not been jealous of Mrs. Beale, she admits that she has been without having realized it before, James also tells us that she had "embraced the implication of a kind of natural divergence between lovers and little girls." In his notebook he recorded that Maisie offered herself to Sir Claude "as a rescue from the temptation, the impropriety of Mrs. Beale," and as late as the preface he commits himself to the proposition that her role in the book was that of "keeping the torch of virtue alive in an air tending infinitely to smother it" and "drawing some stray fragrance of an ideal across the scene of selfishness."[24]

If the illicit nature of the tie between Sir Claude and Mrs. Beale has created the problem Maisie faces at the end, it must be understood both that she is not yet fully aware of all the implications of this and that her judgments, unlike those of Mrs. Wix, do not rest upon a strictly legalistic basis. By this time her "moral sense" has developed beyond that of her preceptress, whom she now needs only for mothering. James says that at last she knew what she wanted; I should say rather that she knows what she *needs*.[25] There is more intuition than reason in her judgments, and being still a child, she could not be expected to explain them fully. But she *has* learned that people go together in twos, not threes, and (as her conversation with the Captain shows) that a dignifying and satisfactory relationship can exist only on a basis of permanency and fidelity. These qualities may be lacking, of course, in legalized as well as unlegalized relationships, as, notably, in those which Maisie has known thus far. She has already been disillusioned about Mrs. Beale, and she is in the process of being disillusioned about her erstwhile knight in shining armor, Sir Claude. In a sense, the proposition she places before him, is, whether she realizes it or not, part of a testing process. She has no desire to become part of a setup which would share the characteristics of those of which she has already seen far too much. As Sir Claude himself finally realizes, "it wouldn't do . . . we can't work her in. It's perfectly true—she's unique. We're not good enough—oh no!"[26]

*The Awkward Age* was written between September and December 1898 and serialized in *Harper's Weekly* between October 1, 1898, and January 7, 1899. Heinemann published the book in London in April 1899 and Harpers in New York in May. Although the magazine paid James $3,000 for it, it was successful neither as a serial nor as a book. The first English printing comprised two thousand copies, the American only one, and there were many unfavorable comments. Aside from William Dean Howells, who praised it warmly, its principal admirer seems to have been the author, and if James was ever complacent about his own work, it was about *The Awkward Age*. "The thing carries itself to my maturer and gratified sense," he wrote in the New York preface, "as with every symptom of soundness, an insolence of health and joy," and he thought the composition of the chapters leading up to and including the big scene at the end of Book VIII, "with all the pieces of the game on the table together and each unconfusedly and contributively placed . . . triumphantly scientific."

Like its two immediate predecessors, it was conceived as a short story, but this time the beginning was not an anecdote or a situation but merely an idea and what must strike us today as a trifling, snobbish, and hypocritical idea at that. What happens to the "good talk" in the fashionable drawing room when the adolescent daughter, having outgrown the nursery, begins to "sit downstairs" but being still unmarried, is not supposed to know what her elders are talking about? Must the good talk be so expurgated to avoid bringing what Mr. Podsnap called the blush to the cheek of the young person? If so, what becomes of the level of sophistication? And if not, what becomes of her innocence? In France the problem could not arise, for the girl would be in a convent school until she was married and so passed at a bound from knowing nothing to knowing everything, nor yet in America, where talk was never "good" in the sophisticated English fashion.[27]

Cargill invoked George Sand's *Valentine* and Marcel Prévost's *Lettres de femmes* and *Les Demi-vièrges* as possible influences on *The Awkward Age*, and it has also been suggested that James may have derived ideas from a series of magazine articles published in England in 1894. But whether or not he had a source, he did avow a model in the light, sophisticated, and (to some) shocking novels in dialogue by the French novelist who called herself Gyp (Sibylle Gabrielle Marie Antoinette Riquetti de Mirabeau, Countess de Martel de Janville) and her disciple Henri Lavedan. What he wanted was to do in English something like that.[28]

Nanda Brookenham, who is nearly nineteen, has grown up in a kind of noncreative Bloomsbury group of which her mother, always called "Mrs. Brook," is the shining light. Her father is a cipher, and her brother, Harold, is about as close to complete worthlessness as a human being can be. Since their means are insufficient to support the way of life they affect, the Brookenhams manage by "sponging" on their friends. Gustavus Vanderbank ("Van"), who has charm but little money, and "Mit-

chy," who is ugly but very wealthy, are the principal
ornaments of the circle. Mitchy loves Nanda, who,
in turn, is in love with Van.

Enter a wealthy bachelor, over fifty-five, Mr.
Longdon, a high-minded man, faithful to the standards of an earlier, cleaner age, who had vainly
loved Mrs. Brook's mother, Lady Julia, and before
that had been interested in Van's mother. He is
overcome by the uncanny physical resemblance between Nanda and Lady Julia as she had been in the
days of her youth, and Nanda is also much drawn
to him, but the contrast between Lady Julia's genteel reserve and Nanda's much freer modern manners presents him with a problem. Because of his
money, Mrs. Brook wants Mitchy for her daughter,
but since Nanda will have none of him, he pleases
her by marrying Little Aggie, the sheltered daughter
of the Duchess, a distant relative of the Brookenhams and the widow of a European. Knowing of
Nanda's love for Van, Mr. Longdon offers to endow
her so that that limp young man can afford to marry
her. But Van cannot make up his mind, and Mrs.
Brook would like to retain him among her hangers-
on. In the big scene at the end of Book VIII, she
goes to the length of humiliating her daughter in the
presence of practically all the other characters and
unmasking the corruption of the Brookenham circle
in the hope that Mr. Longdon may be sufficiently
shocked to take Nanda out of it by virtually adopting
her, which he does.[29]

*The Awkward Age* represents the height of
James's interest in "method," and his satisfaction in
it seems to have derived from the conviction that he
had so triumphantly brought it off. It is divided into
what Cargill calls "ten books or acts and thirty-eight
scenes" (James planned it all out almost mathematically), and there is no central reflective con-

sciousness. Instead each book is named for one of
the characters, intended to furnish what James calls
a "lamp" to illuminate the action. The author
boasted to Mrs. Humphry Ward that although he
went behind "right and left" in *The Princess Casamassima*, *The Bostonians*, and *The Tragic Muse*
and singly in *The American* and *Maisie*, he did this
"never at all (save for a false and limited *appearance*, here and there, of doing it a little)" here.[30]

James's austerity has not pleased all his readers.
Joseph Wiesenfarth, for example, finds the "rigor-
ous symmetry" of the book inorganic and prolix
rather than intense and accuses James of having ov-
erburdened the reader and wastefully expended
both time and space to achieve an objectivity not
worth what it costs (the book fills 545 pages in the
New York Edition as against *Maisie*'s 363). In his
fine study of *The Awkward Age*, Arnold E. Davidson
remarks that "an external narrator objectively views
the behavior of all characters" and that James "res-
olutely requires the reader to assess not only what
'events' might mean, but even what those 'events'
actually are." Yet James did realize that a novel like
Gyp's, wholly in dialogue, would not be accepted
in English, and he did furnish guidance of sorts,
although, as Walter Isle has observed, the portions
of the book that do not stand between quotation
marks do not give much more than a dramatist like
Shaw provides through stage directions or than
"ideal acting" might supply in performance. Characters are carefully described upon their first appearance, and their placement and shiftings of position on the stage are indicated, as well as the tone
of their speeches and the reactions of their companions. Sometimes they fail to understand each
other and ask for explanations, and sometimes, to
recur to Davidson, we are told what "an acute ob-

server" or "a suppositious spectator" might have noticed had he been present. Nevertheless, when two
speakers are in close harmony with each other, the
dialogue may well become "an allusive shorthand
broken only by longer analytical statements or sum-
maries by one or the other."[31]

Isle also finds the characters static and un-
changing, citing Nanda's statements about herself:
"I shall never change—I shall always be just the
same" and again, "What I am I must remain. I
haven't what is called a principle of growth," and
explaining this by reference to the narrow time span
of the book, only a little over a year, "so that there
is not the long period of growth and change observed in Maisie." I should wish to exempt at least
Mr. Longdon from this generalization; it is remarkable that the oldest person in the book should have
been the most successful of all its characters in ad-
justing himself to changed conditions; he begins
caring for Nanda because she resembles Lady Julia
and ends by accepting her for herself.

In the predecessor of this novel, James had tormented his readers with the riddle of what Maisie
*knew*. Here we are not so much concerned with
that (Nanda obviously knows everything) as with
whether she has been corrupted by what she knows
and her contacts with immoral people, and even
more with what must be the effect of all this upon
her eligibility as a *parti* in the marriage market.
Since nobody has ever suggested that she is either
dishonest or unchaste, this may well strike modern
readers as even more much ado about nothing than
the basic problem or situation with which James
began. The only thing Nanda is ever convicted of
in the course of the action comes when her mother
forces her to admit that she had read what was considered an indecent French novel, and since she did

that only to find out whether it was fit to be read by her friend Tishy Grendon, who certainly needed no protection from her, this act shows her up as rather naive than corrupted.[32]

If innocence is to be equated with ignorance, as some critics still seem surprisingly to assume, Nanda cannot be defended. But as she says, "Girls understand now. It has got to be faced," and she even asks, "Doesn't one become a sort of little drain-pipe with everything flowing through?" This is not the way she thinks it ought to be, however. She would like to be the way her grandmother was or like Little Aggie, who had been brought up in the old way by an aunt more corrupt than Mrs. Brook. Or, rather, like what Little Aggie seemed to be, since as soon as she is married to Mitchy, she kicks over the traces and becomes involved with her aunt's lover, probably the most degraded person in the book. James deliberately deglamourizes Nanda. She has "no features" unless she has "two or three too many," and it is a question whether she is pretty at all. She lacks not only her mother's grace but humor and brightness also; at one point Mrs. Brook calls her "as bleak as a chimney-top when the fire's out." But her loyalties are absolute; degradation in others does not repel her; neither does she resent slights that have been shown to herself. Nanda does not love sinners for their sins but because they need loving. Her plea to Van not to desert her mother because "she's so lovely" and "so fearfully young" is even more touching because she is more fully aware of what she is saying than Maisie in her plea to the Captain. She pleads for Aggie with Mitchy on the ground that she is only trying to find out what kind of person she is. "How can she ever have known? It was carefully, elaborately hidden from her." She even begs Mr. Longdon to see to it that

Van shall not lose financially by having turned down the endowment Mr. Longdon proposed to supply him with because he could not bring himself to take her along with the money! And it is quite clear that young as she is, she is going to be a mother to Mr. Longdon quite as much as he will be a father to her.[33]

Mitchy's marrying Little Aggie to please Nanda would be more at home in a book like *Wuthering Heights*, where Cathy marries Linton to help Heathcliff, than in the at least outwardly realistic *Awkward Age*, but although Mitchy is not so "pure" as Nanda, he does share her charity, and she puts her finger on their kinship when she says, "You're so good that nothing shocks you." Van is another story; for all his charm, his behavior at the end leaves room for nothing but contempt. Mrs. Brook had known from the beginning that he would "never come to the scratch," but his difficulty runs deeper than constitutional indecisiveness. Although he quite lacks Gilbert Osmond's capacity for deliberate cruelty, he is like him in his hopeless conventionality and his inability to distinguish between the real and the apparent, and Dorothea Krook may well be right when she suggests that he would not be capable of living with a woman whose judgment and sense of values were superior to his own. What he really likes is the old-fashioned girl, but it is his pride, not purity, that causes Nanda to repel him; he could not bear to mate with a girl coming out of her environment so precious a creature as himself.[34]

One of James's most surprising self-judgments is his special enthusiasm over Mrs. Brook, whom he told Henrietta Reubell he considered the best thing he had ever done, and some of the critics have been eager to outdo him on this score, comparing her to the great ladies of Restoration comedy and seeing her as an artist molding her environment into a work of art. It is true that Mrs. Brook is not the worst member of her circle; I agree that she is almost certainly not an adulteress (most of the adultery in this novel is committed by characters on the border of the circle); neither is she personally unsympathetic or cruel. But the higher one rates her potentialities, the deeper must be the condemnation she incurs for her useless life; indeed, as she herself perceives at one point, the fact that passion is absent even deprives her of an excuse she might otherwise have had. Surely those who have praised the intellectuality of her circle are easily impressed in this area. The only justification for such a judgment is that these people are all immensely preoccupied with analyzing each other's motives and reactions, often in disreputable situations. There is never the slightest suggestion that any of them ever had what could be called an idea in their lives or that they had ever manifested any interest in anything affecting the vital interest or general welfare of mankind. Mrs. Brook is greedy and morally indifferent (she even wants her daughter's life "to be as much as possible like my own") and her only real concern is to keep intact a circle of friends, if you can call them that, most of whom are even more useless than herself.

The basic idea for *The Sacred Fount*, suggested to James by Stopford Brooke and first recorded in his notebook on February 17, 1884, posited a marriage between a young man and older woman, after which she bloomed and he languished, growing progressively older and weaker as she grew younger, stronger, and prettier. James promptly considered combining this with the experience of a second pair of this time unmarried lovers, exhibiting a once dull man who has drained the wit from a clever woman, the transformation in both persons being the means through which the liaison comes to light. According to Edel, the author began his work in the spring of 1900 and sent the manuscript to his agent, apparently in early summer, describing it as "fanciful, fantastic—but very close and sustained, and calculated to minister to curiosity."[35] There was no serial publication, but Pinker sold book rights to Methuen in England and to Charles Scribner in New York; the American connection thus established outlasted James's lifetime. Both firms published in February 1901, and the nature of the book being what it was, the first printings were surprisingly large: 3,000 in America and 3,500 in England. James collected advances totaling $3,500.

The faithful Howells, who not only admired the novel but coyly announced that he had mastered its secret but would, for the time being, keep it to himself, was virtually alone in his admiration. Scribner's distinguished reader, W. C. Brownell, confessed that he could not follow the story and had found the effort "acutely exasperating," as if he were trying to make out illegible writing. He added that his spine curled up, his hair roots prickled, and he wanted "to get up and walk around the block." The book also made Bliss Perry feel "insufferably stupid" and wanting to swear, even though he read it on the Sabbath.[36] John Hay was "greatly troubled," and Henry Adams, to whom he communicated his agitation, wrote Elizabeth Cameron, whose relationship with Adams himself has been conjectured by some of James's more venturesome critics as possibly having been glanced at in the novel, acknowledging James's brilliance but concluding that he ought soon to take a vacation, along with Adams himself and many others, "in a cheery asylum."[37] Nor are the author's own few recorded comments much more admiring (since *The Sacred Fount* is the only novel written after *The Bostonians* excluded from the New York Edition, we have no preface). Touched by the Howellses' having read the book *en famille*, James conjectured that they must have found it "chaff in the mouth" and confided that he would have "chucked" it when he had written fifteen thousand words if he could have afforded to waste that much work and did not have a "superstitious terror" of leaving a tale unfinished, and in letters to the Duchess of Sutherland and Mrs. Humphry Ward he called his novel a "profitless labyrinth," "the merest of *jeux d'esprit*," "a small fantasticality," and "a consistent joke," although he also assured Mrs. Ward that "its own little law of composition" had been applied to it "constructively."[38]

There is no literary source so far as the story is concerned, but there are many literary echoes and allusions. The references to Tennyson ("The Palace of Art"), Poe ("The Raven"), *As You Like It*, and the Cinderella story are obvious. One critic has invoked *The Faerie Queene*, and any reader of Hawthorne must be aware that the basic idea of the tale would be congenial to him. The most rewarding studies in this area are those of James Reaney and William F. Hall.[39] Reaney not only cites echoes of Plato, Dante, Malory, and classical mythology but also relates the fable to "the legendary world of magic fountains and wells of life" and "those sagas where there are shape-changers and heroes and magic doubles." Seeking the source of the image which is the title (the passages in Isaiah, Ecclesiastes, and John which had previously been cited do not furnish very close parallels), Hall spreads a net wide enough to take in both "that which stands in mediaeval, Renaissance, and eighteenth-century

paintings, in the middle of the garden of secular love
. . . and derives ultimately from the religious em-
blem of the fountain of Paradise from which flowed
the four rivers of Eden" and the Great Elm Tree
and Fountain in the Crystal Palace erected for London's Great Exhibition of 1851; he even suggests
that James may well have been thinking of Cran-
ach's *Golden Age*, which could be echoed in Chapter 8, and that the mask in the painting described
in Chapter 4 may reflect contemporary interest in
the Japanese theater.[40]

*The Sacred Fount* resembles *The Awkward Age*
in being developed largely in terms of a series of
dialogues but differs from it in that these inter-
changes are both linked and interpreted by the unnamed narrator (it is the only novel by James, as
distinguished from many short stories, written in the
first person). This aids our understanding if we are
willing to be guided by him but increases our difficulty if, with his antagonist Mrs. Brissenden (generally called Mrs. Briss), we think or pretend to
think him crazy or, with some of the critics, envisage
James as a concocter of puzzles who entrusted his
readers only to guides who might lead them astray.
Although J. A. Ward goes entirely too far when he
tells us that we cannot even be sure whether the
narrator is a man or a woman, it is true that we receive no information that has not been filtered
through his consciousness; we have only his word
not only for what the others do but for much of what
they say, for he tells his story in retrospect and, as
he informs us, sometimes paraphrases.

The book opens on the afternoon the narrator,
Mrs. Briss, and Gilbert Long travel by train to the
house party at Newmarch, and it ends after midnight
on the following night. Since what intervenes is less
an action than what Walter Isle calls "the explora-

tion of a situation," the book is considerably more static than even *The Awkward Age*. The scene is a great country estate, where guests wander through splendid empty rooms, opening one into another, or grounds of surpassing loveliness, where couples "change, shift, or vanish as in a nightmare sequence"; no wonder Laurence Holland called it surrealistic.[41] Besides the narrator, the characters who count are Mrs. Briss; the youthful, now withered husband, at whose expense the narrator suspects her to have renewed her youth; Gilbert Young, the dull man supposedly brightened by the ravaged May Server; the painter Fred Obert, with whom the narrator compares notes up to a point; and the brassy Lady John, who was at first mistakenly conjectured to have been the source of Long's strength. The other guests are mere names at best, and some of them not even that. We are told that a host is present at the dinner, but we do not see him or hear his voice, and although everybody is well served, the servants are invisible to the reader; it is merely "implied that unseen powers waited on our good pleasure and sat up for us." Not even the surpassingly beautiful description of the Newmarch grounds in Chapter 8 involves the slightest relaxation of attention, for this surely is the only kind of half-real environment in which such a novel could be set.

There was a general shade in all the lower reaches—a fine clear dusk in garden and grove, a thin suffusion of twilight out of which the greater things, the high treetops and pinnacles, the long crests of motionless wood and chimnied roof, rose into golden air. The last calls of birds sounded extraordinarily loud; they were like the timed, serious splashes, in wide, still water, of divers not expecting to rise again. I scarce knew what odd consciousness I had of roaming at close of day in the grounds of some castle of enchantment. I had positively encountered nothing to compare with this since the days of fairy-tales and of the childish imagination of the impossible. *Then* I used to circle round enchanted castles, for then I moved in a world in which the strange "came true."

*The Sacred Fount* is generally regarded as James's most difficult novel, and even some of his admirers have called it unreadable. The only scholar who has written a book-length study of it dedicated the volume "For my dear husband Eric, who has steadfastly refused to read *The Sacred Fount*."[42] The difficulty has been much exaggerated, however. It arises not from the style, which is clear enough, but from the intense concentration demanded[43] and from James's insistence that readers interpret for themselves phenomena which admit of more than one interpretation instead of depending upon the author to do it for them. Consequently, the novel has been read as a vampire story (James did write such in "De Grey: A Romance," "Longstaff's Marriage," and "Osborne's Revenge"), a spiritual detective story, and a study of how fiction is created, this last sometimes running over into the absurd notion that the author is burlesquing himself. We may of course agree with Ora Segal as to the possibility of James's emphasis having shifted "from the 'nominal' protagonists to their observer, who becomes 'a usurping consciousness'" so that the book develops into what is essentially his "quest-story," but we had better not ignore Edward Sackville-West's warning that just "because it was in the characters' interest to obscure the issue as much as possible," we have no excuse for supposing that "James himself did not know what it was." As Dorothea Krook has remarked, *The Sacred Fount* is "not a parody but an analysis, an elucidation, an anatomy."[44]

If there is any one thing in the novel that is more obscure than everything else, it is the haunting, sinister picture of "The Man with the Mask" in Chapter 4:

The figure represented is a young man in black—a quaint, tight black dress, fashioned in years long past; with a pale, lean livid face and a stare, from eyes without eyebrows, like that of some whitened old-world clown. In his hand he holds an object that strikes the spectator at first simply as some obscure, some ambiguous work of art, but that on a second view becomes a representation of a human face, modeled and coloured, in wax, in enameled metal, in some substance not human. The object thus appears a complete mask, such as might have been fantastically fitted and worn.

This surely is an impressive use of symbolism which might well hold the key to the meaning of the book, but if so, neither the characters nor the critics have been able to turn the lock.[45] The people looking at the picture seem agreed at least that the man looks like "poor Briss" and the mask like May Server, but there is no agreement as to whether the man is life and the mask death, if that is what they mean, or vice versa; Mrs. Server takes the first view, and the narrator the second. In any case the scene has a strange and eerie power. It seems odd that the reader should be so much affected by something so opaque—unless indeed that is the very reason.

The unnamed narrator is by all means the most important character, and since we know about the others only through him, perhaps it is not surprising either that there should be such a wide range of opinion about him or that so many should have made a pretty good job out of judging themselves through attempting to judge him. The range is indeed extraordinary, stretching all the way from the notion of a sneaking, sniveling Paul Pry or voyeur,[46] through a deluded, pride-blinded fool attempting to play providence, or even, as Mrs. Briss, almost certainly insincerely, puts it at last, a lunatic, to an embodiment of the creative spirit of the artist.

Whatever else may be said of the narrator, he is certainly an unusually observant and sensitive man, introspective, comparatively lonely, with a burning desire to understand himself and those about him. "Most people, don't you see? don't in the least know what has happened to them, and don't care to know. That's one way, and I don't deny it may be practically the best. But if one does care to know, that's another way." He is well aware of his inclinations in this regard, and at times what he calls his "extraordinary interest" in his "fellow creatures" achieves an annoying naiveté: "I have more than most men. I've never really seen anyone with half so much." At present, convinced that Mrs. Briss has stolen her renewed youth and vitality from her languishing young-old husband, he is trying, if only in the interest of symmetry, to find the woman from whom Gilbert Long has acquired his wit.

The narrator is nowhere said to have been an author (which has not prevented some critics from calling him one). He does, however, use the materials which life brings him as an artist; in his mind he operates upon these materials and manipulates the people involved much as a novelist molds the materials of his fictions. "I was positively . . . proud of my work," he remarks at one point. "I had thought it all out, and to have thought it was, wonderfully, to have brought it. . . . It was exactly as if she [May Server] had been there by the operation of my intelligence, or even by that—in a happier way—of my feeling." He speaks of his private amusement, joy, triumph, elation, and even madness, but he seems rather more inclined to use painterly and scientific rather than literary terminology. "I only talk as you paint," he tells Fred Obert. He also invokes working hypotheses, collateral evidence, postulates, and demonstrations, and his search for the facts he needs to support or invalidate his theories is conducted along lines that any scientist should be able to understand.[47]

In view of the intense antagonism he awakens in some readers, I am surprised that nobody seems to have compared him to Iago, the supreme example in literature of the amoral manipulator who develops his plot with living beings rather than imagined characters. "Pleasure and action," he cries, as Othello and Desdemona sink deeper into his toils, "make the hours seem short." But although the narrator knows how easy it is to be carried away by a hypothesis—and look the other way when a damaging fact approaches—he is fully aware that theory is one thing and demonstration another. "Things in the real," he says, "had a way of not balancing; it was all an affair, this fine symmetry, of artificial proportion." He anticipates everything his worst enemies have said about him as he tries to distinguish between "psychologic evidence," which he regards as legitimate because the unexamined life is not worth living and because without it we can understand neither ourselves nor our fellows, and the methods of "the detective and the keyhole," spying out the secrets of the human heart without sympathy and thus committing what both Hawthorne and James regarded as the unpardonable sin. Since he knows that he is a human being, subject to human fallacy, he realizes also that he does not always succeed in keeping his distinctions clear. So he alerts himself against "reading into mere human things an interest so much deeper than mere human things were in general prepared to supply." No one, he thought, had really any business to know what he knew. He even admits to himself that his sense of his "superior vision may perfectly have gone a little to my head."

If such passages play into the hands of those critics who seek to convict the narrator out of his own mouth, they also weaken their case. Those who speak of his hubris have not sufficiently noted that his self-exaltation is very nicely balanced by his self-doubt. In his final encounter with Mrs. Briss, he even gives her opinion that he is crazy a calm, un-impassioned, almost amused consideration which would certainly be impossible for a man really in danger of mental unbalance, and those who see him as a vampire should remember that he comes out of his investigation quite as much drained as draining; when Mrs. Briss figuratively shouts him down, he feels about as old as her husband looks. All in all, his admissions of guilt and inadequacy serve about the same function as the self-exhortatory utterances of Hamlet, which the dramatist uses to remind the audience that he has not forgotten his task and not to indicate that he is a coward or "a man who could not make up his mind" or any of the other nonsense to which Romantic critics and their belated succes-sors have subjected us.

Although at one point the narrator feels suffi-ciently attached to his "precious pearl of an inquiry" to harden his heart against other considerations, he never actually does this. It is only after he is con-vinced that both May Server and "poor Briss" are beyond saving that he tries to comfort himself by guarding "to the last grain of gold, my precious sense of their loss, their disintegration and their doom," for he knows that sympathy and understand-ing have a value of their own even when they are borne down by the brash "tone" of the world so perfectly incarnated in Mrs. Briss. As soon as he is convinced that May is the woman Mrs. Briss has identified as Gilbert Long's abandoned lover, his desire to protect her replaces his passion for ferreting out the facts of the case, and as he continues to observe her misery, his sympathy for her increases until he has nearly fallen in love with her. Even such an enemy of the narrator as Mrs. Blackall does not deny this; indeed, if I read her rightly, she faults him, among other things, because he does not declare himself to May. Clearly, he is no Ethan Brand, for he never forgets his own vulnerability, and at the end he sympathizes almost as intensely with "poor Briss," whom he certainly does not fall in love with, as with May. "Fred Obert has since told me," he writes, "that when I came back to him," after witnessing Briss's final humiliation, "there were tears in my eyes."

Our attitude toward the narrator necessarily determines what we believe about his antagonist, Mrs. Briss, and our interpretation of the interview between them which fills the last three of the book's fourteen chapters. To me nothing is clearer than that Mrs. Briss is another of James's great evil women and that in this scene she is completely mendacious and insincere. She denies everything she had previously affirmed and affirms everything she had previously denied. She now describes Gilbert Long as the same "poor fool" he had always been, although she had remarked the change in him even before the narrator noticed it, and denies that May Server had ever had any connection with him; instead, she declares, May has been making love to "poor Briss"! Long's real connection was with Lady John, a view which both Mrs. Briss and the narrator had previously found untenable, and this she affirms in spite of the fact that if it is true that Long has not changed, no lady at all need be posited. Mrs. Briss begins the scene by denying that May is the woman in Long's life and does not proceed until later to deny that he has changed; thereafter she seems driven, as if in desperation, to one unsubstantiated assertion after another. She offers no evidence to support what she claims to have learned about May from her husband, but the whole tragedy of their relationship for him is suggested by her assertion that although he is "peculiar," he can still have value "if one uses him." Moreover, James's letter to Mrs. Ward states specifically that for Mrs. Briss the interview is "all an ironic *exposure* of her own false plausibility, of course," and he is about as sharp as he ever gets in denying Obert's statement that Mrs. Server is "all right" at the end; how, he asks, did Mrs. Ward ever get that idea into her head.

If the narrator is right in his hypothesis that May Server has been used as badly by Long as "poor Briss" has been used by his wife, that the two victims have now turned to each other for comfort while the two victimizers have embarked upon a fresh liaison with each other (which would be as neat a piece of Jamesian symmetry as anything in *What Maisie Knew*), and if Mrs. Briss now feels reasonably certain that the narrator is in the process of figuring all this out (he has certainly been giving her daring though ambiguous hints in this direction for some time), she has abundant reason for seeking the midnight interview with her antagonist, for her complete change of front when she encounters him, and for her bad manners toward him. Otherwise the whole situation is inexplicable.

But why, then, it may be asked, the contrived ambiguity of the ending? Why especially the last two sentences: "I *should* certainly never again, on the spot, quite hang together, even though it wasn't really that I hadn't three times her method. What I fatally lacked was her tone." This need not necessarily mean anything more than, as Ora Segal suggests, that "all the narrator admits is that he cannot match her brashness, insolence, and effrontery."[48] Joan of Arc, I suppose, lacked the "tone" of the tribunal that sent her to the stake, but that did not prove them right nor her wrong. We must face the fact that there are many circumstances under which the children of light cannot look for anything but defeat by the children of darkness, simply because there are weapons that the children of light cannot use without undoing themselves. As James Reaney has well observed. "The 'condition of light' doesn't need a confession or a vulgar triumph to reveal its splendors," and since the narrator has already limited himself to "psychological evidence," James could not very well end his story with a "material clue."[49]

# 8

# The Masterpieces, I: *The Ambassadors*

After *The Awkward Age* and *The Sacred Fount*, a contemporary admirer of Henry James might have been pardoned for wondering whether the author was not in some danger of falling under Santayana's condemnation: "Nothing is so poor and melancholy as art that is interested in itself and not in its object." To be sure, there is meaning in these books as well as method, but there is no denying that method looms large. If James was in danger, he beat a triumphant retreat in the three great novels with which he developed his art to its utmost capacity, for *The Ambassadors*, *The Wings of the Dove*, and *The Golden Bowl* take the reader to a high tableland flooded with light unmatched in kind in the whole terrain of American fiction. There is method here too, of course, but only a very dull reader could see it as all-embracing, which is not to say that none have been able to accomplish this.

*The Ambassadors* was written before *The Wings of the Dove*, between the autumn of 1900 and the late spring or early summer of 1901, but because the Harpers dragged their feet on the serial, it appeared later. They finally ran it in 1903 through the twelve numbers of *The North American Review* rather than in the more widely circulated *Harper's Monthly Magazine*, and it was the last novel James

ever got serialized anywhere. Methuen published
the book in England in September 1903 and Harper
& Brothers in New York in September.[1]

Probably no novel of comparable length and
complexity ever made do with a simpler fable than
*The Ambassadors*. Lewis Lambert Strether lives in
Woollett, Massachusetts (by which James meant to
indicate a city about the size of Worcester, Hartford,
or Providence), where he edits a green-covered review, subsidized by the town's leading citizen, Mrs.
Newsome, an intense, idealistic, straightlaced lady
who is expiating in good works the fortune built up,
by none too scrupulous means, by her late husband
in the manufacture of a domestic article with whose
identity James teases the reader without ever pin-
ning it down.[2] Strether, a widower of about fifty-
five, oppressed by the sense that he has accomplished little and has never really lived, goes to Europe to disentangle Mrs. Newsome's only son,
Chadwick, the heir to the business, from whatever
it may be that has caused him to linger in Paris far
longer than his mother thinks explicable on any
other hypothesis than that he has fallen into the
clutches of a worthless woman. It seems to be
understood, although it apparently has never been
spelled out, that if Strether succeeds in his mission,
he and Mrs. Newsome will be married.

Strether fails, yet ironically he succeeds too,
since at the end it is clear that the young man will
return, but although he is indeed involved with a
woman, Marie de Vionnet quite fails to conform to
Mrs. Newsome's and Strether's preconceived idea.
She is a French aristocrat, separated from her brute
of a husband under circumstances which, in her milieu, preclude the possibility of divorce; moreover
she deeply loves Chad and has, as it appears to
Strether, so improved him that in appearance and

demeanor he now bears little resemblance to the somewhat loutish youth whom Strether remembers. She has an exquisite young daughter, Jeanne, and until Strether learns that a marriage is being "arranged" for this girl in the aristocratic French fashion, he rather naively supposes that the daughter, not the mother, forms Chad's focus of interest, but even after he learns that this is not the case, he takes literally, in the only interpretation Woollett could tolerate, the assurance vouchsafed by Chad's friend, Little Bilham, that what exists is a "virtuous attachment." Indeed he does not really see the situation as it is until nearly the end of the novel, when, in an exquisite Renoir-like scene, he accidentally encounters the lovers in the country under conditions which make it inescapably clear that they are staying at the inn together.

Long before this, Mrs. Newsome, whose faith in her ambassador has been shaken by his delay and his unsatisfactory reports, has, in effect, replaced him with another embassy, comprising her daughter, Sarah Pocock, a massive lady, as straightlaced as her mother but quite lacking in her mother's grace, consideration, and intelligence; Sarah's husband, Jim, to whom Paris is the Moulin Rouge and the Folies Bergère; and Jim's sister, Mamie, whom Woollett considers the perfect bride for Chad. But even after Sarah has broken off with Strether, the latter refuses to jettison his hard-won understanding of the difference between true and false morality or reality and appearance. Now completely convinced that Madame de Vionnet is victim rather than victimizer, he tells Chad that he will be a brute if he leaves her. The last page of the novel finds Strether preparing to return home to give an account of his stewardship to Mrs. Newsome, live with his new insights, and accept his losses.

James's preface to *The Ambassadors* is one of his frankest pieces of self-evaluation; he judges the work as "quite the best, 'all round,' of all my productions" and records that he felt "no moment of subjective intermittence" during its composition, "never one of those alarms as for a suspected hollow beneath one's feet." For this novel, alone among his works, we are fortunate to possess a twenty-thousand-word scenario submitted in advance of serialization to the Harpers,[3] and a careful comparative study of scenario and finished work affords valuable insights into a great novel in the making.

It was not unusual for James to find the germ of a book in an anecdote orally communicated, but this time the germ was more moral than anecdote, for Strether's famous outbreak to Little Bilham in Gloriani's garden (Book Fifth, Chapter 2)—"Live all you can; it's a mistake not to," etc.—echoes Jonathan Sturges's report to James of what Howells had said to him in Whistler's garden.[4] Of the literary influences involved, those emanating from Balzac were probably the most important, although Richard Poirier found "interesting similarities" of plot with *La Dame aux Camélias* and also compared Strether to Hawthorne's Coverdale. That Strether's first two names come from Balzac's *Louis Lambert* is pointed out in the novel itself, and Adeline R. Tintner has brought both "Madame Firmiani" and "Une Fille d'Ève" into the consideration.[5]

Austin Warren invoked *The Tempest* in a search for precedents not only for *The Ambassadors* but for all James's late novels, and this idea was developed, not too convincingly, by Ronald Wallace, but the Shakespeare play that has attracted most attention in connection with *The Ambassadors* is *Antony and Cleopatra*. Richard Chase mentioned it without actually urging indebtedness, and Robert Garis brought it up again, but it remained for U. C. Knoep-flmacher to try to work out parallels between the two works in an article which seems to me a monument of wasted ingenuity.[6]

Writers and writings mentioned by James himself in the course of his narrative are Victor Hugo, Guy de Maupassant, *The Vicar of Wakefield*, "Kubla Khan," and *Pendennis*. Although Jonathan Sturges may have influenced Little Bilham, Cargill is certainly right in deriving his name from George du Maurier's *Trilby*. Cargill also suggests that Strether's hesitating between Jeanne de Vionnet and her mother as the focus of Chad's interest may have been suggested by Henry Esmond's relations with Beatrix and her mother. His attempt to establish Ibsen's *Rosmersholm* as a major source of *The Ambassadors* seems to me forced, however, and I might be more impressed by Edel's finding Mark Twain's personality in Waymarsh if he did not also find William James and Henry Adams. The chain-smoking Miss Barrace, with her everlasting "wonderful" and "Oh, oh, oh!", strikes me as a horror, but since James is said to have based her on Henrietta Reubell, whom he seems to have liked, he probably did not intend this reaction. Joyce's *Ulysses* was of course neither a source nor an influence, but Stephen Spender draws an interesting comparison between it and James's novel.[7]

*The Ambasadors* has been generally accepted as James's most extended and concentrated exercise in establishing and maintaining a "point of view," or, as he says in the preface, "employing but one centre and keeping it all within my hero's compass." But because he rejected the autobiographical method, declining to make Strether both "hero and historian" and scorning "the terrible *fluidity* of self-revelation," he established, as Albert Stone ex-

presses it, his perspective "outside of the protago-
nist's consciousness." Percy Lubbock, who, in the
early period of James criticism, was almost an "of-
ficial" interpreter, tells us that

all the other people in the book face toward [Strether],
and it is that aspect of them, and that only which is shown
to the reader; still more important, the beautiful picture
of Paris and spring-time, the stir and shimmer of life in
the Rue de Rivoli and the gardens of the Tuileries, is
Strether's picture, *his* vision, rendered as the time and
the place strike upon his sense.

We assist at no scenes in which Strether does
not participate, and we never see even Chad and
Marie together except when he is with them. Nobody has ever seriously faulted the beautifully symmetrical development of this novel, in which there
are no loose ends but everything is perfectly tied
together. "Ficelles," most importantly Miss Gostrey, serve the needs of exposition perfectly, and
such scenes as Strether's sighting of Madame de
Vionnet in Notre Dame and of her and Chad together on the river reveal their full meaning with
ease.[8]

In 1958, however, James E. Tilford, Jr., sharply
challenged both James and his early interpreters.
The author, he argues, was far from limiting himself
to what Strether alone sees, knows, and feels. "Our
friend" occurs more than sixty-five times, sometimes twice on a single page, and James also uses
"I" and "we." Sometimes he is "almost as affably
omniscient as Thackeray," and occasionally his "intimate chat with the reader almost makes us think
. . . that we have unwittingly strayed into George
Eliot." Thirteen years later, William B. Thomas, replying to Tilford, called these lapses "trivial and
inconsequential," directing attention to themselves

"only in the light of such minute and painstaking devotion to technical perfection as has become a fetish in the twentieth century. Both internal and external evidence," he concluded, "shows that James intends us to read *The Ambassadors* in its entirety as Strether's experience, *registered* by him, and relayed by him."[9]

Yet though Tilford may have overplayed his hand somewhat, his interpretation is not really either revolutionary or denigratory; he merely did a much more thorough job than his predecessors. Nor did Thomas overthrow his findings. Even Lubbock had admitted that in the "scenic dialogues . . . we seem to have edged away from Strether's consciousness. He sees and we see with him; but when he *talks* it is as though we were outside him and away from him altogether." When James determined to tell his story from Strether's point of view but write it in the third person, he made it possible for himself to introduce many equally convenient and subtle shifts which could not have appeared in a first-person narrative. Sometimes these shifts are made obviously, even naively, and sometimes very subtly. Probably the general reader is never more troubled by them than Shakespeare's audiences have been by the fact that he has two contradictory time schemes running through both *Othello* and *The Merchant of Venice*. There is no harm in admitting or even admiring such sleight of hand, but we should remember that it *is* sleight of hand and that, all in all, both Shakespeare and James have achieved their objectives.

John Little Bilham, Waymarsh, and Maria Gostrey are the important utility characters. Bilham, the artist manqué who gives Strether information and misinformation about Chad and his Parisian milieu, has affinities with Hyacinth Robinson of *The Prin-*

*cess Casamassima* and Gabriel Nash of *The Tragic Muse*, but Strether, who likes him much, does not give up hope of encouraging him to play a more active role in life, for he not only urges him to "live" but also to marry, first, Jeanne de Vionnet and, later, Mamie Pocock. Waymarsh, an old American friend of Strether's, who looks like Daniel Webster and is nicknamed Sitting Bull because of his portentous disappoval of everything European, especially the Catholic Church, suggests Henrietta Stackpole in *The Portrait of a Lady* and the Reverend Benjamin Babcock in *The American*, but he parts company with both when he turns sinister and betrays his friend. Although she would surely have grasped the situation without his help sooner or later, Waymarsh apparently notifies Mrs. Newsome of her ambassador's defection, and after the Pococks arrive he forms a close alliance with the terrible Sarah. Miss Gostrey, whom James described in his project as "clever, independent, humorous, shrewd, a little battered, a little hard, both highly unshockable and highly incorruptible, and many other things besides," is much more important, a remarkable example of a "ficelle" who develops a complex independent interest of her own. An American with a charming home in Paris, she is a kind of one-woman travel agency before the travel agency had been invented, who occupies herself by acting as a kind of courier, adviser, and confessor to her countrymen abroad. Far sharper and more worldly-wise than Strether, she is his confidante from the beginning of the book to the end, and many readers have been frankly disappointed in his failure to take up the closer relationship with her that she clearly desires at last.[10]

Of the Newsome–Pocock clan, Mrs. Newsome is incomparably the most substantial, She has "a large, full life," but she is also "delicate, sensitive, highstrung," perhaps not quite at ease in her enjoyment of the wealth her late husband accumulated, and the review Strether edits for her is her "tribute to the ideal." Although she never comes to Paris, James wanted her to be "no less intensely than circuitously present" through the whole action there, and no critic seems to have doubted that he succeeded. She looms across the Atlantic for the reader as she did for Strether, and though her looming may suggest that of "some particularly large iceberg in a cool northern sea," she is always treated with respect. Her son Chad is no authority on the nuances of human character, but he is surely right when he rates her as worth fifty of her daughter.

Sarah herself may best be vulgarly described as a "battle-axe," narrow-minded and essentially cruel in her judgment of everything she does not understand. Of her husband Jim Pocock enough has been said already. His sister Mamie is the surprise. Not only is she excessively pretty, she is also tolerant, generous, and, alone of her family, intelligent enough to know what is going on. Nevertheless, James seems to take pains to undercut her in comparison with Jeanne de Vionnet. Although he was an expert at inventing ugly names for his girls, he surely never did better along this line than "Mamie Pocock," and he deals her a cruel blow when he tells us that she will be fat at thirty. Nevertheless, if Chad should still fulfill the family hopes by marrying her after they have returned to Woollett, he will be getting better than he deserves.

Because Chad deserts Marie de Vionnet in the end (Strether is shocked when he denies being "tired" of her "almost as he might have spoken of being tired of roast mutton for dinner"), it has been urged that she did not do so very much for him after all and that Strether's finding him so wonderfully improved is only another example of the observer's naiveté. But Little Bilham sees the change too, although he suggests that Chad has become somewhat unnatural and that he was more attractive in his original, uncultivated state. The young man reveals his essential selfishness as early as Book Fourth (he does not enter until the end of the third), when he tells Strether that if he wanted to go home, no entanglement could hold him, and Miss Gostrey sizes him up correctly when she tells her friend, "He's not so good as you think!" The truth of the matter seems to be that although Marie has done her best, she has been so handicapped by the material she has had to work with that she has only been able to improve Chad as a "social animal," and his helping her find a husband for her daughter has been the supreme testimonial to his sophistication. Since we know with what contempt James regarded what is now known as "Madison Avenue," it is surely not without significance that one reason why Chad decides to go home and take his place in the family business when he does is that he has had a vision of the great potentialities of the new "science" of advertising!

Some critics feel that Strether is too tender toward Marie de Vionnet and not sufficiently so toward Mrs. Newsome. Thus Robert Marks says bluntly that Marie "had no claim on Chad, and the young man's total circumstance is such that to refuse to jettison her on grounds of morality is at best to do a little justice only in terms of a greater injustice."[11] But surely to have established intimate relations with another human being does involve a moral obligation, whatever the legal standing of the relationship involved. The best case one can make for Chad is to point out that he has suffered himself to be maneuvered into a position in which he can make no move without hurting somebody. Moreover, he is not an artist, and he has no talent. If he remains in Paris, there is nothing for him to do there except make love to Marie, and he simply does not care enough for her to count the world well lost for her sake; even if she does have touches of Cleopatra in her, he is no Antony. If he had stayed, the time would certainly have come when he would have been of no more use to her than to himself. He has had a fling in Paris, but at heart he is a true son of Woollett, and his final decision is as inevitable as Strether's own.

Probably no novelist ever pulled out all the stops wider to glorify a woman than James does to permit both Marie de Vionnet and her daughter to enthrall his readers. "Here is a woman," wrote Henry Seidel Canby of the mother, "who, if France were overrun with barbarians, might still explain the incomparable values of French culture—and yet as human and as emotionally imagined as James's American girls."[12] Marie makes her first appearance in Book Fifth, Chapter 2, and we see her in formal splendor in the third chapter of Book Sixth.

Her bare shoulders and arms were white and beautiful; the materials of her dress, a mixture, he supposed, of silk and crape, were of a silvery grey so artfully composed as to give an impression of warm splendour; and round her neck she wore a collar of large old emeralds, the green note of which was more dimly repeated, at other points of her apparel, in embroidery, in enamel, in satin, in substances and textures vaguely rich. Her head, extremely fair and exquisitely festal, was like a happy fancy, a notion of the antique, on an old precious medal, some silver coin of the Renaissance, while her slim lightness and brightness, her gaiety, her expression, her decision, contributed to an effect that might have been felt by a poet as half mythological and half conventional. He could have compared her to a goddess still partly engaged in a morning cloud, or to a sea-nymph waist-high in the summer surge. Above all she suggested to him the revelation that the *femme du monde*—in these finest developments of the type—was, like Cleopatra in the play, indeed various and multifold.

And Jeanne, surely, is the essence of all the loveliest *jeunes filles* of literature and of life:

She was fairly beautiful to him—a faint pastel in an oval frame; he thought of her already as of some lurking image in a long gallery, the portrait of a small old-time princess of whom nothing was known but that she died young. Little Jeanne wasn't, doubtless, to die young, but one couldn't, all the same, bear on her lightly enough. . . . She was fluttered, fairly fevered—to the point of a little glitter that came and went in her eyes and a pair of pink spots that stayed in her cheeks—with the great adventure of dining out and with the greater one still, possibly, of finding a gentleman whom she must think of as very, very old, a gentleman with eye-glasses, wrinkles, a long grizzled moustache. She spoke the prettiest English, our friend thought, that he had ever heard spoken, just as he had believed her a few minutes before to be speaking the prettiest French. . . . She trusted him, liked him, and it was to come back to him afterwards that she had told him things. She had dipped into the waiting medium at last and found neither surge nor chill—nothing but the small splash she could herself make in the pleasant warmth, nothing but the safety of dipping and dipping again.

No wonder even Miss Gostrey thought at first that it was Jeanne who had attracted Chad; after reading such a description of her, one cannot but wonder what was wrong with him that she did not.

Marie de Vionnet is ten years older than Chad, and Strether is at first disappointed to find her so charming and refined; if she were only "worse," he

could see his way more clearly! Although he is immensely taken with her, he has great difficulty in
making her out. Her marriage plans for her daughter, so foreign to American ways of doing, are a
shock, and since readers have no means of knowing
whether the young man chosen is as worthy of the
girl as her mother claims, they are in no better position to judge this act than Strether himself. With
her ability to speak "as if her art were all innocence"
and again "as if her innocence were all an art,"
Marie de Vionnet puzzles Strether no end, yet as
late as when he encounters her in Notre Dame, he
is innocent enough to ask himself why, unless her
relationship with Chad was innocent, she could
"haunt the churches."[13] After she has confronted
Sarah Pocock, who can ask Strether, "Do you consider her even an apology for a decent woman?"
both he and the reader are constrained to love Marie
for the enemies she has made, but it is not until the
end, when, now knowing that he knows the truth,
she asks him to come to see her and he finds her
spiritually naked, realizing that she has lost Chad
yet pathetically anxious not to lose Strether's respect as well, that he realizes the full depth of his
commitment to her.

She is soiled now, a sinner whose pitiful tribute
to decency was to try to deceive him about her sin.
She is also "visibly less exempt from the touch of
time" than he had seen her before, and although
she is still "the finest and subtlest creature" he has
ever seen, she has also become vulgar in the way
of common humanity, like "a maid servant crying
for her young man." "What I hate is myself," she
says, "when I think that one has to take so much, to
be happy, out of the lives of others, and that one
isn't happy even then. . . . The only safe thing is to
give. It's what plays you least false." And it was

because of her desolation, because of her need, in a sense even because of her vulgarity and her sin, that Strether now knew "he was serving her to the end." She had done more for him than for her lover. More than any other human being, she had brought him to spiritual maturity, not sloughing off his decency but moving definitely away from judgment and out of the seat of the scornful. At the end of the book, Lambert Strether is on his way to embrace the accomplishment with which John Buchan credited Scott, to gather "all things, however lowly and crooked and broken, within the love of God."

Stephen Spender thought Strether idealized Madame de Vionnet and Chad too, seeing both in the enlargement of vision Paris had brought him. However this may be, the lady and the city are so closely connected for him that they can hardly be disentangled. Surely there is no other novel more clearly pervaded by the feeling of a great city, and it is clear that James drew upon his own memories of Paris in evoking its spell. Henry van Dyke's lines certainly hold good for Strether:

> Oh, London is a man's town, there's power in the air;
> And Paris is a woman's town, with flowers in her hair.[14]

Yet James was fearful of using this setting at first, remembering that even if it is true that all good Americans go to Paris when they die, the pleasures they seek out when they go there in this life are often the reverse of heavenly. In *The Ambassadors* this type of American is represented by Jim Pocock, who sees even Marie in this light and is therefore as much attracted by her as his wife is repelled. As Robert Marks has said, Woollett knows but two levels of activity—"the strenuous upper and the abandoned lower"—while Paris has "a state of civili-

zation providing for the beauty and dignity of art."
Strether senses "a civilization intenser" there even
before he reaches the city and before he has learned
to discriminate between true and false art, taking
for "comparatively divine" the London theater that
the more sophisticated Miss Gostrey brands "impossible." The preparation for his conversion is
made very carefully, even in such a matter as Miss
Gostrey's gown being cut lower than any Mrs. Newsome would have worn at dinner or the red velvet
band around her throat, where Mrs. Newsome
would have worn a ruff, as if to mark the difference
between Mary Queen of Scots and Queen Elizabeth
I. Yet, although Madame de Vionnet is glorified by
being associated with classical and Renaissance art
and the splendor of the First Empire, yet, since neither Strether nor James can accept even Paris un-
critically, "the evil of the past" cannot all be left
out, and there is something "covertly tigerish" even
in Gloriani's garden and in the sculptor himself.[15]
The First Empire and what led up to it was encrusted with blood, whose remembered odor blends
subtly with more agreeable scents in Paris, and if
there are suggestions of Cleopatra about Marie, in
her desolation at the end she seems more like Madame Roland on the guillotine.

Strether's refusal to close with Miss Gostrey's
virtual offer of marriage and his determination to
return to America at the end of the novel and complete his mission by reporting to Mrs. Newsome has
caused some readers to associate him with the life-
denying John Marcher in "The Beast in the Jungle."
Yvor Winters speaks for these when he calls the act

a sacrifice of morality to appearance; there might, con-
ceivably, have been more Christian humility in considering the feelings of Maria Gostrey and in letting his reputation in Woollett go by the board. The moral choice,

here, appears to be of the same strained and unjustifiable type as that of Fleda Vetch, or as that of Isabel Archer.[16]

But the question is not what Yvor Winters would have done—or thought it right to do—nor yet what the reader would do nor even what Henry James would have done. The question is merely what the character James has created and presented to us would have done under the circumstances posited, and any sensible consideration of these matters must begin with a frank admission that may well make all other considerations irrelevant. Strether simply does not love Maria Gostrey. As James specifically explains in his project, her charm "gratifies some more distinctively disinterested aesthetic, intellectual, social, even, so to speak, historic sense in him." The project alone would not be conclusive, of course, but on this point the whole development of the novel bears it out. If at the end Strether loves anybody, it is Marie de Vionnet, but it can hardly need saying, even apart from all moral considerations, that for him, at this point, to take on Chad's leavings would be an offense against good form which neither he nor his creator could have been expected to countenance.

For E. M. Forster was wrong when he found in *The Ambassadors* an hourglass pattern in which Chad and Strether exchange positions, like Thaïs and Paphnutius (called Athanaël in Massenet's opera) or Madame Cavallini and the Reverend Thomas Armstrong in Edward Sheldon's *Romance*. Strether does not work his way out of the Woollett straightjacket only to have himself fitted with an elegant new Parisian model. Having learned that there is more than one set of standards in the world and more than one kind of human being, he casts off provincialism and intolerance and learns how to rest his weight on his own backbone. From now on his allegiance will be to his own standards, held tentatively and pragmatically and tested in the fires of experience. As Sallie Sears says, the book "has for its framework not one but two . . . codes in radical opposition, neither of which in the final analysis completely triumphs or is completely defeated," and Richard Poirier sees its hero as "a man whose capacities for appreciation create a world—alternative both to Paris and to Woollett and more compelling in the duties it demands from him than either place could be."[17]

These considerations must be kept in mind too if we are to understand that when Strether tells Little Bilham to "live all you can," he is not advising, or at least not simply advising, him

> To sport with Amaryllis in the shade,
> Or with the tangles of Neaera's hair,

for there is quite as much emphasis here on seeing as on doing. Critics who have a passion for finding self-portrayal in James's novels are in luck when they come to *The Ambassadors*, for he himself told Jonathan Sturges that there was a marked mental, though not physical, resemblance between himself and Strether.[18] James had always been a person "in whom contemplation takes so much the place of action." The adventures he relished most were those of "the visiting mind," and he never forgot that "a man might have . . . an amount of experience out of all proportion to his adventures." Strether knows very well that what he might have done but failed to do in his youth could not be made up for now and that the best he could hope for along this line would be "a little supersensual hour in the vicarious freedom of another," but he knows too that his "perceptual" type of experience, though different from Chad's, is no less real.[19] He tells Miss Gostrey, "I

seem to have a life only for other people," and he
defines his own way of both living and giving quite
correctly when, during their last interview, Marie
de Vionnet says, "What's cheerful for me is that we
might . . . have been friends. . . . You see how, as I
say, I want everything. I've wanted you too," and
he replies, "Ah, but you've *had* me!" So, in spite of
what he tells Miss Gostrey, he has not come out of
his European adventure empty-handed. He has had
a large imaginative experience; his sympathies have
been widened and his understanding deepened. It
is more than anybody else has been able to carry
away.[20]

# 9

# The Masterpieces, II: *The Wings of The Dove*

The first mention in James's notebook of what became *The Wings of the Dove* occurs on November 3, 1894, with the vision of a wealthy "young creature . . . preferably a woman," facing death and pitied by a young man she loves, himself engaged to another girl whom, because of financial need, family opposition, or whatever, he cannot presently wed. His fiancée wishes him to "be kind" to the invalid, and he himself longs desperately to "make her taste of happiness, give her something that it breaks her heart to go without having known," but a sexual entanglement is ruled out not only by the girl's physical condition but because it would be too banal, too ugly, too incongruous, and too nasty.

Four days later James returned to the theme, seeming "to get almost a little 3-act play—with the main part for a young actress," but now both the young man and his fiancée are less disinterested, pondering the possibility of his marrying the dying girl "*in order to come into her money and in the certitude that she will die and leave the money to him.*" Through a discarded suitor of the fiancée, the intended victim learns of the plot, but her love survives betrayal and disillusionment; she dies and leaves her money to her betrayer. Then, "in the light of how exquisite the dead girl was he sees how little exquisite is the living"; he gives her the money but refuses to marry her. And only now did James see the victim as "perhaps an American."[1]

In *Henry James: The Master* (1972), Leon Edel stated that the author began dictating *The Wings of the Dove* at Lamb House on July 9, 1901, but four years later, in an immensely detailed account of the writing, publication, and revision of the novel, Sr. Stephanie Vincec wrote that he "began to write it as a serial some time before November 1899 and he worked at it occasionally thereafter until September 1900." In July 1901 he returned to his task and continued sporadically until mid-October and intensively in November and from Christmas until January 1902, but it still required a "final burst of activity from 27 April to 21 May 1902" to finish the work. According to Edel, James sent off five hundred pages of manuscript to Constable in January 1902 and was "reading proof of the book even while writing the final sections." Publication came at the end of August by Constable in London and Scribners in New York.[2]

The deepest roots of the *Dove* lie not in literature but in life—and death. As James tells us in the very first sentence of the preface, he could "scarce remember the time when the situation on which this long-drawn fiction mainly rests was not vividly present to me." Milly Theale, the doomed, life-hungry girl, derives ultimately from James's cousin Minny Temple, who died of tuberculosis in 1870 and had already in some degree influenced Isabel Archer in *The Portrait of a Lady*. James had cared for her intensely, and although there had been no "romance" between them, if he had ever, in any sense, "loved" any woman, it was she; as he says in the moving last chapter of *Notes of a Son and Brother*, he thought of her death as marking the end of both his and William's youth. Now, at last, he sought "to lay the ghost by wrapping it . . . in the beauty and dignity of art."[3]

Yet there was no real lack of influences from literature. The basic image of the dove comes from Psalm 55, which also inspired Mendelssohn's "Hear My Prayer"—"Oh that I had wings like a dove! for then I would fly away and be at rest"—but it is often forgotten that the Psalmist wishes to escape from a false and treacherous friend and that in Psalm 68 the dove's wings are "covered with silver, and her feathers with yellow gold."[4] Since Cargill's interesting speculations about the possible derivation of the story from the romance of Tristan and Iseult[5] do not seem to have found wide acceptance, it is probably still safe to see the most important influence from secular literature in the figure of "Hilda the Dove," attended by her flock of doves in *The Marble Faun*,[6] but James himself compares Milly and Kate, "in the twilight that gathers about them" in Chapter 3 of Book Seventh, to "the likeness of some dim scene in a Maeterlinck play," and the novel certainly contains dialogue that sounds much like Maeterlinck. The preface also mentions Edmond About's *Germaine*, and Edel adds references worth considering to Balzac's *Seraphita*, Blake, and *The Varieties of Religious Experience*. Nor should one forget Matthiessen's acute observation that the whole idea of the novel is in harmony with Poe's idea that the death of a beautiful woman is the most poetic subject in the world.[7]

The notion that Ford Madox Hueffer was the original of Merton Densher seems to have occurred only to that gentleman himself, but a better case can be made out for the journalist Morton Fullerton, who, according to R. W. B. Lewis, became the lover of James's friend Edith Wharton. James had visited the Palazzo Barbaro in Venice, where Milly dies, when Isabella Stewart Gardner and other tenants inhabited it, and there may be an echo of Mrs. Gardner's famous pearls, immortalized in Sargent's painting of her now at Boston's Fenway Court, in the pearls Milly wears at her fete. A number of possible originals have been suggested for Milly's physician, Sir Luke Strett, including, not very plausibly, James himself.[8]

Although, as has already been pointed out, *The Wings of the Dove* was written after *The Ambassadors*, it displays less interest in "point of view" than either that work, which preceded it in order of composition, or *The Golden Bowl*, which followed it. The narrative shifts freely from the consciousness of one character to another, and it is even more difficult than it usually is with James to distinguish clearly between these persons and an unnamed narrator or hypothetical impartial observer.[9]

The most striking peculiarity of the narrative method is that Milly, the character about whom the action revolves and for whom both the author and his readers care most, is the one we see least of and whose angle of vision is the most sparingly employed. As Sr. M. Corona Sharp has remarked, James's "whole point" is to "press hard" on the consciousness of the others, Kate, Densher, and Susan all having "blocks" focused upon Milly, while she herself gets "only one book [the fifth] and part of two others."[10] James writes in his preface that we get Milly chiefly through "watching her, as it were, through the successive windows of other people's interest in her." She does not appear at all in the first two of the ten books into which the novel is divided nor yet in the last two, and we are in London with Kate, Densher, and Mrs. Lowder when she dies in Venice, attended by her friend Susan Stringham and Sir Luke Strett.

Howells once spoke of "that wonderful way of Mr. James's by which he imparts a fact without stating it, approaching it again and again, without actually coming in contact with it."[11] Whether this "way" is "wonderful" or not must depend on the reader's taste, but there can be no doubt of the accuracy of the description (James once playfully rebuked Hugh Walpole for having dared to suggest that he ever did anything so vulgar as to "state"). Milly's position in the *Dove* is indeed anomalous. Although her ardent temperament qualifies her supremely for living an active life, her illness and the plot of the novel combine to force her into a position where she is acted upon rather than acting, yet it is what she does offstage at the end that determines the fate of Kate and Densher. It seems altogether appropriate, therefore, that we should see her mainly through the others and in terms of her effect upon them, and it may well be that she moves us best in this way. James told Hueffer that he cued us in on her final interview with Densher only in retrospect because he did not wish his novel to become a Hall Caine tearjerker, and that if he had described the scene in which Lord Mark brings her the tidings that break her heart and cause her to "turn her face to the wall," he would either have had to funk it or else allow himself a much more overwhelming expression of emotion than the novel could have accommodated at that point.

Nevertheless, one cannot but feel that James's method of handling Milly was altogether congenial to his temperament. Indirectness and suggestion always appealed to him. Of Mrs. Lowder's dinner party in Book Fourth, Mary Doyle Springer remarks amusingly that "it must be the most barren banquet table ever set: there is a point at which Lord Mark 'crumbled up his bread,' and that is *all* the food presented in the twenty-three page duration of the dinner."[12] It has been said of Meredith, whom James considered a difficult writer, that his first rule for narrative was that when you had a really big scene to describe, you must leave it out, and there are times when James resembles him in this regard.

James himself regarded the *Dove* as the most glaring example of his incorrigible tendency to overdevelop the first half of his narrative so that he was obliged to scant the rest in order to keep the whole within bounds. "A thing of my own, too longwinded and minute a thing, but well-meaning," he called it to Howells, and he told Mrs. Cadwalader Jones that "the centre . . . isn't in the middle, rather, isn't in the centre, but ever so much too near the end, so that what was to come after it is truncated."[13] But I think most readers are likely to be more troubled by the necessity laid upon them to pause every now and then to ask themselves whether all the finespun motivations they encounter and the larger-than-life sensibilities to which they are exposed are completely convincing. Some of these things, no doubt, might be more at home in the poetic or romantic drama than in what we generally think of as realistic fiction; the way Sir Luke Strett keeps Densher dangling in Venice before finally telling him that Milly wishes to see him resembles the way the Duke handles Isabella toward the end of *Measure for Measure*. But we must also remember that Matthiessen was never more penetrating than when he observed that for James, "particularly toward the end of his career, realistic details had become merely the covering for a content that was far from realistic."[14]

Matthiessen pioneered too in the appreciation of James's imagery, which in the later novels becomes so rich and complex that the line of demarcation between prose fiction and lyric poetry wavers dangerously, and also of his use of a sympathetic nature background.[15] The Shakespeare of *King Lear* would have been quite at home with the way James uses the storm to express Densher's desolation when Milly shuts him out in Venice as well as with the comparative calm which succeeds upon Sir Luke's coming, and the scene in which Milly is introduced, perilously perched upon her eminence in the Alps, certainly communicates a kind of physical sensation which James is not popularly given credit for having been able to command.

The novel began, as has been noted, with Milly's pathetic figure soliciting James's imagination, but since the action is initiated by Kate Croy and the (at this point) subservient Densher, we necessarily begin with them. In Book First, Kate's situation is explored through her encounters with her father and sister, hers being the reflecting consciousness. Book Second introduces Kate's lover, Merton Densher, and develops the relationship between them and its reference to Kate's aunt, Maud Lowder. Milly and her traveling companion, Susan Shepherd Stringham, are introduced in Switzerland in Book Third, which closes with their departure for London. Milly had known Densher in America, when he was there on journalistic assignment, and Susan had been at school with Mrs. Lowder long, long ago; thus the way is naturally prepared for Milly's social success in London and her friendship with Kate, both of which themes are developed in Book Fourth. Milly now becomes aware that Densher loves Kate but has no idea that his passion is reciprocated.

Although Howells spoke of "that terribly frank, terribly hard English gang" in *The Wings of the Dove*, Kate is at the beginning a wholly sympathetic character. She has two terrible millstones hanging around her neck. Like Milly's disease and the nature of the manufactured article in *The Ambassadors*, just what her father did to get himself banished from decent society is never spelled out, but if there is a more utterly shameless and contemptible human being in literature, I have not encountered him; if that grand old word "naughty" had survived in its Elizabethan sense of indicating the complete negation of all moral qualities, it would suit him perfectly. As for Kate's widowed, whining sister, Marian Condrip, her courage has been sapped by her misfortunes to such an extent that she can only look to Kate for both moral and physical support. Kate's offer to take these people on is heroic, whether or not it is totally believable. Her father turns it down because he thinks his chances for material reward may be greater if Kate accepts the offer of Mrs. Lowder, who sees in her handsome niece an opportunity to improve her own social position, virtually to adopt her, even though that "Britannia of the Market Place" has insisted that if Kate comes to her, she must forego all future contacts with the rest of the family.

Mrs. Lowder and Lord Mark take their places with the "bad" characters in the novel, while Susan Stringham and Sir Luke Strett rank emphatically with the good. Lord Mark bears the immediate responsibility for causing Milly to "turn her face to the wall," and it is one sign of the ironic subtlety of the book that, as Pelham Edgar long ago observed, he is the one person who tells the complete truth! He would be willing to marry either Kate or Milly, and Dupee compares Kate's rejection of him with

Isabel Archer's of Lord Warburton. Whether he was trying to help his own suit when he told Milly that Densher was secretly engaged to Kate or was merely intent on making mischief we are not told; under the circumstances posited, his action was indefensible upon any hypothesis, and he remains the "idiot of idiots" that Susan calls him. Mrs. Lowder is one of James's overweening "unscrupulous and immoral" older women—"majestic, magnificent, high-coloured, all brilliant gloss, perpetual satin, twinkling bugles and flashing gems." She is not at all immoral in the usual sense; she merely will not permit anybody with whom she is associated to control his own life, and her management of others is so masterly that it sometimes even creates the impression of benevolence. "She was vulgar with freshness, almost with beauty, since there was beauty, to a degree, in the play of so big and bold a temperament." She being what she is, there is black humor in her monstrous sentimentality at the close, where she announces that "our dear dove . . . has folded her wonderful wings." One cannot but think of Shaw's remark about the soft cruel hearts in the world and the hard kind ones.

James uses humor again, and more daringly, in his portrait of Milly's devoted companion, Susan Shepherd Stringham, the New England magazinist who adores Guy de Maupassant, reads the Boston *Evening Transcript* in Europe, wears a Tyrolese felt hat, and aims to take New England local color writing out of the kitchen. Susan is a wholly unselfish friend, whom Milly trusts and esteems, although she is too intelligent not to be aware of her romantic exaggerations, and James expects the reader to value her the same way. Yet as Ellen Leyburn observed, "James keeps his own adoration of Milly from being oversolemn by letting it come through

Susan Stringham, whose solemnities he can under-cut by humor,"[16] thus eating his cake and keeping it too. Except for that beautiful, beneficent being Sir Luke Strett, the most distinguished physician in England, Susan is the only real friend Milly has. Sir Luke has been called the wise old man of the fairy tales, and if Susan is a shepherd, James surely did not give him the name of Saint Paul's beloved physician for nothing. After her first visit to him, Milly felt "as if I had been on my knees to a priest." "You can depend on me for unlimited interest," he tells her, and nobody ever more nobly kept his word. He even went to Venice to see her, and he was with her when she died.

Unfortunately, when Mrs. Lowder takes Kate in hand, she insists not only that she must give up her family but also that she must relinquish the idea of marrying Merton Densher. This is not at all because she does not like him, for she does, and even welcomes him to her house as a guest, but simply because she is sure that he will never have any money and she plans a distinguished marriage for her niece, perhaps to Lord Mark. The lovers have literally no place to meet as lovers except in the park. The description of their early encounter on the Underground is charming; James is uncommonly direct in telling us that Densher's attraction for the girl on the score of his qualities of mind is all to her honor, and her pledge, "I engage myself to you for ever," has the true romantic ring.

Yet both these people have faults to match their virtues. J. A. Ward calls Densher "the nonheroic yet perceptive man, driven to self-understanding by his weakness of will and horror of ugliness" with whom we have become more familiar since James's time.[17] But there are many with whom he has an affinity both in James's other novels and in Edith Wharton's.

Up to his final disillusionment, he would have been willing to challenge fate by marrying Kate at any time, but she wishes to "try for everything," and except on the one occasion in Venice when he refuses to go on with the plot against Milly unless Kate pledges her faith by coming to his rooms to spend the night with him,[18] he follows where she leads. She is the executive member in their partnership, "a whole library of the unknown, the uncut," and when he deceitfully tells Milly that he does not really feel he knows Kate, there is a sense in which he is telling the truth. Material things speak to her; she is not Maud's niece and Lionel's daughter for nothing. She is not a materialist in the Lowder sense, for she has taste and aspirations, but she fails to realize that the achievement she desires must be undercut by the means she employs to encompass it, and despite her superior fineness, she attempts to devour both Milly and, in a different way, Densher as she sees that Mrs. Lowder was devouring her.

If Kate and Densher had married, he would always have been in a sense subservient to her, but they would have been happy enough so long as he could have kept unsoiled the image of her he had cherished since the beginning of their acquaintance. For it must be remembered that in the beginning, Kate's scheme had looked like a plot against Mrs. Lowder rather than Milly. Milly was known to be interested in Densher; if Aunt Maud could be made to believe that Densher was coming to Lancaster Gate to see her, the deception would prove a convenient cover for him and Kate. It is not until the beginning of Book Sixth that Densher even begins to grasp the full significance of his lover's designs (it is from this point that Kate becomes a definitely unsympathetic character), and it is not until nearly the end of Book Eighth that the whole thing is blurted out: "Since she's to die I'm to marry her?" and "So that when her death has taken place I shall in the natural course have money?"

Kate is capable of a brutal directness, but she is also adept at wrenching the false cause the right way. She does not, she admits, like the idea of lending Densher to Milly, but she is thankful that she is capable of doing what she does not like for a consideration. She is right of course in positing that she is giving Milly what Milly wants, and if that were all there was to it, there would be a perverse kind of benevolence in her actions. What vitiates the thing is her greed; she would not dream of giving up her lover to the other girl except for material reward; indeed, she even admits that she would not care nearly so much for Milly herself if Milly were not rich. Thus, although it is true that she is not so bad in the novel as in the notebook entries, James never permits the reader to excuse either her or Densher or absolve them from responsibility because of the difficult position they occupy. Like the worst of Dante's sinners, Kate betrays her friend, and thus in the end she loses her highest and purest aim, the life she had planned with the man she loves, and once more the devil is an ass.[19]

Since there can be no question that James intended Milly as his supreme tribute to the memory of Minny Temple, that the reader was intended to admire her is not debatable.[20] Not all critics have found the characterization equally successful, however. Matthiessen called her "the most resonant symbol for what [James] had to say about humanity," and Edmund Wilson found her "a personality independent of the novel, the kind of personality, deeply felt, invested with poetic beauty and unmistakably individualized, which only the creators of the first rank can give life to," but Marius Bewley, F. R. Leavis, and others have hardly been willing to grant that she is characterized at all. The basic difficulty with these critics seems to be that they are too much at home with modern realistic literature to be able to understand anything that has been created in an older, more idealistic mold.[21]

Yet it is difficult to see how any competent reader could fail to perceive that though she rises at the end to a Christlike capacity for forgiveness and self-abnegation, Milly is plentifully endowed with individual characteristics and human limitations. She is an enormously rich, tragically orphaned American girl, a "slim, constantly pale, delicately haggard, anomalously, agreeably angular young person of not more than two-and-twenty summers . . . whose hair was somehow exceptionally red even for the real thing, which it innocently confessed to being, and whose clothes were remarkably black even for robes of mourning, which was the meaning they expressed." She has "rather too much forehead, too much nose and too much mouth, together with too little mere conventional colour and conventional line," and her "curious and splendid coils of hair" are "'done' with no eye whatever to the *mode du jour.*" There is "something helpless in her grace and abrupt in her turns."

Some readers have questioned her intelligence because she allows herself to be deceived. She may be plot-ridden here; obviously, she cannot be victimized if she is to be suspicious from the beginning. But she loves both Densher and, in a different way, Kate, and it is certainly neither unbelievable nor reprehensible that she should possess a trusting nature. At the same time, James takes care that we shall not judge her stupid unless we are stupid ourselves. She knows Susan's limitations despite Susan's devotion to her and her own love for Susan, and she sees through both Mrs. Lowder and Lord Mark from the beginning, sensing that the former was "a person of whom the mind might in two or three days roughly make the circuit" and that the latter was blasé but not enlightened, "familiar with everything, but conscious really of nothing," because destitute of imagination. And much as she admires her, she suspects that Kate has a secret, senses a latent capacity for brutality in her, and compares her to a panther as she paces the room before her. So when all is said and done, Densher is the only person by whom Milly is really deceived, and Densher has also deceived himself.

Since Minny Temple died of tuberculosis (or "consumption," as it was generally called at the time), the great girl killer of the nineteenth century, this would seem the most likely candidate for Milly's complaint, but James does not specify, and since there are certainly nonphysical elements involved in her turning "her face to the wall," he does gain in this instance by his lack of specification. Matthiessen seems to be the only critic who ever really committed himself to the hypothesis of tuberculosis. Kate tells Densher that it is "not lungs, I think" and suggests that it may finally become a case for surgery, and Susan tells Mrs. Lowder that "she hasn't what she thought" and that when Sir Luke examined her he found something else, but Susan didn't know what it was. Indeed, Sir Luke treats her throughout more like a psychiatrist or a Christian Science practitioner than a regular physician, which seems to suggest, if it suggests anything, that her case was medically hopeless from the beginning and that what he was trying to do was to make the time she had left as pleasant and comfortable as possible.

Although the scene in which Milly is introduced to the reader, brooding over the vast panorama spread out before her from her perch in the Alps, inevitably suggests Christ's temptation in the wilderness, renunciation is far from being the note here. Minny Temple had religious problems which she hoped, without notable success, that Phillips Brooks could help her solve, but nothing is said about this in connection with Milly. She is no devotee, and she opts for living, not learning. I see no sense in the suggestion made by the generally perspicacious Dorothea Krook that she makes her doom inevitable by excessive pride; she does everything Sir Luke tells her to do, and stoical concern in facing sickness is not generally accounted a fault. What she does have is a tremendous and, in her condition, a self-consuming zest for life, a Marie Bashkirtseff kind of appetence: "her doom was to live fast." Such hunger is characteristic of tuberculosis patients, and Marie of course *was* a consumptive. Milly is capable of human passion also, as her love for Densher shows, and she displays a mild human resentment of Kate's indifference toward Susan, as if it were a kind of insult to her that one she values should not be good enough for her friend.

Milly's two great scenes are her confrontation at Matcham of the Bronzino portrait she is supposed to resemble and her appearance at the fete she gives in her palazzo on the only occasion when she discards her mourning for white. The Bronzino scene is as impressive in its way as the portrait scene in *The Sacred Fount* and far more poignant, for Milly recognizes the resemblance but is impressed, more than anything else, by the fact that the woman in the portrait is "dead, dead, dead"; "I shall never be better than this."[22] But the fete is the doomed girl's hour of glory; even for Densher, Kate's splendor is dimmed: "As a striking young presence she was practically superseded."

Milly revels in the social success she meets in England, and if she is ever complacently self-conscious, it is in the way she accepts and enjoys the dove image that Kate fastens upon her. Basically the dove is a religious symbol, in the Christian religion exemplifying the Holy Spirit, but James's use of the image is not simple. When first employed it suggests merely innocence and vulnerability, like that of a lamb, but by Book Eighth Densher at least realizes that doves have "wings and wondrous flights . . . as well as tender tints and soft sounds" and that they "spread themselves for protection." Milly's wings do spread themselves at the end ("they cover us"), but they spread themselves in power, the power of the terrible meek, and although Milly never foresaw or desired such a result, they separate the lovers forever.[23]

After his last interview with Milly, Densher returns to London, but he has been there two weeks before he even comes near Kate. "The essence was that something had happened to him too beautiful and too sacred to describe. He had been, to his recovered sense, forgiven, dedicated, blessed; but this he couldn't coherently express." Since Milly's love had been great enough to survive her knowledge that she had been wronged, so that she had not only forgiven but enriched him, thus making it possible for him to marry the girl with whom he had joined to betray her, it is highly appropriate that the news should reach them both at Christmastime. Some critics have been repelled by what they see as Densher's cruelty to Kate at the close and his testing her, and there is no denying that there is a certain priggishness and self-righteousness here, but essentially when Densher tells Kate that she can have the money without him or him without the money but not both, he is only submitting to the inexorable logic of life. "He had brought her there to be moved, and she was only immoveable—which was not moreover, either, because she didn't understand. She understood everything, and things he refused to; and she had reasons, deep down, the sense of which nearly sickened him." When he gives her Milly's letter, she burns it unopened and unread. "You will have it all . . . from New York," she says, "all" being the bequest, which is all that matters to her, and when the American letter arrives and he brings it to her, she disappoints him by opening that.

She understands everything in the sense that she stands alone in a kind of heroic, Satanic impenitence, cleaving unmoved to her own selfishness and greed. She knows as clearly as he does that by practicing a perfect nonresistance Milly has made their marriage impossible: "We shall never be again as we were!" Yet in a deeper sense she understands nothing; there is no work of art extant in which stupidity is more mercilessly identified with evil than *The Wings of the Dove* or in which we come closer to Dante's definition of damnation as losing "the good of the understanding." But Kate's stupidity is not at all lack of intelligence but rather moral insensitiveness. She was stupid to begin with by leaving Densher with Milly in Venice, to be acted upon by her goodness without any countervailing influence from Kate's own presence, and she was stupid in never grasping the growing male resentment which festers in him as he is reduced to merely carrying out her orders. But what really sickens him at the end is that even now she thinks that everything has gone well, that their situation is "perfect" and "quite ideal," and that she is so far from repenting having told Lord Mark that she was engaged to Densher ("Would you have liked me to give him an answer that would have kept him from going?") that she wonders only why Densher could not have remedied the situation by lying to Milly about it. The one thing that troubles her is that she would like to be assured that Densher is not in love with Milly's memory. She has won her game but lost her lover. Whether she takes the money or not we are not told, nor is there any reason why we should be, for it does not matter except to her.

# 10

# The Masterpieces, III: *The Golden Bowl*

One of the stories they tell about Henry James is that during his last visit to Boston, he was waiting one day for the traffic to change and permit him to cross Copley Square, when a policeman came to escort him across the street. Not knowing that he had been recognized, he was astonished when the officer asked, "Mr. James, which of your novels is your favorite?" "Why," he replied, "I think I like *The Golden Bowl* best." "Oh, thank you, sir," said the blue coat. "That is my favorite too."

The story is very likely apocryphal, playing up to or ridiculing Boston's reputation for culture, but the reply indicated is one that James might well have made. In what Millicent Bell called "the great triple range of his 'major phase,'"[1] *The Ambassadors* is the most beautifully symmetrical and *The Wings of the Dove* the richest in spiritual beauty and suggestiveness, but *The Golden Bowl* is the most elaborately developed and consummately "done." Here is the final reach of James's "later manner."

At the beginning Maggie Verver, the only daughter of a fabulously wealthy American tycoon now retired from business and committed to collecting on a grand scale and looking forward to the establishment of an art museum in "American City," is in London preparing for her marriage to an Italian prince, Amerigo, a *gentiluomo* of impressive lineage but unimpressive means. Maggie's close friend, Charlotte Stant, of Florentine birth but American descent, arrives unexpectedly from America for the wedding and makes an appointment with the Prince to go shopping for a wedding gift for Maggie. In an out-of-the-way shop they find a golden bowl (actually a crystal bowl gilded) by which Charlotte is much taken, but Amerigo detects a crack in the crystal, and they turn it down.

What Maggie and her father, Adam Verver, do not know is that Charlotte and the Prince had been lovers who did not marry only because both were too poor. This is known, however, to Fanny Assingham, their friend, who is also Charlotte's friend and the Prince's friend. The tie between Maggie and her father, which is uncommonly warm and close, is not weakened by her marriage or the birth of her son (the "Principino"), but Maggie feels that Adam would be less lonely if he were to marry again, and their choice falls upon Charlotte Stant. Since Maggie and her father are by nature stay-at-homes while Charlotte and Amerigo have outstanding social gifts, they increasingly come to "do the 'worldly'" for the whole quartet, and as they are thrown more and more together a liaison develops, although James is evasive on whether it goes to the full length of adultery.

Chance leads Maggie, searching for a birthday gift for her father, to the very shop where Charlotte and Amerigo had inspected the golden bowl. She buys it and takes it home, but the dealer, suffering qualms of conscience over having overcharged her for a defective article, comes to offer restitution. Upon seeing photographs of Charlotte and the Prince in Maggie's house, he tells her about his former customers. Maggie then tells Fanny Assingham that she is now sure her husband and Charlotte are having an affair, and Fanny smashes the bowl in what is supposed to be a decisive symbolic gesture. Amerigo walks in upon the scene, and Maggie makes him aware that she now understands the situation but gives him no indication of what she intends to do.

Throughout the remainder of the long novel, Maggie's apparently doing nothing puts unbearable pressure on the lovers. When Charlotte, unable to stand the strain any longer, takes the initiative by boldly asking her whether she has a grievance, she denies it. Finally, Charlotte persuades her husband to return with her to America, where they can both devote their energies to the museum, and Maggie is left with her Prince, who can now "see nothing but *you.*"

The original idea for *The Golden Bowl* was recorded in James's notebook on November 28, 1892, when, as usual, he thought it might make a short story. In the outline, the setting is Paris, the husband is English or French, and the father's marriage is arranged for at an earlier stage than in the book and not at the daughter's instigation. The relations between the daughter and her husband are much less happy than in the novel, and father and daughter commiserate with each other over their unhappy state. There was at this stage no idea of dividing the material between "The Prince" and "The Princess," and there was no golden bowl. In December 1895 James thought that he might use his idea for one of the "short 'International' novels that Harpers want" and regretted that he had used up the title "The Marriages" on a short story.[2]

Leon Edel has James beginning to write the novel "early in 1903" or "in the early summer of 1903," and on May 20, 1904, James wrote his agent

that he had "been working on the book with un-
remitting intensity the whole of every blessed
morning" since beginning it "some thirteen months
ago." In New York, Scribners published it in two
volumes on November 10, 1904, "in very charming
and readable form, each vol. but moderately thick
and with a legible, handsome, large typed page."
James was much less pleased with the "fat, vile,
small-typed, horrific, prohibitive" single volume
which followed from Methuen in London next February and refused to send copies of this to his
friends. The American edition astonished both author and publishers by going into its fourth printing
while James was still in the United States. He had
told Pinker that it was "the best book, I seem to
conceive, that I have ever done" and the Scribners
that it was "the most composed and constructed and
completest" and "the solidest" of his works, and
probably the impressive American sale did not tend
to cause him to modify this judgment. In the preface
to *The Ambassadors*, however, he would, as we
have seen, call that "frankly, quite the best, 'all
round,' of all my productions," and when, in 1911,
Edith Wharton, surprisingly in view of her criti-
cisms of it, asked him for another *Golden Bowl*, he
waved away the suggestion and called the composition of this novel "the most arduous and thankless
task I ever set myself."[3]

James could hardly have written *The Golden
Bowl* without thinking of Ecclesiastes 12:6—"Or
ever the silver cord be loosed, or the golden bowl
be broken, or the pitcher be broken at the fountain,
or the wheel broken at the cistern"—nor yet of
Blake's

> Can wisdom be kept in a silver rod,
> Or love in a golden bowl.

Cargill has pointed out striking resemblances (as

well as striking differences) between the *Bowl* and two novels by Paul Bourget, *Cosmopolis* and *A Tragic Idyll*. Mildred S. Greene has dealt similarly with *Les Liaisons Dangereuses* of Choderlos de Laclos, and both Scott Byrd and Miriam Allott have brought George Eliot into the consideration. The novel itself contains important references to Keats's Cortez sonnet and to Amerigo's interest in Poe's *Narrative of Arthur Gordon Pym*. Passing from literature to life, it may be noted that at Christmastime 1902 James saw an actual golden bowl that had been presented by King George I to the Lamb family of his own Lamb House. Edel suggested that Maggie's close relationship with her father may have derived something from what James knew about Lizzie Boott, her father, and her husband, Frank Duveneck. Adeline R. Tintner has now shown both that Fanny Sitwell, who married Sir Sidney Colvin, may have been drawn upon for Fanny Assingham, and that in all likelihood Prince Amerigo was influenced by the Marchese Simone de Peruzzi de Medici, who married the daughter of the sculptor William Wetmore Story, whose biography James wrote; in another fascinating and richly illustrated article she illuminates James's many veiled references to the furnishings, objets d'art, and surroundings of Waddeston Manor, the residence of Baron Ferdinand de Rothschild. I cannot help wondering also whether he may not have thought about Marian Hooper (Mrs. Henry) Adams, whose association with her father had been very affectionate and whose suicide may have been triggered in part by the strain of nursing him through a long terminal illness.[4]

Structurally, *The Golden Bowl* is divided into two unnumbered parts (corresponding to the two volumes of the New York Edition) called, respectively, "The Prince" and "The Princess." The first part comprises Books First through Third and the second Books Fourth through Sixth. These books are of uneven length; Book Fourth fills considerably more than half the second volume.

In Book First Maggie's wedding has been arranged, Charlotte comes from America, and she and Amerigo go shopping. Book Second opens on the married life of the Prince and the Princess, who have returned from America, where their son has been born. Mr. Verver is now being pursued by undesirable females, and Maggie thinks that he should wed. While she and Amerigo are in Rome, he proposes to Charlotte, who, after consideration, accepts him. In Book Third the liaison gets under way.

In Book Fourth Maggie first suspects and then, after the visit of the antique dealer, knows her husband's infidelity. In Book Fifth she silently drives Charlotte to her decision to escape to America, and Book Sixth is taken up with their preparations for departure and the final complete reconciliation between Maggie and the Prince. There are time intervals, not always precisely indicated, to allow for developments, especially in the first half. The last half is more concentrated, and the action, if it can be called that, moves more simply and directly.

In the preface to the *Bowl*, James discusses at length his addiction to "point of view" and, exempting only the scenes assigned to the Assinghams, declares that "the Prince, in the first half of the book, virtually sees and knows and makes out, virtually represents to himself everything that concerns us" and that "the function of the Princess in the remainder, matches exactly with his," and most commentators have taken this at face value. It is far from being wholly true however, although it works better for the second half than for the first. The Prince is absent through all of Book Second, part of

which is surely from Mr. Verver's point of view, and
James is, as usual, very skillful in introducing authorial comment and guidance, muted or disguised,
sometimes even from the standpoint of an imaginary
observer who would have functioned thus and so,
had he been present.

The narrative method is often highly idiosyn-
cratic. James was fond of reporting the experience
of his characters as it was looked back on. In the
*Bowl* he tends to give us dialogue in chunks, separated by long stretches of unbroken narrative that
is actually more analysis than story.[5] Sometimes he
reports what was *not* said (although it may have
been thought). In Book Fourth, Chapter 10, just
after the Prince has walked in on the smashed bowl
and the reader expects a clash, nine pages of nar-
rative-analysis intervene before he and his wife are
permitted to talk to each other. Charlotte receives
the telegram the Prince sent her upon learning of
her engagement to Verver on page 239 of the first
volume of the *Bowl* in the New York Edition. She
daringly offers to show it to her fiancé, knowing full
well that he is too much of a gentleman to take her
up on it, and it is not until pages 290–91 that we
learn what Amerigo wrote. But the most extreme example of this sort of thing comes in the same volume, where the man-chasing Mrs. Rance opens the
door of the billiard room on Mr. Verver at page 129
but does not reach his side until page 151. Throughout the interval James and his readers explore Verver's mind, and although Mrs. Rance remains with
him until the others return from church, no word
that passed between them has been reported.

Whatever discounts may be taken, however, the
book remains a wonderful tour de force. "If I'm both
helpless *and* tormented," says Maggie, "I stuff my
pocket-handkerchief in my mouth. I keep it there,

for the most part, both night and day, so as not to be heard, indecently moaning," and much of her nerve-tingling tension communicates itself to the reader, which is an amazing thing to be able to say about a narrative so lacking in what is ordinarily thought of as action. Aside from the smashing of the bowl, which I think miscarries, the "big scene" is the splendidly successful one in Book Fifth, Chapter 2, in which, on a summer night, Maggie paces the terrace watching the others playing bridge inside and at last Charlotte tries to brazen it out by coming to her to ask whether she has offended her. This does not sound like a world-shattering confrontation, yet we are on tenterhooks.

*The Golden Bowl* is so rich in imagery that many passages read like lyric poetry. Gold, wealth, conquest, water, sailing and exploration, architecture, games, and animals (especially beasts of prey in connection with Charlotte) are all drawn upon, and I certainly would not suggest that these images, often running over into symbolism, fail to reveal the minds of the characters or deny that they add greatly to the charm and distinction of the book. I must confess, however, that I have distinct reservations concerning both the pagoda image at the beginning of Book Fourth and that of the bowl itself.

Since it is used only once, the pagoda image is much the less pervasive, but in itself it is far the more elaborate, which is exactly my difficulty; it seems to me strained and artificial, like the worst excesses of the metaphysicals.[6] As to the bowl, it is effective enough at the outset if we are to take it as suggesting the flaw in Maggie's marriage, but it is made to suggest so much in the course of the narrative—or critics have read so much into it[7]—that it ends by effectively figuring forth none of these things. Its destruction by Fanny Assingham is pre-

pared for as early as the end of Book First, but it
seems to me as melodramatically unbelievable as
everything that leads up to it. The melodrama begins with Maggie's inadvertently visiting the same
shop where Charlotte and Amerigo had been and
hitting upon the same article (as the Prince remarks,
this is "the sort of thing that happens mainly in novels and plays"), and it ends when he walks in upon
the shattered bowl. I do not believe that the shop-
keeper, having overcharged Maggie, would come to
her house afterward to offer restitution and there
encounter the photographs of Charlotte and the
Prince (Maggie's careful explanation of his motives
to Fanny is alone enough to show that both she and
James knew how all this would strain credulity), and
Mrs. Assingham being the cautious worrier she is,
and her relationship to the Ververs being what it is,
it is simply unbelievable that she should take it
upon herself to destroy Maggie's property for the
sake of a theatrical gesture. *The Golden Bowl* is neither a parable by Hawthorne nor a melodrama by
Sardou, and though I must surely have made it clear
by this time that I am well aware that much in James
is made up of fairy-tale motifs disguised, the point
is that here they are not disguised; the realistic ve-
neer simply sloughs off. Moreover, even if we are
willing to waive all such considerations, the scene
does not work as symbolism. Whatever the flaw in
Maggie's marriage, to destroy it would be the last
thing Fanny could desire.

"What," Edith Wharton once asked James,
"was your idea in suspending the four principal
characters in 'The Golden Bowl' in the void?" to
which he replied, "My dear, I didn't know I had."[8]
It is true that both the author and his characters here
achieve an unusual degree of concentration upon
their personal concerns, and it is to this fact that

much of the claustrophobic power of the book is due; one can well understand why its economy in dramatis personae and unity of action and (almost) place should remind Dorothea Krook of the Greek drama. Yet the stage is considerably less narrow than it has sometimes been represented as being. Although we remain for the most part in upper-class London, both Italy and America are spiritually present, and the characters live in the same world the rest of us inhabit.[9]

For all the concentration of the novel upon the Ververs and their *sposi*, one other couple are important in it: Fanny Assingham, who, having no children and little money, has nothing but the affairs of her friends to interest her, and her husband, Colonel Bob. Fanny almost "made" the marriage between Maggie and the Prince; she is his confidante in the first half and, with reservations, Maggie's in the second; she is also a close friend of Charlotte's, and after the liaison gets under way, she spends much of her time worrying about it, denying it to Maggie in order to spare her feelings, and talking it over with her husband, for she is a confidante with a confidant. Edith Wharton played the devil's advocate here also—"This insufferable and incredible couple spend their days in espionage and delation, and their evenings in exchanging the reports of their eavesdropping with a minuteness and precision worthy of Scottland Yard"—and although critics have shown that the function of the Assinghams is considerably more complex than Mrs. Wharton perceived, it is no doubt still possible to argue that they are bores or that they are not worth the space James gives them. Most of this goes into Fanny's observations and analyses. Wegelin called her "a caricature of the Jamesian clairvoyante," but she might almost as well be called a caricature of James him-

self as a novelist, with a husband who, as Matthiessen observed, is about "the staunchest anti-Jacobite
on record" and who interrupts his listening with
occasional trenchant commonsense comments,
some of which his wife considers coarse.[10]

Of the four leading characters Adam Verver is
the least clearly defined and, judged by ordinary
standards, the least successful; even at the end,
when he leaves with his wife for American City, we
are not quite sure whether he knows what has been
going on behind his back. Estimates of his character
and personality embrace the whole spectrum; those
who see Maggie as a Christ figure would make him
God the Father, while others load him with all the
sins of the economic order. Crews calls him "cap-
italism almost in the abstract," sees even in his collecting "the American irresponsibility toward Europe," and makes him "almost something of the
villain of the drama," and Caroline Gordon seems
to stand alone in viewing him as James's "arch-cre-
ation."

His outward aspect is that of "some precious
spotless exceptionally intelligent lamb," and he
seems almost as much Maggie's child as her parent.
When they lived alone together, they thought of
themselves (quite without Freudian overtones,
either on their part or the author's) as married to
each other or as "paying visits, playing at 'Mr.
Thompson and Mrs. Fane,' each hoping that the
other would really stay to tea." Verver's past as a
tycoon is only vaguely indicated, but his present
phase as a collector is more vivid: "It was the
strange scheme of things again: the years of darkness had been needed to render possible the years
of light." It is natural that those whose standards in
these matters have been derived from Dreiser's portrait of Frank Cowperwood should find him unbe-

lievable, but might they not have been similarly affected by the outward aspect of John D. Rockefeller, who looked even to Sargent's painterly eye very much like a saint? Maggie believed "that he was simply a great and deep and high little man, and that to love him with tenderness was not to be distinguished a whit from loving him with pride," but Fanny Assingham, who calls him "Charlotte's inconceivably funny husband," cannot figure him out at all. He might be "too inconceivably great" or he might be "stupid"; on the other hand, he might be "sublimer even than Maggie herself."[11]

If there is any one thing about Adam Verver more ambiguous than everything else, it is his relations with his wife. That he admires her and expects to spend the rest of his life with her there can be no question, nor can it be doubted that he is a pleasant husband who, in a material way, gives her everything she wants. Whatever he may or may not know concerning her relations with Amerigo, we may be sure that he will never reproach her, and when she makes the move to go to America at the end, he accepts it at once even though it necessitates his separation from his beloved daughter.

His only serious fault in this connection is that he married Charlotte more to please Maggie than either himself or her. He "collected" her even as he "collected" the Prince for his daughter, and not even the fact that both persons were fully consenting parties can quite take the bad taste of these transactions out of our mouths. It may also be that he is impotent; if this is not what Charlotte means when she tells the Prince that she and Verver tried to have a child but were unable to do so and that this was not her fault, the passage is seriously misleading. There is nevertheless a pretty good case to be made for the view that before the end, and in spite of her

physical or spiritual adultery, Adam comes to value
Charlotte for herself and not merely for what the
Ververs can make of her. Even in their last conference together, Verver and Maggie never suggest to
each other that Charlotte had a fault.

Among James's "bad" heroines, Charlotte's
closest affinity is with Kate Croy, but although both
these girls are very attractive, Charlotte seems built
on a larger scale. She has strength, intelligence,
dignity, presence, style, high efficiency, and outstanding social gifts; from the beginning she impresses Maggie as "great." She is poor, she has not
had a sheltered life, and circumstances have taught
her both boldness and aggressiveness. She can face
danger without flinching and is confident of her
ability to swim in almost any sea. She and Kate are
alike in that both betray a friend, but the suspicion
of adultery attaches only to her. Both are single-
mindedly faithful in love; Kate never wanted anybody but Densher nor Charlotte anyone but the
Prince. That we may not be smug or self-righteous
in our judgment of them, James places both in
highly extenuating circumstances, but that we may
not decieve ourselves, he is also careful not to justify
what they do.[12]

If Charlotte's motives upon returning to England for Maggie's wedding are not wholly innocent,
neither are they criminal; she has no immediate
plans beyond spending one hour alone with the
Prince. Although Mrs. Assingham thinks that Amerigo never really loved her because she was too easy,
I cannot go along with Dorothea Krook's idea that
what bound them was not love but lust; as it develops after the Prince's marriage, their connection
was unlawful, but I see no reason to suppose that
the attraction was base in itself. They would have
married if lack of means had not stood in the way,

and Charlotte would surely have become a faithful wife. Except that she does not show Verver the Prince's telegram, she is honest in her examination of both his motives and her own when he asks her to marry him and she seems to me to hold the reader's sympathy fairly well up to the end of the first volume. Both she and the Prince are highly aesthetic, if not always highly moral, people, and the one thing they never violate is the "forms" which, as Mrs. Verver assures her husband, are "two-thirds of conduct."

Charlotte is dishonest with herself, however, when she poses as a fatalist whose circumstances have placed her in a position where she cannot do anything except—well, except exactly what she does and obviously wishes to do. The Prince is the passive one, and she dominates him as clearly as Kate Croy dominates Merton Densher.[13] Her comparative hardness appears clearly in their respective attitudes toward Fanny Assingham. The Prince worries over what she may think of them, but the only thing that interests Charlotte is that Fanny is not in a position where she can do them any harm. After his awakening, Amerigo calls Charlotte "stupid," but her stupidity, like Kate Croy's, is a moral, not an intellectual, shortcoming. Even in the first volume she admits that she cannot understand Maggie, who had always thought of herself as a little mouse compared to Charlotte. But once her eyes have been opened to the situation she confronts, Maggie *does* understand Charlotte, whereupon she proceeds to manage her affairs so successfully that her rival is driven from the field.

Amerigo's aestheticism and his passiveness are, then, clearly established. Dorothea Krook calls him "James's quintessential Aesthetic Man," and to John R. Theobald, his worst enemy, he is not only a "sensitive exquisite" but a dilettante, gigolo, and wastrel.[14] He realizes that the tendencies he has inherited from his aristocratic, sometimes criminal ancestors leave something to be desired, but he makes a distinction between his ancestors and himself, and though he realizes that he lacks the "moral sense" as Americans understand it, he insists that he entered into his engagement with Maggie in complete good faith. He is a complete snob, but though he does not so much look down upon his social inferiors as simply fail to see them, he does not wish to hurt anybody. "My dear friend," the gentle hedonist tells Fanny Assingham, "it's always a question of doing the best for one's self one can—without injury to others." If there are waste places or empty places in his nature, he recognizes their existence and hopes to fill them in, for his shortcomings are balanced by his humility. But it is Colonel Assingham who, in quite the most perceptive thing he ever says, puts his finger on his heaviest handicap when he exclaims, "What in the world did you ever suppose was going to happen? The man's in a position where he has nothing to do."

It is clear that James believed him to be redeemable and worth fighting for, not only because Maggie passionately loves him but because he carried within himself the seeds of growth, and if the reader does not share this impression, the book's ending must be unsatisfying or unconvincing. Actually, Amerigo plays an important part in saving his marriage and Charlotte's too. If he had not recognized and responded to his wife's superiority to his actual or potential mistress, nothing that anybody else could have done would have saved his marriage; it was when she learned that he had not told Charlotte what she had discovered that Maggie knew she was within sight of her goal. When, at the

end, the Prince "sees" only Maggie, he learns, perhaps for the first time, that both vision and intelligence are helplessly moral. In *The Imagination of
Loving*, Naomi Lebowitz sees the *Golden Bowl* situation in terms of "The Frog Prince": "The young
Princess must win her Prince who, under an evil
spell, has become a Frog. She must conquer him by
love and knowledge, enter the carriage with her
Frog-Prince, transformed once more back to his old
self, and ride away from the realm of the Father-
King." Only this time it is the Father-King who rides
off with the Wicked Witch, tamed and hopefully
transformed, while the Prince is not so much
changed "back to his old self" as given the hope of
becoming something he never was before.

The most important character in the *Bowl*, the
Princess, Maggie Verver, has been conceived (or
misconceived) by critics as everything from a Christ
figure to a monster. The second view is too silly to
require serious refutation,[15] but it should be understood that the first is also inadmissible. James certainly glorifies his heroine by using religious imagery in presenting her, but he does not confine
himself to such; neither does he ever permit his
book to become an allegory. Maggie's effort, though
eminently praiseworthy, is not self-sacrificing; her
aim is to save her own as well as her father's marriage and regain the man she loves. She is a winner,
not a loser, and unlike Milly Theale, she does not
die for the sins of others, although they certainly
cause her great suffering.[16]

When we meet Maggie, she is a "funny" little
person, lovable but lacking in poise, not wise in the
ways of the world, "a small creeping thing" who
"lives in terror" and is quite incapable of the "style"
of which Charlotte is past mistress. She has the kind
of innocence James was likely to associate with

Americans, but in her case this is accented by the fact that her father's wealth had sheltered her not only from evil but from all the shocks and conflicts of life.[17] "She wasn't born to know evil," says Mrs. Assingham. "She must never know it." The power of the great card party scene which Peter Brooks well describes as illustrating both "the threat of melodramatic outburst and its transcendence"[18] inheres in Maggie's "horror of finding evil seated all at its ease where she had only dreamed of good; the horror of the thing hideously *behind*, behind so much trusted, so much pretended, nobleness, cleverness, tenderness. It was the first sharp falsity she had known in her life."

Great as the shock is, she does not flee from it. Against the grain of her nature, she sets to work to conquer it, and she succeeds so well that at last Fanny calls her "amazing" and "terrible." Her unwillingness to involve her father in her hurt deprives her of her natural ally and thrusts her into a position where she must keep not only her own counsel but even, on occasion, his. Her balance, her equilibrium is perilous. James compares her to a dancer, a trapezist, an actress, and even a dramatist, and if it be objected that an actress must *act*, whereas it is Maggie's cruel lot that she must refrain from all overt acting, we ought to remember that sometimes the very greatest actors seem to do nothing but *will* the audience to see what they want them to see. Her victory is measured by the extent to which at last she can bear anything "for love."

"My idea is this, that when you love only a little you're naturally not jealous—or are only jealous a little, so that it doesn't matter. But when you love in a deeper and intenser way, then you're in the very same proportion jealous; your jealousy has intensity and, no doubt, ferocity.

When however you love in the most abysmal and unutterable way of all — why then you're beyond everything and nothing can pull you down."

There is no denying that she comes before the end to feel her power and enjoy feeling it, for James tells us that "she rose of a sudden to the desire to possess and use" the others, "even to the extent of fairly defying, of directly exploiting, or possibly quite enjoying . . . the felt element of curiosity with which they regarded her," and since we all know the truth of the saying that all power corrupts and absolute power corrupts absolutely, she is to that extent corrupted, not selfless, not the Christ figure her more sentimental admirers would have her.

It is also true of course that although the Prince has shared Charlotte's sin, he gets off much more lightly than she does and seems unpleasantly superior toward her once he has escaped from her toils. But if she is exiled, so is the husband who probably knows that she has been at least spiritually unfaithful to him, and if she has lost the Prince, her husband has been separated from his daughter. Moreover, nobody is compelling Charlotte to go to America with Verver, any more than anybody compelled her to marry him; if she goes, it is because she prefers, even under the circumstances posited, to be the wife of a multimillionaire rather than return to her premarital state. It should also be noted that such images as that of the "silken halter looped round her beautiful neck" by which Matthiessen and others have been so shocked, come not from James but from Maggie. "It's always terrible for women," she says, another indication that she understands and feels for Charlotte as Charlotte never does for her.

The cornerstones of Theodore Roosevelt's for-

eign policy were that you must never speak of another nation as a "potential enemy" of the United
States and that if you are going to make a demand,
it must be made in such a way that the other party
can back down without losing face. Save that her
demand is never more than implied, this is the way
Maggie treats Charlotte. When she lies to her and
allows her to pretend that she is going to America
of her own free will, she is simply saving Charlotte's
pride. Even at the end, when Amerigo wishes to
strip her of her defenses, she will not have it. "'Correct' her?" she asks him. "Aren't you rather forget-
ting who she is?" Unless Maggie's critics think she
ought simply to have acquiesced in the liaison and
done nothing about it, it is difficult to see how she
could have treated Charlotte more considerately
than she does.

Both Maggie and her father *are* open to criticism, however, for their failure adequately to realize
and admit their responsibility not for what Charlotte
and the Prince do but for their own share in giving
them the opportunity to do it. No man should marry
one woman as a service to another, and surely the
stupidity of the Ververs became culpable at the
point where they called Charlotte in "as a specialist
might be summoned to an invalid's chair" and threw
her and Amerigo together as they did. Even at the
end Maggie tells the Prince that it is as if Charlotte's
unhappiness "had been necessary to us—as if we
had needed her, at her own cost, to build us up and
start us," and she also tells Fanny that the difference
between her separation from her father and that between Charlotte and the Prince is that "for them it's
just, it's right, it's deserved, while for us it's only
sad and strange and not caused by our fault." The
Ververs are not always so blind as that, since as early
as Book Fourth, Chapter 5, they wonder whether

they have not lived too selfishly and secludedly. Nevertheless, the passages I have quoted make it clear that although James does not obscure ethical values, he also eschews blind partisanship and is less concerned to judge than to understand.

# 11
# Addenda: *The Outcry; The Ivory Tower; The Sense of the Past*

It seems a pity that the last novel Henry James had a chance to publish during his lifetime should have been so inconsequential a piece as *The Outcry*. Like *The Other House*, it was a novelized play, but it is far more insignificant than that work.

The whole thing begain in 1909 with Charles Frohman's ambitious plan for a repertory season in London enlisting James along with such famous playwrights as Barrie, Shaw, Galsworthy, and Granville-Barker. On July 19 James wrote Mrs. W. K. Clifford that

I am interesting myself deeply in the three act comedy I have undertaken for Frohman—and which I find ferociously difficult—but with a difficulty that, thank God, draws me on and fascinates. If I can go on *believing* in my subject I can go on treating it, but sometimes I have a mortal chill and wonder if I ain't damnably deluded.

He finished it on December 17, but the work of preparing it for production was delayed by a long and serious illness which began in January, and when the death of King Edward VII on May 6, 1910 closed the theaters, Frohman canceled his plans and paid James a forfeit of £200. On April 19, 1911, the author wrote C. E. Wheeler that he had turned the play into a novel "so as not to have to view it as merely wasted labour on the one hand and not have sickeningly to hawk it about on the other," and on October 5 the novel was published by Methuen in London and Scribners in New York. To James's astonishment it sold very well. As we have seen, he had had difficulty *"believing"* in his subject even while trying to write the play, and by November he was blushing to tell Edith Wharton that the insignificant novel was "on its way to a fifth edition" while *The Golden Bowl* was even yet only in its third.[1]

There is no indication in the notebooks or elsewhere that *The Outcry* had any literary sources, and there are no noteworthy differences between the play and the novel. The three books of the novel correspond to the three acts of the play, and the dialogue is virtually the same in both versions. Both dialogue and narrative are definitely "late James," and one might reasonably suppose that many readers willing to give *The Wings of the Dove* or *The Golden Bowl* the concentration they demand might still balk at approaching such a trifle as *The Outcry* with similar care, a circumstance which adds to one's wonderment about the good initial sale.

The outcry is the fuss engendered in London over the fear of England's art treasures being snapped up and whisked out of the country by "filthy rich" American collectors. Lord Theign's need of money has been caused by his worthless elder daughter, Kitty Imber, who has piled up enormous gambling debts that he must cover or allow her to be exposed. Breckenridge Bender is the wealthy American on Lord Theign's trail, representative of "such a conquering horde as invaded the old civilisation, only armed now with huge

cheque-books instead of with spears and bat-
tleaxes." Lord Theign will not let him have the Reynolds portrait of an ancestor at any price, but he
would be willing to sell him a prized Moretto for
ten thousand pounds. Bender, however, is not interested in "ten thousand pound pictures" but only
in deals that will create a sensation. Hugh Crimble,
a budding art connoisseur who has become a friend
of Lord Theign's charming younger daughter, Lady
Grace, suspects that the Moretto is really a Montavano,[2] one of only eight examples known, which
would increase its value to about a hundred thousand pounds, a figure that *would* interest Bender,
but its certification awaits more expert opinion.

Meanwhile Crimble, whom Lord Theign regards as an impudent upstart, and Lady Grace have
begun to fall in love, and both set their faces against
art treasures leaving the country. This unfortunately
leads to an estrangement between Lord Theign and
his daughter, and when the picture is publicly ex-
hibited, the young people's cause is taken up by
press and public. Grace has another suitor, favored
by her father, "his awful mother's son," the odious
Lord Jim (the mother is the duchess to whom Kitty
is in debt). Once Lord Jim has told the Prince of
Wales that Lord Theign plans to give his picture to
the nation and the prince has announced his intention of calling to thank him, there can no longer be
any question of selling to Bender. At the end, the
visit of His Royal Highness impends, and we are
given to understand that Grace and Hugh will make
a match of it and that the widowed Lord Theign will
do the same with Lady Sandgate, a mature woman,
the owner of another valuable portrait sought by collectors, who has served as a kind of confidante to
both him and Grace all through the story.

Many complications characteristic of Edwardian drama are introduced, and there is more forming and re-forming than we often find in longer and more elaborate works. James manages it all as well as most contemporary dramatists did, and the dropping of the final curtain upon the company awaiting the arrival of the prince is a clever teasing device, but there is no reason to suppose that *The Outcry* would have been any more of an ornament to the English stage than it became a milestone in the development of the English-American novel. On the "cause" to which Crimble and Lady Grace commit themselves, James does not seem to take a definite stand. Although in life he did express some doubts over the extensive collecting of his friend Mrs. Gardner, he did not condemn Verver in *The Golden Bowl*, and he is careful to include a reference to England's own rape of the Elgin Marbles in *The Outcry* itself. In any case, there are so many more urgent causes now that it seems unlikely any American reader will commit himself to the thesis that it is immoral to purchase European works of art for American collections or that American museums should display only American work. All the characters in *The Outcry* are adequately handled (the tempery but basically kind Lord Theign is the best), but none are much more than that, and although seasoned readers will recognize a number of them as familiar Jamesian types, their appreciation is likely to be tempered by the thought that it had all been done better before.

When the novelist died in 1916, he left two unfinished novels of much greater potential: *The Ivory Tower* and *The Sense of the Past*. Edited by Percy Lubbock, they were published as he had left them, along with his "Notes," by Collins in England and

Scribners in America in September and October 1917 and were also added to the New York Edition, bringing the total number of volumes to twenty-six.

As we have seen in Chapter 1 of this book, James undertook his American tour of 1904–1905 because he was hungry for new material for fiction, but illness, death in the family, and the necessity of borrowing time to write *The American Scene* and the autobiographical works and to prepare the New York Edition, with its extensive prefaces and revisions, threw up many roadblocks in the way of getting at *The Ivory Tower*, the first novel he had attempted with an American setting since *The Bostonians*. On December 3, 1908, he wrote Howells of having "broken ground on an American novel," but Lubbock did not index this as a reference to *The Ivory Tower* in his collection of James's letters, and it probably refers to what James was first calling "The 'K. B.' Case" and then "Mrs. Max." Whatever may have been written of this work has not survived, but James used a number of names from it in *The Ivory Tower*, which, as we have it, seems to have been begun, as Lubbock says, "early in 1914."[3] Although James did not know it, it had been in a sense subsidized by Edith Wharton, who persuaded Scribners to offer him an advance of $8,000, secretly diverting the funds from her own account with them. But when the agony of the war came upon him, he found that he could not go on with it. "Black and hideous to me is the tragedy that gathers, and I'm sick beyond cure to have lived to see it." The trouble was that to him "the subject-matter of one's effort has become *itself* utterly treacherous and false—its relation to reality utterly given away and smashed. Reality is a world that was to be capable of *this*—and how represent the horrific capability *historically* latent, historically ahead of it?" It was true that he had lived through "the age of the mistake,"[4] but he had never shared in the mistake, at least not since the days of the Spanish-American War, which, like William James, he had hated; touching as these utterances are, it is astonishing that he should have failed to perceive that the world he was depicting in the *Tower* was just the kind of world that might have been expected, sooner or later, to produce the horror in which it now wallowed.

Even in its fragmentary state, *The Ivory Tower* has been warmly, even extravagantly, praised by good critics; perhaps Elizabeth Stevenson goes furthest when she calls it and *The Sense of the Past* "both potentially greater than anything that had preceded them."[5] But to make such a statement it is necessary to take a good deal on faith and to rely as much on James's notes as on the portion of the novel he finished, for it reaches only the first chapter of the fourth book out of a contemplated ten, and although the author speaks of his "planned compactness, absolutely precious and not to be compromised with" and his "intensities of foreshortening," it moves exceptionally slowly even for him through a prose about as dense as he ever achieved in fiction.

As far as we get, Graham Fielder, son of Frank Betterman's late, estranged half sister, comes back to Newport from Europe to become the heir of his dying uncle. Rosanna Gaw, whom he had known as a child, the daughter of Betterman's embittered former business partner, Abel Gaw, who has succeeded in effecting a partial reconciliation between the two old men, rejoices in "Gray's" good fortune because it has troubled her that it was partly upon her advice that he had refused a previous overture from Betterman. Gaw and Betterman die on the same day, and the way is now open for the finan-

cially innocent Fielder to get into the clutches of
the unscrupulous Horace ("Haughty") Vint, to
whom he feels indebted for having once saved his
life in Switzerland and to whom he now entrusts
the management of his fortune. From the "Notes,"
which are not the kind of thing we have for *The
Ambassadors* but rather a series of self-communings
in which James ruminates over the problems he
faces and tries to work out solutions for them, we
learn that Vint would betray his trust and Fielder
behave as magnanimously as Milly Theale, but we
do not know how James planned to end the story
nor, though Rosanna obviously loves Gray, whether
they would finally be united.[6]

We do know, however, that the action was intended to cover a year and that it was to move from
Newport to New York to Lenox, Massachusetts
(James had flirted with the idea of both Boston and
California). Each book was to focus on a single character, "treated from its own centre, as, though with
qualifications [in] The Awkward Age." The principal image or symbol is the ivory tower itself, the
Indian cabinet which Rosanna presents to Gray, one
of whose drawers contains a letter to him, written
by her father shortly before his death. Gray had appealed to Betterman primarily because of his complete detachment from "business," and "ivory
tower" must surely here carry something of its usual
meaning, but we do not know what the letter contains nor when, if ever, Gray opens it.[7]

In spite of James's desire to write a thoroughly
American novel, the Newport setting he knew so
well is indicated only in a very general way. We
know from *The American Scene* that he had returned in 1904 to that loved spot only to find it quite
blighted by the vulgar display of people who had
much more money and much less culture than was

good for them, and no proletarian novelist ever painted a more devastating picture of the very rich than James does here. Abel Gaw has been almost wholly dehumanized by money lust and the cruel exigencies of the marketplace, and if, as his name unsubtly suggests, Betterman is not quite so bad, it is principally because we do not meet him until after he has experienced a kind of awakening and turned away in a kind of repentance. "I've *been* business," he says, "and nothing else in the world."

Except for Rosanna, who is hopelessly at odds with her environment and who hates every dollar of the twenty million her father's sins have saddled her with,[8] the young people are no better; in their idle frivolity they are even worse. "We're all unspeakably corrupt," says Vint, and on that subject if none other he may be regarded as an authority. Perhaps there may still be some hope for Davey Bradham, but his wife, Gussy, is "crude and hard and blatant" as well as "vulgar," a "portentous woman." James had long thought of American women and girls as the custodians of American culture; now, in the midst of overwhelming vulgarity, the burden has apparently become too heavy for them to bear. Even the lovely Cissy Foy, who appeals to Gray on his aesthetic side (the morally impressive Rosanna having "no more taste than an elephant"), is allied with the swindler "Haughty" Vint; like Kate and Densher and like Charlotte and the Prince, they would marry if they could afford it. Surely, if James intended to suggest the future which is our present, he could hardly have done better than have Gray see the house he has inherited "very much as he might have eyed some monstrous modern machine, one of those his generation was going to be expected to master, to fly in, to fight in, to take the terrible woman of the future out for airings in."

James had often described Americans as innocents abroad, pitted against European sophisticates;
here the process is reversed, and the Americans
themselves become corruptionists, for Graham
Fielder, though of American ancestry, is essentially
a product of European culture. On his return to
America he is like James himself: "Everything
played before him, everything his senses embraced;
and since his landing in New York . . . the play had
been of a delightful violence." After his own awakening, Frank Betterman leaves his money to Gray
because, as Elizabeth Stevenson puts it, this is the
only thing he can do to try to place "elemental
power in America back into the hands of the gentle
and sensitive,"[9] and he succeeds so well that Gray
not only resists not evil in his relations with Horace
Vint but even shares with Rosanna the feeling that
"the black and merciless things that are behind the
great possessions" they now control could not be
purged away even by devoting them to benevolent
purposes, for they have been "so dishonored and
stained and blackened at their very roots, that it
seems . . . they carry their curse with them. . . ."
The most impressive figure in the book is Abel
Gaw, who is presented with almost Gothic vividness. "The effect" of his activities in the money market, as Rosanna observes, "has been to dry up his
life." He was "incapable of thought save in the sub-
limities of arithmetic," and after his daughter has
built a bridge between him and his former partner
and enemy, he squats on Betterman's veranda, "like
a ruffled hawk, motionless but for his tremor, with
his beak, which had pecked so many hearts out, visibly sharper than ever." He sits "in a low basket-
chair which covered him save for little more than
his small protrusive foot, crossed over a knee and
agitated by incessant nervous motion," with never

a thought of opening a book, seeking a chance to talk, taking "a step of exercise," or giving "in any manner a sign of an unsatisfied want." He is waiting impatiently for Betterman to die so that he may gloat over him and find out how much less than himself he had been "worth," and when he is informed, mistakenly, that Betterman has rallied sufficiently since his nephew's coming so that there is now hope of his recovery, the shock and disappointment kill him.

When James gave up *The Ivory Tower* because he did not believe himself able to get on with it under wartime conditions, he turned back to *The Sense of the Past*, apparently hoping that a fantasy might provide refuge from a reality grown so dark and grim. It was not a wise choice, for the subject bristled with difficulties that would have challenged all his powers when he was physically and mentally at the top of his bent. Even in *The Golden Bowl*, I think, there is no such minute shading as he projects here, and his "Notes," which pose at least as many problems as they offer solutions, fairly make the reader's head swim, not this time by the prose, which is clear enough, but rather by the difficulties inherent in the situations themselves.

*The Sense of the Past* had been begun before the century. After the success of "The Turn of the Screw," Frank Doubleday, apparently prompted by Rudyard Kipling, had asked James to supply him with something in kind, but by the time he had written thirty thousand words in January 1900, the publisher had lost interest. If he had wanted another "Screw," it is easy to see why, for atmospherically *The Sense of the Past* is, as James was aware, "different and less ghostly and merely apparitional." In June, Howells, who had formed an alliance with Clarke and Company of Chicago, approached his friend about doing a fifty thousand-word "international ghost" for newspaper syndication, and James embraced the project eagerly, although he feared that the "damnable *difficulty*" of the job he had undertaken for Doubleday would very likely prevent his using that idea, "international" though it was. Since Howells was to withdraw from his association with Clarke in July, this project too died aborning, and the thirty thousand words James had set aside apparently lay undisturbed until the late autumn of 1914. Then he sent Theodora Bosanquet down to Lamb House to fetch the manuscript to him in London, and while awaiting her return he drew up the "First Statement (Preliminary)" which now appears in *The Notebooks of Henry James*. The later, more elaborate "Notes" printed with the text of the novel were drawn up after he had revised what he had written in 1900. As it now stands, *The Sense of the Past* runs to about seventy-five thousand words. According to Percy Lubbock, in his preface to the 1917 book, James continued to work on it "at intervals until the autumn of 1915 . . . and was preparing to return to it" when he suffered his stroke on December 2.[10]

The hero, Ralph Pendrel, an American, is another of James's sensitive young men, the author of "An Essay in Aid of the Reading of History" which has attracted the suffrages of good judges. "He was by the turn of his spirit oddly indifferent to the actual and the possible; his interest was all in the spent and the displaced—in what had been determined and composed roundabout him, what had been presented as a subject and a picture, by ceasing—so far as such things ever cease—to bustle or even to be." He yearned "to remount the stream of time"; "he wanted the very tick of the old stopped clocks"; according to the young American widow with the obviously symbolic name, Aurora Coyne, whom he wished to marry, "the sense of the past" was, before anything else, *his* sense. Aurora herself has no sympathy with such things; she wants a man of action who is committed to doing something in his own country, and unless Pendrel is willing and able to slough off the lure of Europe and the past, she can give him no hope in his suit.

Just now Pendrel has special reason for yielding to this lure, for an English kinsman has died, leaving him a fine eighteenth-century house in Mansfield Square, and "on opening the door" of the house with his latchkey, Ralph "lets himself into" or "disappears into the Past," exchanging identities with another Ralph Pendrel of some ninety years before who had come from America to wed Molly Midmore and who comes down from his portrait in the house to greet him.

When he steps into his predecessor's shoes, the 1910 Ralph Pendrel steps into his situation also, yet to say that the two have "exchanged" identities is an unwarranted simplification of a condition almost unstatably complicated. "The point is that I'm not myself," the 1910 man tells the American ambassador to whom he talks in an attempt to clarify the situation. "I'm somebody else." And so he is, yet, strangely and irreconcilably, without also ceasing to be himself. "Enormous, however, as the assimilation may be," so James put it in his "Notes," "it is not absolutely perfect," for he is both the other man and not the other man, being just sufficiently the other, "his prior, his own, self, not to be able to help living in that a bit too."

The inevitable dislocation is devastating. Ralph knows a great deal that he could not possibly have known in 1910, but there are curious, disconcerting gaps in his knowledge, and he is himself quite as strange to the Midmores as they are to him. "I'm not a prophet or a soothsayer," he says, "and don't pretend to the gift of second sight. Therefore perhaps it is that these things glimmer upon me at moments from a distance, so that I find myself in the act of catching them, and am liable to lose them again." It is hard to separate the haunted from the haunters in this story or determine whether the dead haunt the living or the living the dead, and the action, such as it is, is involved with and/or determined by what happened ninety years before. Two things do stand out clearly, however. The first is that the Midmores are at least as much interested in Ralph's fortune as they are in him, and the second is that he has engaged himself to the wrong girl. His real mate is "sweet Nan," the younger sister, "a slight, fine, concentrated little person," the only member of the family who, not being repelled by his strangeness, is capable of achieving rapport with him but whom they are in the process of sacrificing to the detestable Sir Christopher Bland, a creature "with a small sort of reaffiné Horace Walpole atmosphere about him," whom, as James's "Notes" make clear, she regards with horror. As far as the novel goes, Nan hardly appears, but the plan was that Molly should finally break off and Nan return Ralph's affection but sacrifice her own happiness to help him return to Aurora and his own time.

Although there is nothing about Aurora to make the reader satisfied to regard her as a suitable replacement for the lost Nan, this is undoubtedly the right, the only possible, ending, for a third thing that is clear about *The Sense of the Past* is the testimony it bears to James's own essential modernity. He had little feeling for history and no interest in the historical romances so popular in his time, and the only past in which he delighted was one recent enough to be "visitable." When John L. Balderston and J. C. Squire made *The Sense of the Past* into the distinguished play *Berkeley Square*, in which Leslie Howard performed so impressively on both stage and screen, they carried the action back into the eighteenth century, but James had not ventured farther back than 1810. For all the desire Ralph had entertained to "remount the stream of time," it was not only because he did not wish to be trapped in the past with the wrong woman that he failed to find himself at home there. His instantaneous, delighted tribute to Nan, upon his first glimpse of her, is, "Why, she's modern, *modern!*" and in his "Notes" James speaks of her as "the exquisite, the delicate, the worthy-herself-to-be-modern younger girl."

In what may well be the most careful study of *The Sense of the Past* that has been made, David W. Beams sees James as creating in it "perhaps the most brilliant structure of any of his novels."[11] This seems an odd thing to say of a novel of which only four books were written, with the last longer than the first three together and obviously different in style and method. Like *The Ivory Tower*, however, it is certainly one of James's most original works, and source hunters can pin down positively only two things. We have James's own word for it that he intended the American ambassador for a loving portrait of James Russell Lowell, and he could not possibly have used the business of the portrait without thinking of *The Castle of Otranto* (if evidence is needed here, we may find it in his reference to Horace Walpole in connection with Nan's unwelcome suitor). Such works as Hawthorne's *The House of the Seven Gables* and "Edward Randolph's Portrait" may also have been in his mind, and the time-traveling element may have been connected with *A Connecticut Yankee in King Arthur's Court* by Mark Twain and *The Time Machine*, more recently published by James's friend H. G. Wells.[12] (It is interesting and suggestive that James's sympathies are more undividedly "modern" than Mark Twain's.) As it stands, James's novel is by no means his most successful story of the supernormal or supernatural, but it certainly stands as his most ambitious enterprise in this field. I doubt that either he or anybody else could ever have solved all the problems which would have had to be resolved in order to mold it into a really satisfying work of art, but anybody who could have done so would have had a masterpiece on his hands, and even as it stands, it will always cast its spell over those who care for the mystical overtones in literature or in life.

# 12
# Significances[1]

Henry James's novels were written from the standpoint of an observer, not an actor, in the theater of life. His was the "visiting" mind, operative from "the rim of the circle." Such a temperament may lead its possessor to confront life merely with a claim for exemption; on the other hand, it can mean an ability to live vicariously, almost selflessly, in others' lives. Like his own Rowland Mallett, James had "sympathy as an active faculty." But an age which understands the contemplative life so little as our own must experience difficulty in understanding such things, and widespread obfuscations concerning the character of James's works have been the natural result.

Setting aside the noncreative sensation of physical pain, probably the most intense forms of experience that human beings can know are sexual intercourse, mystical contemplation, and aesthetic creativity. James seems never to have known either the first or the second, although he comes pretty close to having achieved a transfer of the latter from the devotional to the aesthetic plane in his rapturous communings with his muse. The third, however, he knew as well as any man who has ever lived.

He is, before all else, the novelist of experience imaginatively apprehended. He wanted to understand life, not merely to fling himself into it, and for understanding a certain detachment is requisite. He embodies, therefore, the principle that experience itself is worthless until it has been adequately interpreted by the mind and its significance assessed. This is the answer to those who feel that James could not be a great novelist because he never "lived." With him as with Lambert Strether, observation itself became the most intense possible form of activity. Nothing was taken for granted. Everything must be "looked at and listened to with absorbed attention, pondered in thought, linked with its associations" and never released "until the remembrance had been crystallized in expression, so that it could be appropriated like a tangible object."[2] The process increased in intensity—and became progressively more wearing—throughout his lifetime, and when, after 1914, he applied it to the harrowing business of the war, it may well have killed him.

In the light of these considerations, James's addiction to the use in fiction of a reflecting consciousness emerges as of something larger than technical interest. "I see you as you are," says Ralph Pendrel to Aurora Coyne, "and you don't see me; so that after all I've in a manner the advantage." If it is "high lucidity" that you are after, obviously you must tell your story from the standpoint of somebody who can understand. So *The Spoils of Poynton* would not "come" until Fleda Vetch had been born in the author's imagination to comprehend the significance of what must take place.

All these considerations have been ignored by those who, early and late, have bewailed James's residence abroad. He did not, as the man in the street has often supposed, love Europe and hate America. Many of his finest characters are Americans; he was conscious of poverty and suffering in Europe long before he wrote *The Princess Casamassima*, and he saw the chink in England's armor before it had begun to split. It is quite true, however, that he ceased, in a manner, to be an American without ever really becoming a European. But since he did not write the kind of fiction that depends on immersion in a particular environment, this is comparatively unimportant; if he was detached from America, he was also detached from politics, from business, and from much else besides. Of course this is not to say that he paid no price for his detachment but simply that it was not due primarily to his European residence; he would have been detached from the American scene even if he had never laid eyes on Europe. Like all artists, but more than most because more completely the artist, he was a stranger and pilgrim upon earth.

Yet James was not a philosophical novelist; it is ironical that so much should have been made over the difficulty of reading a writer whose books are so free of "ideas" and who was never really an intellectual except in his attitude toward fiction. Even in the arts his range was comparatively narrow. He had a competent knowledge of painting, and his own work has often been compared with that of great painters, especially Veronese, Sargent, and Renoir. But music—and even poetry—meant comparatively little to him, and even as a critic he was hardly at home with anything except nineteenth- and twentieth-century fiction in French and English. There are not many male novelists who concentrate to his extent upon personal relationships. Humanity spoke to him as nature speaks to the Romantic poet, and in *The Question of Our Speech* he declares bluntly that "all life comes back to the question of our relations with each other."

There are dangers involved in such concentration, and James did not escape them all. As we have seen, there are unbelievable situations in his books and unthinkable observations and concentrations. But he was always saved from the excesses of the narcissists by his objectivity. He is the most objective of all "psychological" novelists, and although he is committed to the consideration of problems, it is not his own problems with which he deals. This is the "classical" element in James's art.

He did not stress the importance of either learning or formal philosophy for the understanding of life; he probably would have matched his mother's understanding against anybody's. What was indispensable was "awareness." The best thing ever said about him is Joseph Conrad's description of him as the "historian of fine consciences," but the fineness of his characters is not exclusively moral. Consequently, they are forever making distinctions which the anti-Jacobites regard as merely exercises in hairsplitting; consequently again, the reader who has really entered into James's world pays the price of always being tempted to consider most other novelists underdeveloped in comparison.

Exceptional persons are by definition rare; committed as he is to "the superior case," it is not surprising that James should have seemed to many to be standing out of the novelistic mainstream. And since the logic of the situation obliged him to set his people free from ordinary domestic and economic cares so that he—and they—might concentrate on the spiritual problems which are the main concern of his fiction, he was obliged to choose many of them from the leisure class. So he has been accused of trifling and of snobbery; neither of these charges can be sustained. There are humble, simple souls in his books who are lovingly presented; he

generally refuses to give them the center of the stage
not because he does not value them but simply because they cannot provide him with the material he
needs for his subtle and analytic art. In his pages
the world of "society" merely provides a theater for
a searching consideration of spiritual realities, a
search which he conducted with a sense of values
as sound as any that can be found in fiction.

He wanted the largest, most passionate, most
deeply significant human themes possible for his
work, and he insisted that novels must have charm
even when they deal with dispiriting subjects.
When his own fictions seem to lack breadth, his
basic modesty seems the cause. For all the monstrous "development" of which he was capable, he
was still, in his own way, an unpretentious writer.
He had an idea that there is no point in carrying a
heavy lamp where a light one will do, that any
theme is a large theme if it is adequately handled
and any subject dignified if it is treated in a dignified manner; thus Maisie, Fleda, and the heroine
of "In the Cage" ennoble the degraded concerns
with which they have to do.

What people generally mean when they find
James deficient in vitality is that he leaves out the
fire in the members, but even aside from the fact
that there is, as we have seen, plenty of sex and to
spare in the late novels, it is dangerous to isolate
James's treatment of sex or of anything else. When
Graham Greene accuses him of evasiveness in indicating the nature of the accident which he claimed
incapacitated him for the Civil War, he overlooks
not only that we now know the injury in question
to have been an injury to James's *back* but, more
important, that literal recording is hardly the note
of any of James's autobiographical writings. When
Bernard Smith objects to his intellectualizing of sex

and his lack of interest in copulation as such, one can only point out that James treats all other human activities in exactly the same way. Deny the legitimacy of an oblique aesthetic method, and the whole Jamesian novel world falls to the ground.[3] It *is* important, however, to remember that James is a pre-Freudian novelist. His range is that of the conscious, not the subconscious, mind. Although he has had some influence on the "stream-of-consciousness" novel, he would not have cared for it. Like Katherine Mansfield, he might well have felt that making everything equally important, it made everything equally unimportant, and he would certainly have thought that lacking form, it must also lack art.

The principal difficulty with James's later books from the point of view of the uncultivated reader is of course the difficulty of the method and the style. But there was no quest for mystification on James's part: Philip Guedalla got the thing exactly wrong when he divided the novels under James the First, James the Second, and The Old Pretender. On the contrary, James is committed to clarity up to the hilt, determined to leave nothing to chance, and so determined to explain everything that he sometimes becomes obscure through his very anxiety.

This final style has been variously described. William James, who did not like it, called it "the method of narration by interminable elaboration of suggestive reference" and "complication of innuendo and associative reference on the enormous scale." Mr. Dooley wanted James to "pit it right up into Popper's hand," and Mrs. Humphry Ward spoke of "this involution, this deliberation in attack, this slowness of approach toward a point which in the end was generally triumphantly rushed."

Several writers have invoked musical parallels; among these, James Huneker actually found "simplification" in James's final manner. What he meant was that James omits much of the framework which other novelists think necessary. But the omission of these noncreative guideposts, upon which the reader has been taught to rely, do not make for easy reading; indeed, James's omissions are quite as likely to give trouble as what seems to some the overdevelopment of what he chooses to give. His habit of concentration on the results of actions rather than the actions themselves was, however, an inevitable concomitant of his search for meaning.

At times the objective world seems almost to have disappeared from James's later novels. He concentrates absolutely upon the subject in hand—refusing to allow either himself or the reader a moment of relaxation—but the resultant intensity is sometimes secured by shifting the action to a plane where the author's own limitations of knowledge and experience do not matter. In addition to all this, he sometimes seems to be giving over the standard novelistic practice of differentiating between characters by supplying each with distinctive speech patterns. This is not because he is trying "to make everybody talk like Henry James" but rather because he is going in for a "surface" as smooth and finished as that of the great tapestries.

If the world of James's fiction is not a philosopher's world, it is, nevertheless, a world of values. James was not formally religious, and he did not pretend to be able to explain the mystery of life, but such tales as "The Altar of the Dead" show that he had a deep and abiding sense of the sacred, and he tells us specifically that the origin of the idea for that story could not be isolated for the very reason that the feeling had always been there.

Such a man would obviously subscribe to no unnecessary creedal baggage. So far as doctrine goes, James comes closest to committing himself to the hope of immortality.[4] Unlike recent, deterministic novelists, he also affirms the freedom of the will. He knew that this can never be demonstrated, but he held that even if it were an illusion, we must cling to it, if for no other reason then because the moral life (and the art of fiction which portrays it) can exist only on the basis of this postulate.

James is pragmatic also on the great question of the livableness of life. He knew that we live in a world in which, time and again, the spoils go to the impercipient and the undiscerning, but he knew too that even in defeat, their opponents win a dark victory which they alone among the sons of men can know. James would not have cared much for Samuel Butler's novels, but he would surely have agreed with Butler that the question "Is life worth living?" was a question for an embyro rather than a man.

Of late years much has been made of his sense of evil. Graham Greene went so far as to find it "religious in its intensity" and the ruling fantasy which drove him to write, which seems a bit melodramatic. Socialistically minded critics, on the other hand, have been inclined to exaggerate his social consciousness, although there is no denying that he was aware of something "tigerish" in the world and that he saw widely spreading corruption encrusting civilization itself.

Except in "The Turn of the Screw," however, evil in James is not something that has crawled out of the pit. It wears the best clothes and moves in the best society; it may even fail to recognize itself as evil. With a start, Isabel Archer realizes that she has encountered it in the charming Madame Merle. For James as for Hawthorne, to treat a human being like a thing is the unpardonable sin, and no trouble that one can take to understand another can be too great. And certainly salvation is as difficult in his world as in the New Testament.

Although he valued intelligence, sensitivity, and fine manners, simple love and fidelity were what he cherished most—the love that accepts and forgives and refuses to accept defeat; the love that will not claim even a just reward, lest one should seem, even to oneself, to have wrought pure deeds for love of gain; the good will which reaches out and saves and redeems those who, like Prince Amerigo, are redeemable and which nobly disdains but does not punish those who, like Newman's antagonists in *The American*, are not. Maggie Verver's is the classical statement: "When . . . you love in the most abysmal and unutterable way at all—why then you're beyond everything and nothing can pull you down." Among other things, such love necessarily involves fidelity, and the essential point about James's sexual ethic is not, as has sometimes been said, that he regarded the sexual act as "wrong" but that he believed that in order to have human dignity, a sexual relationship, once established, must endure.

"To be completely great," Henry James wrote in an early review, "a work of art must lift up the heart," and his own novels do this to an outstanding degree. "Here," cries Howells, "you have the work of a great psychologist, who has the imagination of a poet, the wit of a keen humorist, the conscience of an impeccable moralist, the temperament of a philosopher, and the wisdom of a rarely experienced witness of the world." It ought, one feels, to be enough. More than sixty years after his death, the great expatriate who sometimes professed to have no opinions stands foursquare in the great Christian humanistic and democratic tradition. The men and women who, at the height of World War II, raided the secondhand shops for his out-of-print books knew what they were about. For no writer ever raised a braver banner to which all who love freedom might adhere.

# Notes

The following abbreviations are employed in the references given in the notes.

HJ      Henry James
J       James

## Novels by Henry James

| | |
|---|---|
| AA | *The Awkward Age* |
| Am | *The American* |
| Amb | *The Ambassadors* |
| B | *The Bostonians* |
| C | *Confidence* |
| E | *The Europeans* |
| GB | *The Golden Bowl* |
| IT | *The Ivory Tower* |
| O | *The Outcry* |
| OH | *The Other House* |
| PC | *The Princess Casamassima* |
| PL | *The Portrait of a Lady* |
| R | *The Reverberator* |
| RH | *Roderick Hudson* |
| SF | *The Sacred Fount* |
| SPa | *The Sense of the Past* |
| SPo | *The Spoils of Poynton* |
| TM | *The Tragic Muse* |
| WD | *The Wings of the Dove* |
| WMK | *What Maisie Knew* |
| WS | *Washington Square* |
| WW | *Watch and Ward* |

## *Publishers*

| | |
|---|---|
| CUP | Cambridge University Press |
| HM | Houghton Mifflin Company |
| HUP | Harvard University Press |
| L | J. B. Lippincott Company |
| M | The Macmillan Company |
| Me | Methuen & Co. |
| OUP | Oxford University Press |
| PUP | Princeton University Press |
| S | Charles Scribner's Sons |
| UCP | The University of Chicago Press |
| UNCP | University of North Carolina Press |
| YUP | Yale University Press |

## *Periodicals*

| | |
|---|---|
| *AL* | *American Literature* |
| *ALR* | *American Literary Realism, 1870–1910* |
| *AQ* | *Arizona Quarterly* |
| *CE* | *College English* |
| *CL* | *Comparative Literature* |
| *CLAJo* | *College Language Association Journal* |
| *Crit* | *Criticism* |
| *EIC* | *Essays in Criticism* |
| *ELH* | *English Literary History* |
| *ELN* | *English Language Notes* |
| *ES* | *English Studies* |
| *ESQ* | *Emerson Society Quarterly* |
| *HJR* | *Henry James Review* |
| *HLB* | *Harvard Library Bulletin* |
| *JAS* | *Journal of American Studies* |
| *JNT* | *Journal of Narrative Technique* |
| *MFS* | *Modern Fiction Studies* |
| *MLN* | *Modern Language Notes* |
| *MLQ* | *Modern Language Quarterly* |
| *MLR* | *Modern Language Review* |
| *MP* | *Modern Philology* |
| *MQ* | *Midwest Quarterly* |

| MR | *Markham Review* |
| NCF | *Nineteenth Century Fiction* |
| NEQ | *New England Quarterly* |
| NMAL | *Notes on Modern American Literature* |
| NQ | *Notes and Queries* |
| PLL | *Papers on Language and Literature* |
| PMLA | *Publications of the Modern Language Association* |
| PQ | *Philological Quarterly* |
| SA | *Studi Americani* |
| SAF | *Studies in American Fiction* |
| SAQ | *South Atlantic Quarterly* |
| SN | *Studies in the Novel* |
| SR | *Sewanee Review* |
| TSLL | *Texas Studies in Language and Literature* |
| UR | *University Review*, under this name and its original name, *University of Kansas City Review* |
| UTQ | *University of Toronto Quarterly* |
| WHR | *Western Humanities Review* |

Books not included in "Suggestions for Further Reading" are completely described when first cited in the notes, but books fully described there are identified only by author and title the first time they are cited in any given chapter and thereafter by the shortest intelligible reference.

## 1. BIOGRAPHY

1. Percy Lubbock, ed., *The Letters of Henry James*, I, p. 3.
2. Henry James, *Notes of a Son and Brother* (S, 1914), p. 179.
3. Henry James, *A Small Boy and Others* (S, 1913), pp. 4, 37.
4. *Small Boy*, pp. 233–37; *Son and Brother*, pp. 163–72.
5. *Small Boy*, p. 215.
6. *Small Boy*, pp. 25–26.
7. *Small Boy*, pp. 263–64.

8.  *Letters*, I, p. 4.
9.  *Son and Brother*, pp. 2–3.
10. *Letters*, I, p. 8.
11. *Son and Brother*, p. 344.
12. *Letters*, I, p. 12.
13. Henry James, *The Middle Years* (S, 1917), pp. 8–9, 29.
14. Gamaliel Bradford, *American Portraits, 1875–1900* (HM, 1922), p. 175.
15. *Letters*, I, p. 176.
16. *Letters*, I, p. 180.
17. *Letters*, I, p. 182.
18. *Letters*, I, p. 229.
19. *Letters*, II, p. 9.
20. *Letters*, II, p. 167.
21. *Letters*, II, p. 424.
22. *Letters*, II, p. 388.
23. *Letters*, II, pp. 477–79.

## 2.   THEORY

1.  Henry James, *Partial Portraits* (M, 1895), p. 396. All quotations in this chapter not otherwise credited are from James's prefaces to the New York Edition.
2.  Percy Lubbock, ed., *The Letters of Henry James*, II, p. 15.
3.  *Letters*, I, pp. 103–104.
4.  *Partial Portraits*, p. 402.
5.  *Letters*, I, p. 165.
6.  *Partial Portraits*, p. 390.
7.  *Letters*, II, p. 43.
8.  *Partial Portraits*, p. 389.
9.  *Letters*, I, p. 333.
10. *Partial Portraits*, pp. 375–76.
11. *Letters*, I, p. 249.
12. *Letters*, II, pp. 236–38.
13. *Letters*, II, p. 488.
14. *Letters*, I, p. 347.
15. *Partial Portraits*, p. 406.

## 3. BEGINNING

1. James had no standard length for his fictions, his ideal being to accord each subject the development it needed. He began with short stories and brought out a number of collections during his lifetime: *A Passionate Pilgrim* (1875); *The Madonna of the Future* (1879); *Tales of Three Cities* (1884); *The Author of Beltraffio* (1885); *The Aspern Papers* (1888); *A London Life* (1889); *The Lesson of the Master* (1892); *The Real Thing, The Private Life,* and *The Wheel of Time* (all 1893); *Terminations* (1895); *Embarrassments* (1896); *The Soft Side* (1900); *The Better Sort* (1903); and *The Finer Grain* (1910). All his short stories, collected and uncollected, are now available in Leon Edel, ed., *The Complete Tales of HJ,* 12 volumes (L. 1961–64). There are also works of intermediate length, such as "In the Cage" and "The Turn of the Screw," which latter was published with "Covering End" in *The Two Magics* (1898).

2. *HJ—The Lessons of the Master,* especially pp. 107–12.

3. J. A. Ward, "The Double Structure of *WW*," *TSLL,* 4 (1962–63), 613–24, is the fullest study of the sexual overtones of the novel. See, further, B. R. McElderry, Jr., "J's Revision of *WW*," *MLN,* 67 (1952), 457–61, and Charles Fish, "Form and Revision: The Example of *WW*," *NCF,* 22 (1967–68), 173–90.

4. Leo B. Levy, "The Comedy of *WW*," *Arlington Quarterly,* Vol. I, No. 4 (1968), pp. 86–98, sees this as a realistic departure from most novels of the genre represented.

5. Recent critics manifest a tendency to view Lawrence unfavorably; cf. Lee A. Johnson, "'A Dog in the Manger': J's Depiction of Roger Lawrence in *WW*," *AQ,* 29 (1973), 169–76.

6. Cf. "That Mallet was without vanity I by no means intend to affirm"; "as a rapid glance at his antecedents may help to make the reader perceive"; "The document was voluminous, and we must content

ourselves with giving an extract"; "Mary Garland's letter was so much shorter that we may give it entire"; "We shall not rehearse his confession in detail." At times, too, James comes close to pretending that he is writing history rather than fiction.

7. Viola Dunbar's "A Source for *RH*" is in *MLN*, 63 (1948), 303–310. Oscar Cargill discusses *L'Affaire Clemenceau* in *The Novels of HJ*, p. 32, which see also for some of the other possibilities named. For Veeder, see especially pp. 33 and 115ff. Leon Edel nominates Elena Lowe as the original of Christina in *HJ: The Conquest of London*, pp. 112, 179; for other nominations, see Edward Wagenknecht, *Eve and Henry James*, p. 55n. There is further discussion of Turgenev in Daniel Lerner, "The Influence of Turgenev on HJ," *Slavonic and East European Review*, 20 (1941), 28–54; Viola Dunbar, "The Problem in *RH*," *MLN*, 67 (1952), 109–113; and Dale E. Peterson, *The Clement Vision: Poetic Realism in Turgenev and J* (Kennikat Press, 1975). Because James began his novel the same year he reviewed Turgenev's *A King Lear of the Steppes*, John A. Cook, "The Fool Show in *RH*," *Canadian Review of American Studies*, 4 (1973), 74–86, tries, unconvincingly I think, to show Shakespearean influence. See, further, Paul A. Newlin, "The Development of *RH*: An Evaluation," *AQ*, 27 (1971), 101–23; Robert L. Gale, "Roderick Hudson and Thomas Crawford," *AQ*, 13 (1961), 495–504; and Charlotte Goodman, "HJ's *RH* and Nathaniel Parker Willis's *Paul Fane*," *AL* 43 (1971–72), 642–45. But the best and fullest study of all these matters now is in Adeline R. Tintner's masterly article "*RH*: A Centennial Reading," *HJR*, 2 (1980–81), 172–96, which deals not only with sources in the narrower sense but places the novel in the whole context of the influences from art and literature operative in its time. Cf. also her references, which give much more than can be included here.

8. Joseph Warren Beach, *The Method of HJ*, p. 196, re-

sented having the facts about Roderick filtered through the much less interesting consciousness of Mallet, and T. S. Eliot thought James had been taken in by Rowland and failed to see through him. Recent critics, however, have shown a tendency both to disparage Rowland and at the same time see him as the leading character. Perhaps the most extreme statements are those of John Scherting, "*RH*: A Revaluation," *AQ*, 25 (1969), 101–119, who also believes that Roderick and Christina planned an elopement and that, on one occasion, they had physical relations, and Paul Surgi Speck, "A Structural Analysis of *RH*," *SN*, 2 (1970), 292–304, who argues that Christina was in love with Rowland. Sacvan Bercovitch, "The Revision of Rowland Mallet," *NCF*, 24 (1969–70), 210–21, finds the character less sympathetic in the New York Edition. See also Quentin G. Kraft, "The Central Problem in J's Fictional Thought: From *The Scarlet Letter* to *RH*," *ELH*, 36 (1969), 416–39; Peter J. Conn, "*RH*: The Role of Observer," *NCF*, 26 (1971–72), 65–82; and, for revision, Helène Harvitt, "The Revision of *RH*," *PMLA*, 39 (1924), 203–27, and Raymond D. Havens, pp. 433–34.

9.  This is a kind of combination of Marguerite's two fleeting appearances in the first two acts of Gounod's *Faust*, as Roderick himself remotely suggests by saying that Stenterello may be a phantom "like the black dog in *Faust*." In his essay on *RH* in Lyall H. Powers, ed., *HJ's Major Novels*, Edward Engelberg suggests plausibly that *Faust* may have influenced the novel in other aspects.

10. Christina suggests charity, but does Light stand opposed to darkness or indicate instability? Was James perhaps thinking of the equally enigmatic Queen Christina of Sweden?

11. It has been urged that when Christina does this she is still hoping to mate with Roderick, and this may well be true, for she admits that she has two motives and prefers to keep one of them to herself, but surely

it is more important to note that her basic need is to
satisfy herself by standing well in her own account.

### 4. CONTINUING

1.  The stylistic qualities of *The American* have been
    well described by William Veeder, *HJ—The Lessons
    of the Master*, and Richard Poirier, *The Comic Sense
    of HJ*. Poirier's is the most detailed discussion of the
    book's humor, but cf. Veeder, pp. 117–19, on how,
    although the rendezvous Newman arranges with
    Mrs. Bread to obtain the letter of the marquis is sex-
    ually innocent, the language employed is that of se-
    duction in the popular Rake and Servant Girl ro-
    mances. Some interpreters cannot cope with
    Jamesian subtlety even in so straightforward a book
    as this; thus John Clair's "*Am*: A Reinterpretation,"
    *PMLA*, 74 (1959), 613–18, is a detailed discussion of
    the book James did *not* write. For Clair the only fault
    of the old marquise and her son is a somewhat ex-
    cessive formality, and they treat Newman quite
    fairly. Not only was Mrs. Bread the mistress of the
    late marquis, she is the mother of both Claire and
    Valentin, and the threatened revelation of Claire's
    illegitimacy (which would make *Am* a rerun of *RH*)
    is the weapon Madame de Bellegarde uses to break
    up the engagement! Taken in by the Bellegardes,
    Clair has himself taken in Floyd R. Horowitz, "The
    Christian Time Sequence in HJ's *Am*," *CLAJo*, 9
    (1965–66), 234–45, and apparently also Judith Fryer,
    *The Faces of Eve: Woman in the Nineteenth Century
    American Novel* (OUP, 1976), for although she does
    not mention Clair in a discussion in which she both
    states and doubts that a murder was committed, she
    does list his article in her bibliography and, for good
    measure, sees Claire as "literally comdemned to
    hell," presumably because the convent was located
    in the Rue d'Enfer. Fortunately, some critics are bet-
    ter able to cope with subtleties, e.g., James W. Gar-

gano, "Foreshadowing in *Am*," *MLN*, 74 (1958),
600–601, who points out how the performance of
*Don Giovanni* which Newman and the Bellegardes
attend prepares for the unhappy ending, and Edmund Greeth, "Moonshine and Bloodshed: A Note
on *Am*," *Notes and Queries*, 9 (1962), 105–06. These
little articles are full of large matters.

2.  On these sources, see Cargill, *The Novels of HJ*, pp.
42–46. Adeline R. Tintner, "Balzac's *La Comédie
Humaine* in HJ's *Am*," *Revue de Littérature Com-
parée*, 54 (1980), 101–04, explores the Balzac matter
further; see also her "The House of Atreus and Mme.
de Bellegarde," *NQ*, 20 (1973), 98–99. Michael Kot-
zin, "*Am* and *The Newcomes*," *Etudes Anglaises*, 30
(1977), 420–29, sees resemblances between the two
novels.

3.  On the names in *Am*, see Joseph W. Backus, "'Poor
Valentin' or 'Monsieur le Comte': Variation in Character Designation as Matter for Critical Consideration [in HJ's *Am*]," *Names*, 20 (1972), 47–55, which
covers much more than the title promises, also p. 20
in R. W. Butterfield's "*Am*," in John Goode, ed., *The
Air of Reality*, an admirable study of the characters
in the novel and of Newman in particular.

4.  Mutlu Blasing, "Double Focus in *Am*," *NCF*, 28
(1973–74), 74–84, has an elaborate statement of
Newman's shortcomings, sees inconsistencies in
James's presentation of him, and argues that contradictory intentions necessitated reliance on melodrama at the end. Royal A. Gettmann, "HJ's Revision
of *Am*," *AL*, 16 (1944–45), 281–95; Isadore Traschen,
"An American in Paris," *AL*, 25 (1954–55), 67–77;
and Larry J. Reynolds, "HJ's New Christopher Newman," *SN*, 5 (1972–73), 457–67, all see Newman
being made more attractive in the revised version.
Less favorable views of James as revisionist appear
in Robert Herrick, "A Visit to HJ," *Yale Review*, 12
(1923), 724–41; William T. Stafford, "The Ending of
J's *Am*: A Defense of the Early Version," *NCF*, 18
(1963), 86–89; and James W. Tuttleton, "Rereading

*Am*: A Century Since," *HJR*, 1 (1979–80), 139–53, which is also valuable on the symbolism derived from art, literature, music, and mythology as well as other matters. See also *HJ's Am: The Version of 1877, revised in autograph and typescript for the New York Edition of 1907. Reproduced in facsimile from the original in the Houghton Library, Harvard University*, with an introduction by Rodney G. Dennis (London, Scolar Press, 1976).

5.   *The Comic Sense of HJ*, pp. 50ff. It should be pointed out, however, that Madame de Bellegarde is English, the daughter of the Earl of St. Dunstans. I have no idea why James did this. Cf. John V. Antush, "The 'Much Finer Complexity' of History in *Am*," *JAS*, 6 (1972), 85–95.

6.   Isadore Traschen, "J's Revisions of the Love Affair in *Am*," *NEQ*, 29 (1956), 43–54, argues that this novel and James's work in general show that he knew "very little about the more intense moments of love" but that the revisions "reveal the later James to be more deeply *aware* of the sexual aspect of love."

7.   The melodrama too is prepared for. In Chapter 6, Newman tells Tristram that "that dark old house over there looks as if wicked things had been done in it and might be done again"; later he tells Mrs. Tristram that he "shouldn't wonder" if the marquise "had done some one to death—of course from a high sense of duty." To Tristram he adds that "it's like something in a regular old play," and later, when Newman is listening to Mrs. Bread's story, James tells us that he "made almost the motion of turning the pages of a detective story."

8.   Leon Edel, ed., *HJ Letters*, II, pp. 104–07.

9.   F. O. Matthiessen and Kenneth B. Murdock, eds., *The Notebooks of HJ*, p. 100.

10.  George Knox, "Romance and Fable in J's *Am*," *Anglia*, 83 (1965), 308–23, provides a careful, detailed reading in the light of myth, folklore, ritual drama, archetypal imagery, and psychoanalysis. Ronald

mocking work." Darshan Singh Maini's "*WS*: A Centennial Essay," *HJR*, 1 (1979–80), 81–101, includes a useful review of criticism. See also several studies of the novel in Gerald Willen's edition of *WS* (Crowell, 1970).

## 5. ACHIEVEMENT

1. *Notebooks*, p. 16.
2. Sydney, J. Krause's detailed account of "J's Revisions of the Style of *PL*," *AL*, 30 (1958–59), 67–88, includes a list of earlier studies, of which F. O. Matthiessen's "The Painter's Sponge and the Varnish Bottle," *American Bookman*, 1 (1944), 49–68, reprinted in his *HJ: The Major Phase*, was the first of importance. Nina Baym, "Revision and Thematic Change in *PL*," *MFS*, 22 (1976), 183–200, finds that although James did not completely transform *PL* into a late novel, he clouded "the original dynamics of the story" so that the result was "a baffling and problematical work," but quite different conclusions are reached in Anthony J. Mazzella's "The New Isabel," in Robert D. Bamberg's Norton Critical Edition of the novel (1975). See also Simon Nowell-Smith, "Texts of *PL*, 1881–1882," *Papers of the Bibliographical Society of America*, 63 (1969), 304–310.
3. See especially F. R. Leavis, "George Eliot (IV): *Daniel Deronda* and *PL*," *Scrutiny*, 14 (1946–47), 102–31, and George Levin, "Isabel, Gwendolen, and Dorothea," *ELH*, 30 (1963), 244–57.
4. "The Two Isabels: A Study in Distortion," *Victorian Newsletter*, No. 25 (1964), pp. 15–17.
5. The names Gilbert and Osmond both had many sinister literary associations, and the letter M, too, was often associated with evil characters. In the serial version Madame Merle's first name was not Serena, which indicates her smooth surface, but Geraldine, thus recalling the vampire of Coleridge's "Christabel." Osmond is both a Byronic figure and a dandy,

Wallace, *HJ and the Comic Form*, pp. 72–73, expounds the fairy-tale elements in the plot, with Newman as "the humble but honorable lover wooing the lady of high estate who lives in a well-guarded castle." I do not find Gary Lemco's "HJ and Richard Wagner," *Hartford Studies in Literature*, 6 (1974), 147–58, convincing in its depiction of Newman as Lohengrin, but Susan P. Ward's "Painting and Europe in *Am*," *AL*, 46 (1974–75), 566–73, is a suggestive and subtle study of Newman's contacts with and attitudes toward works of art as clues to his character and also as structural devices.

11. Cf. Michael McFee, "The Church Scenes in *Amb*, *Am*, and *WD*," *PLL*, 16 (1980), 325–28.
12. Edward R. Zietlow, "A Flaw in *Am*," *CLAJo*, 9 (1965–66), 246–54, argues that Newman was obliged by both "legal and moral considerations" as well as his obligations to Valentin and Mrs. Bread to turn the evidence in his hands over to the authorities. This seems to me an unwise insistence on introducing the complications of life into the simplicities of art, faintly reminiscent of the nineteenth-century critics who blamed Romeo and Juliet for disobeying their parents and neglecting their duties as citizens. James D. Wilson, "The Gospel According to Christopher Newman," *SAF*, 3 (1975), 83–88, is correct in seeing Newman as a man in need of chastening who learns that he cannot go through the world asking "How much?" but he goes too far when he writes that Newman's values contained "no more innate moral purity than the decadent values and methods of the Europeans." I find Floyd C. Watkins, "Christopher Newman's Final Instinct," *NCF*, 12 (1957–58), 85–88, supersubtle and unconvincing when he sees Newman in the final chapter regretting that he let the Bellegardes go, but see Robert Secor, "Christopher Newman: How Innocent Is J's American?" *SAF*, 1 (1973), 141–53, and Leland Person, Jr., "Aesthetic Headaches and European Women in *The Marble Faun* and *Am*," 4 (1978), 65–79.

13. See F. W. Dupee, ed., *The Question of HJ*, pp. 1–5.
14. *HJ Letters*, II, 192–94 and 189–91.
15. Poirier, *Comic Sense*, p. 100, points out that her names recall "a queen, recently deposed in France, a courtesan, made almost a mythic figure by Dumas *fils*, and the traditional lady of the sorrows." As for Silberstadt-Schreckenstein, it would be quite at home in George Barr McCutcheon's *Graustark*.
16. Edel, *HJ: The Conquest of London*, p. 313; Graham, *HJ: The Drama of Fulfilment*, p. 3.
17. Poirier, *The Comic Sense of HJ*, p. 138. There are thoughtful, convincing interpretations of James's balance in weighing European against American values in Peter Buitenhuis, "Comic Pastoral in HJ's *E*," *UTQ*, 31 (1961–62), 152–63; Deborah Austin, "Innocents at Home: A Study of *E* of HJ," *Journal of General Education*, 14 (1962–63), 103–29; J. W. Tuttleton, "Propriety and Fine Perspective: J's *E*," *MLR*, 73 (1978), 481–93; and Gail Farnham, "'The Alchemy of Art': HJ's *E*," *English Studies in Africa*, 23 (1980), 83–92. Eben Bass has a suggestive, though speculative, interpretation of the scene in which Acton surprises Clifford in Eugenia's rooms in "J's *E*," *Explicator*, 23, Sept. 1969, Item 9. F. R. Leavis, "The Novel as Dramatic Form (III): *E*," *Scrutiny*, 15 (1947–48), 200–21, provides a sympathetic, enthusiastic interpretation of the work as a whole.
18. *Notebooks*, pp. 3–7.
19. *Confidence* is one of the two James novels whose manuscript exists intact, annotated and corrected by the author. Edited by Herbert Ruhm, it was published by Grosset's Universal Library, 1962. See Abigail Ann Hamblen, "*C*: The Surprising Shadow of Genius," *Universal Review*, 36 (1969–70), 15–54.
20. Martha Collins, "The Center of Consciousness in Stage: HJ's *C*," *SAF*, 3 (1975), 39–50, sees the novel as a not wholly successful attempt to combine the "single center of consciousness" method James had used elsewhere with the basically dramatic method of *The Europeans*.

21. See Leo B. Levy, "HJ's *C* and the Development c the Idea of the Unconsciousness," *AL*, 28 (1956–57 347–58, which is undercut, however, by the author determination to see James as a precursor of Freuc
22. *Notebooks*, pp. 12–14. *HJ Letters*, II, 266–68.
23. *HJ: The Conquest of London*, p. 399.
24. Veeder, p. 200. Springer, *A Rhetoric of Literai Character*.
25. See Harold Schlechter, "The Unpardonable Sin *WS*," *Studies in Short Fiction*, 10 (1973), 137–4 and Robert E. Long, "J's *WS*: The Hawthorne R lation," *NEQ*, 46 (1973), 573–90. William Kenne "Dr. Sloper's Double in *WS*," *UR*, 36 (1969–7( 301–306, makes a more startling comparison b tween Sloper and Townsend.
26. "*WS*: A Study in the Growth of an Inner Self," *Stu ies in Short Fiction*, 13 (1976), 353–62. Thaddeus Babiiha, "J's *WS*: More on the Hawthorne Relatior *Nathaniel Hawthorne Journal*, 1974, pp. 270–7 points out resemblances between Catherine in h final phase and Hester in *The Scarlet Letter*. F much fuller discussion of James and Hawthorne, s Babiiha, *The J-Hawthorne Relation: Bibliograp cal Essays* (G. K. Hall, 1980), and Robert E. Lor *The Great Succession: HJ and the Legacy of Ha thorne* (University of Pittsburgh Press, 1978).
27. Two of the most sensitive discussions of *Washingt Square* are Veeder's and Poirier's. Veeder relies marily upon an analysis of style. He dissents fr and, in my judgment, successfully corrects Poiri interpretation at some points, also performing same service for John Lucas's "Marxist-oriente essay in John Goode, ed., *The Air of Reality*. N licent Bell takes a more favorable view of the sc in the Alps than I do in her "Style as Subject: W *SR*, 83 (1975), 19–38, which views the novel a "melodrama which becomes a criticism of the n odramatic principle" and melodrama itself as "o one of the kinds of 'artificial' style that make th appearance in this artistically self-conscious, s

"the ethical hero turned upside down, the Paterfamilias." Veeder discusses popular fiction (*St. Elmo, East Lynne*, the Elsie Dinsmore books, etc.), as well as standard literature and shows that Tennyson's "Isabel" "raises virtually every issue which Isabel Archer will confront through *The Portrait*." Pansy too had been used as the name of a children's magazine of the period with which James's first readers would surely have been familiar. In line with Veeder, see Elsa Nettels's charming article "*PL* and the Gothic Romance," *South Atlantic Bulletin*, 39, Nov. 1974, pp. 73–82, in which, relying especially upon *The Mysteries of Udolpho* and *Uncle Silas*, she shows how the *Portrait* is a kind of Gothic romance both transformed and criticized.

6. *The American Novel and its Tradition* (Doubleday, 1957).

7. I am not convinced, however, by Andrea Roberts Beauchamp's "'Isabel Archer': A Possible Source for *PL*," *AL*, 49 (1977–78), 267–71, in which she modestly and tentatively enters a claim for an undistinguished four-page story by "Professor Alden, D.D." in *The Ladies' Wreath* (1848–49). The name could easily be a coincidence, and the stress on the girl's independence and rejection of advice in making an unfortunate marriage do not seem to me so significant as they do to the author.

8. Joseph L. Tribble, "Cherbuliez' *Le Roman d'une Honnête Femme*: Another Source of J's *PL*," *AL*, 40 (1968–69), 279–93.

9. "The Aesthetic Movement and *PL*," *NCF*, 30 (1975–76), 495–510. Robert L. Gale, "A Possible Source for Elements in *PL*," *SA*, 11 (1965), 137–41, suggests Harriet Hosmer as the original of Henrietta and mentions other possible influences from Louisa Ward and her two husbands, Thomas Crawford and Luther Terry. For Miss Hillard, see Edel, *HJ: The Conquest of London*, pp. 430–32. M. E. Grenander, "Henrietta Stackpole and Oliver Harper: Emanations of the Great Democracy," *Bulletin of Research in the Hu-*

*manities*, 83 (1980), 408–22, makes a strong case for the thesis that James was influenced by a flamboyant female journalist of the 1870s who ran afoul of Swinburne and Bierce. Henrietta, however, is a much nicer woman.

10. See especially Martha Collins, "The Narrator, the Satellites, and Isabel Archer: Point of View in *PL*," *SN*, 8 (1976), 142–57, and cf. Veeder, p. 220.

11. Adeline R. Tintner, "The Centennial of 1876 and *PL*," *MR*, 10 (1980–81), 27–29, comments on the irony of having Isabel recognize "her defeat and her loss of freedom in the very year commemorating the hundredth anniversary of her America's winning its liberty," the only date given in the book.

12. Cf. Sr. Lucy Schneider, "Osculation and Integration: Isabel Archer and the One-Kiss Novel," *CLAJo*, 10 (1966–67), 149–61.

13. Cf., for example, Joseph H. Friend, "The Structure of *PL*," *NCF*, 20 (1965), 85–95, and Fred B. Millett's outline in Cargill, *Novels of HJ*, pp. 93–94. In "The Time-Scheme in *PL*," *AL*, 12 (1960–61), 127–35, M. E. Grenander, Beverly J. Rahn, and Francine Valco work out "a very complicated and elaborate sequence of incidents to span the period from 1871 to 1877. . . ."

14. *Notebooks*, p. 15.

15. Cf. "Perhaps you also might have to pay too much" (Ch. 13); "Take care you're not alone too much" (Ch. 17); "You say you want to put wind in her sails, but aren't you afraid of putting too much?" (Ch. 18); "You think it will prove a curse in disguise. Perhaps it will" (Ch. 20); "I want to be treated with justice. I want nothing but that" (Ch. 21); "Yes, he's very hard to satisfy. That makes me tremble for her happiness" (Ch. 25).

16. Mrs. M. Mukherji, "Role of Pansy in *PL*," *Calcutta Review*, n.s. 1 (1969–70), 589–94, provides the best and most extensive study of Osmond's daughter.

17. *Versions of Melodrama*, pp. 46–52.

18. Cf. J. T. Laird, "Cracks in Precious Objects: Aes-

theticism and Humanity in *PL*," *AL*, 52 (1980–81), 643–48.

19. *Notebooks*, p. 18.

20. The only considerable discussions of Isabel's problem against the background of her times are Veeder's and Mary S. Schriber's, "Isabel Archer and Victorian Manners," *SN*, 8 (1976), 441–57. Among the articles in which her decision is attacked, see Marion Montgomery, "The Flaw in the Portrait: HJ vs. Isabel Archer," *UR*, 26 (1959–60), 215–20; J. M. Newton, "Isabel Archer's Disease and HJ's," *Cambridge Quarterly*, 2 (1966–67), 3–23; Juliet McMaster, "The Portrait of Isabel Archer," *AL*, 45 (1973–74), 50–66; and Victor H. Strandberg, "Isabel Archer's Identity Crisis: The Two Portraits of a Lady," *UR*, 34 (1968), 283–90. Among Isabel's defenders are Vincent F. Biehl, "Freedom and Commitment in J's *PL*," *Personalist*, 42 (1961), 368–81; John Rodenbeck, "The Bolted Door in J's *PL*," *MFS*, 10 (1964–65), 330–40; Thomas P. Smith, "Balance in HJ's *PL*," *Four Quarters*, 13, May 1964, pp. 11–16; Courtney Johnson, "Adam and Eva and Isabel Archer," *Renascence*, 21 (1968–69), 134–44; Sheldon W. Liebman, "The Light and the Dark: Character Design in *PL*," *PLL*, 6 (1970), 165–70 and "Point of View in *PL*," *ES*, 52 (1971), 136–47; and William J. Krier, "The 'Patent Extravagance' of *PL*," *Mosaic*, Spring 1976, pp. 57–65. Isabel's most determined enemies, whose views I find unconvincing, are William Bysshe Stein, "*PL*: Via Inertia," *WHR*, 13 (1959), 177–90; Marjorie Perloff, "Cinderella Becomes the Wicked Stepmother: *PL* as an Ironic Fairy Tale," *NCF*, 23 (1968–69), 413–33; Michael Routh, "Isabel Archer's 'Inconsequence': A Motif Analysis of *PL*," *JNT*, 8 (1977), 128–41; and Dennis L. O'Connor, "Intimacy and Spectatorship in *PL*," *HJR*, 2 (1980–81), 25–35, who probably holds the distinction of being the only reader who has ever seen Madame Merle as "perhaps" more "human" than Isabel. Annette Niemtzow, "Marriage and the New Woman in

PL," AL, 47 (1975), 377–95, studies Isabel's return in the light of Henry James, Sr.'s, ideas. See also Dominic J. Bazzanella, "The Conclusion to PL Re-Examined," AL, 41 (1969–70), 55–63, and Lyall H. Powers, "PL: The Eternal Mystery of Things," NCF, 14 (1959–60), 143–55.

21. See Carla L. Petersen, "Dialogue and Characterization in PL," SAF, 8 (1980), 13–21, on James's use of "differences in language usage" as an element in characterization.

22. A number of articles about the Portrait have been conveniently gathered in William T. Stafford, ed., Perspectives on J's PL (New York University Press, 1967); Peter Buitenhuis, Twentieth Century Interpretations of PL (Prentice-Hall, 1968); and Lyall E. Powers, The Merrill Studies in PL (Charles E. Merrill Publishing Company, 1970), but the extensive collection of new centenary essays edited by Leon Edel and Marion Richmond and scheduled for publication in 1982 was not available in time to be used for this book; there is some account of it in Stafford's "PL: The Second Hundred Years," HJR, 2 (1980–81), 91–100. Other recent articles are Edwin S. Fussell, "Sympathy in PL and GB," HJR, 2 (1980–81), 161–66, and Alden R. Turner, "The Haunted PL," SN, 12 (1980–81), 228–38.

## 6. EXPLORATIONS

1. This chapter also embraces The Reverberator, the shortest novel James included in the New York Edition. Chronologically it falls between The Princess Casamassima and The Tragic Muse, but I have chosen to treat it briefly at the end in order to keep the three somewhat similar novels together.

2. Herbert F. Smith and Michael Painovich, "B: Creation and Revision," Bulletin of the New York Public Library, 73 (1969), 298–308, count nearly 1,200 variants between the serial and the book.

3. For James's own comments, see his *Notebooks*, pp. 46ff. The most specific comments on *L'Evangéliste*, whose influence has often been played down, are by Lyall H. Powers, "J's Debt to Alphonse Daudet," *CL*, 24 (1972), 150–62, and Peter Buitenhuis, *The Grasping Imagination*. For Hawthorne, see Marius Bewley, *The Complex Fate* . . . (Grove Press, 1954); Robert Emmet Long, "Transformations: *The Blithedale Romance* in Howells and J," *AL*, 47 (1975–76), 552–71. For Cargill, see, besides his *Novels of HJ*, his article with Daniel Lerner, "HJ at the Grecian Urn," *PMLA*, 66 (1951), 316–31, whose starting point, so far as *B* is concerned, is Verena's finding in Olive qualities characteristic of Electra or Antigone, but the conclusion, that Olive derives basically from Antigone but that James enriched her personality with traits drawn from other tragic heroines, including Cassandra, making her "almost a synoptic version of the Sophoclean tragic female," seems to me unwarranted. Pastoralism has been invoked by Robert C. McLean, "*B*: New England Pastoral," *PLL*, 7 (1971), 374–81, and R. A. Morris, "Classical Vision and the American City: HJ's *B*," *NEQ*, 46 (1973), 543–57. For Balzac, see Adeline R. Tintner, "J and Balzac: *B* and 'La Fille aux yeux d'or,'" *CL*, 29 (1977), 241–54; the resemblances pointed out are less significant in themselves than the value of the article for its data on James's interest in French decadent literature. Similarly, the prime value of Marcia Jacobson's "Popular Fiction and HJ's Unpopular *B*," *MP*, 73 (1975–76), 262–75, is that it contributes to our understanding of the novel as a picture of American life, even though the reader may dissent from Ms. Jacobson's view of it as a pessimistic, antifeminist document. Howard Kerr's references to Brownson and Taylor are in his *Mediums, and Spirit-Rappers, and Roaring Radicals* (University of Illinois Press, 1972). Sonja Bašič, "Love and Politics in *B*," *Studia Romanica et Anglica Zagrabiensia*, 33–36 (1972–73), 293–303, plays down the public

aspects and sees the real theme of the novel as "the struggle of natural and unnatural human relationships realized with a stunning awareness of the sexual undercurrents."

4. Howard Kerr's extensive, authoritative, and highly entertaining book (see note 3 above) has a long, valuable chapter on *The Bostonians*, but Susan Wallenstein's "Possession and Personality: Spiritualism in *B*," *AL*, 49 (1977–78), 580–91, reaches the unacceptable conclusions that "the real subject-matter" of the book is "the entire mind-process with which William James was concerned" and that Henry "appears to view the human condition as hopeless." Martha Banta's *HJ and the Occult* (Indiana University Press, 1972) also makes some pretty sweeping assumptions. Sara deSassure Davis, "Feminist Sources for *B*," *AL*, 50 (1978–79), 570–87, is an indispensable study, and Graham Burns, *"B," Critical Review* (Melbourne), No. 12 (1964), 45–60, also contributes background material, although it is primarily concerned with the novel as a work of art.

5. For Dr. Mary Walker, see Robert Emmet Long, "A Source for Dr. Mary Prancer in *B*," *NCF*, 19 (1964–65), 87–88. Edel's conjecture is in *HJ: The Middle Years*, pp. 67–68; see also Judith Fryer's discussion of Olive in *The Faces of Eve*, pp. 220–26. For Davis and Kerr, see note 4 above. Kerr's account of Cora Hatch is on pp. 197–203.

6. David Bonnell Green, "Witch and Bewitchment in *B*," *PLL*, 3 (1967), 167–69, acutely suggests that James sought to reinforce the drama being played out by reference to Scott's *Marmion*.

7. David Howard well develops Verena's complexity in his essay in John Goode, ed., *The Air of Reality*.

8. Taking off from Ransom's observation to Mrs. Luna, "You speak as if it were a rendezvous of witches on the Brocken," and relying especially on what he considers influences from *Faust* and "Christabel," Howard D. Pearce, "Witchcraft Imagery and Allusion in J's *B*," *SN*, 6 (1974), 236–47, sees the pres-

ence of this element as a device to heighten the emotional overtones of the book and especially of Olive's attempt to "charm" and "possess" Verena. This article was partly anticipated by Lee Ann Johnson, "The Psychology of Characterization: J's Portraits of Verena Tarrant and Olive Chancellor," *SN*, 6 (1974), 295–303, who finds Verena's characterization unsatisfactory because of James's use of fairy-tale and romantic elements but fails to perceive that he uses the same devices in his portrayal of Olive, which is praised. See also W. R. Martin, "The Use of the Fairy Tale: A Note on the Structure of *B*," *English Studies in Africa*, 2 (1959), 98–109, which unwarrantably idealizes Ransom, and cf. Green in note 6 above.

9.  Charles R. Anderson, "J's Portrait of the Southerner," *AL*, 27 (1955–56), 309–31, is the most detailed study of Ransom. Gerald Haslam, "Olive Chancellor's Painful Victory in *B*," *Research Studies, Washington State University*, 36 (1968), 232–37, is probably the most sympathetic study of Olive. Sara deSassure Davis, "*B* Reconsidered," *Tulane Studies in English*, 23 (1978), 39–60, provides an admirable, detailed consideration of various characters, especially valuable for its destructive criticism of the commentators who have been strangely taken in by Ransom. See also Elizabeth Schultz, "*B*: The Contagion of Romantic Illusion," *Genre*, 4 (1971), 45–59, and Elizabeth McMahon, "Sexual Desire and Illusion in *B*," *MFS*, 25 (1979–80), 241–57. Structural analysis is essayed by Alfred Habegger, "The Disunity of *B*," *NCF*, 24 (1969–70), 193–209, and Barry Menikoff, "A House Divided: A New Reading of *B*," *CLAJo*, 20 (1976–77), 459–74. T. A. Birrell, "The Greatness of *B*," *The Dutch Quarterly Review of Anglo-American Letters*, 7 (1977), 242–64, is an almost ecstatic appreciation which includes a partial review of earlier criticism.

10. See Daniel H. Heaton, "The Altered Characterization of Miss Birdseye in HJ's *B*," *AL*, 50 (1978–79), 588–603.

11.    The groundbreaking study here was Daniel Lerner,
       "The Influence of Turgenev on HJ," *Slavonic and
       East European Review*, 20 (1941), 28–54, which is
       summarized by Cargill, pp. 146ff. See further Eunice
       C. Hamilton, "HJ's *PC* and Ivan Turgenev's *Virgin
       Soil*," *SAQ*, 61 (1962), 354–64; Jeanne Delbaere-
       Garant, "HJ's Divergences from the Russian Model
       in *PC*," *Revue des Langues Vivantes*, 37 (1971), 525–
       46; and Anthony D. Briggs, "Someone Else's
       Sledge: Further Notes on Turgenev's *Virgin Soil*
       and HJ's *PC*," *Oxford Slavonic Studies*, 5 (1972), 52–
       60. For David Seed, cf. "Hyacinth Robinson and the
       Politics of *PC*," *Etudes Anglaises*, 30 (1977), 30–39;
       for Marcia Jacobson, "Convention and Innocence in
       *PC*," *Journal of English and Germanic Philology*, 76
       (1977), 238–54. Seed's suggestion that Miss Pynsent
       is related to Hawthorne's Miss Pyncheon seems only
       a play on names.

12.    See Edel, *HJ: The Middle Years*, pp. 185ff., and Car-
       gill, *Novels of HJ*, pp. 151–52. Lionel Trilling's in-
       troduction to the 1948 Macmillan edition of the
       novel, which was reprinted in his *The Liberal Imag-
       ination* (Viking Press, 1950) is important. W. H. Til-
       ley's *The Background of* PC, University of Florida
       Monographs, Humanities, No. 5 (University of Flor-
       ida Press, 1960) is the most extensive study. Others
       include George Woodcock, "HJ and the Conspira-
       tors," *SR*, 60 (1952), 219–29; Taylor Stoehr, "Words
       and Deeds in *PC*," *ELH*, 37 (1970), 93–134, Mildred
       E. Hartsock, "*PC*: The Politics of Power," *SN*, 1
       (1969), 297–308; and Mark Seltzer, "*PC*: Realism
       and the Fantasy of Surveillance," *NCF*, 35 (1980–
       81), 506–34.

13.    John L. Kimney has an article on "*B* and *PC*," *TSLL*,
       9 (1967–68), 537–46, and another on "*TM* and its
       Forerunners," *AL*, 41 (1969–70), 518–31. He sees *PC*
       as a conscious attempt to avoid the weaknesses of *B*
       and both the first two novels as a trial run for the
       third. Although his is the best study of these novels
       *as a group*, he pushes some of his parallels and com-

parisons pretty hard. Walter Dubler's formalistic "*PC*: Its Place in the J Canon," *MFS*, 12 (1966–67), 44–60, sees the novel as representing the end of early and the beginning of later James. Adeline R. Tintner has a fascinating article, "Hyacinth at the Play: The Play within the Play as a Novelistic Device in J," *JNT*, 2 (1972), 171–85. Taking her point of departure from James's own comparison of Hyacinth to Hamlet, she develops the idea that incidents in *The Prince of Paraguay*, which Hyacinth witnesses with Christina on the occasion of their first meeting, recall the death of Roderick Hudson and foreshadow his own.

14. James is correct in showing anarchism as flourishing among artisans and craftsmen, not those whom Marxians called the proletariat. John L. Kimney, "*PC* and the Quality of Bewilderment," *NCF*, 22 (1967–68), 47–62, acutely points out that in the York mystery plays the sacrifice of Isaac was staged by the bookbinders and cites several references which would seem to indicate that James was aware of this. Reid Badger, "The Character and Myth of Hyacinth: A Key to *PC*," *AQ*, 32 (1976), 316–26, describes the resemblance between the circumstances surrounding the death of Hyacinthus in classical mythology and those of James's hero.

15. See Sr. Jane Marie Luecke, "*PC*: Hyacinth's Fallible Consciousness," *MP*, 60 (1962–63), 174–80. Philip Page's reading of the novel in terms of physical and psychological penetration in "*PC*: Suicide and 'The Penetrating Imagination,'" *Tennessee Studies in Literature*, 22 (1977), 162–69, is interesting but highly subjective. See also Frederick C. Crews's acute discussion of Hyacinth in the first chapter of *The Tragedy of Manners*.

16. It is true that Christina is herself a bastard, but the reader is not often reminded of this. Critics have seen her in almost every possible light. M. E. Grenander's "HJ's *Capricciosa*: Christina Light in *RH* and *PC*," *PMLA*, 85 (1965), 309–19, is an admirable

extended study. D. G. Halliburton, "Self and Sec-
ularization in *PC*," *MFS*, 11 (1965–66), 116–28, is
probably her severest critic; George Monteiro, "The
Campaign of HJ's Disinherited Princess," *ES*, 45
(1964), 442–54, defends her heartily.

17.   Whether or not one accepts his conclusion that
Christina is a dilettante in revolution with a strong
dash of naiveté, Sam Bluefarth's "The 'Radicalism'
of *PC*," *Barat Review*, 2 Spring–Summer 1971, pp.
68–72, is a careful examination of her motives and
commitment.

18.   On Muniment's character see P. K. Grover, "Two
Modes of Possessing: Conquest and Appreciation—
*PC* and *L'Education Sentimentale*," *MLR*, 66 (1971),
760–71; Thomas Hubert, "*PC*: Ideas Against Persons," *AQ*, 32 (1976), 341–52; Mary M. Lay, "The
Real Beasts: Surrogate Brothers in J's 'The Pupil'
and *PC*," *ALR*, 13 (1980), 73–84.

19.   There is an excellent study of Madame Grandoni in
Ellen Douglas Leyburn's *Strange Alloy*, which is
also very good on Hyacinth.

20.   Daniel J. Schneider, "The Theme of Freedom in J's
*TM*," *Connecticut Review*, 7, April 1974, pp. 5–15,
argues that the preface oversimplifies this antithesis
and that critics have followed James too blindly.
Schneider has much to say that is worth considering,
but one can hardly follow him when he suggests that
Nash represents a kind of Jamesian norm.

21.   The fullest discussion of *Miss Bretherton* in its relation to James, Mary Anderson, and the aesthetic
and theatrical controversies of the time is in the
essay by D. J. Gordon and John Stokes, "The Reference of *TM*," in John A. Goode, ed., *The Air of
Reality*. For Cargill, see his *Novels of HJ*; for Sarah
Bernhardt, the chapter on Miriam Rooth in the present writer's *Eve and Henry James* and the study of
Bernhardt in his *Seven Daughters of the Theater* (Da
Capo Press, 1981).

22.   Kenneth Graham, *HJ: The Drama of Fulfilment*, de-

fends Nick against all his critics including James; he also gives extended consideration to Julia and Lady Agnes. James suggests in passing that Miriam might have given up her career for Nick though she would not do it for Peter, but wild horses could not make me believe this; see Graham, pp. 118–19.

23. See Oscar Cargill, "Mr. J's Aesthetic Mr. Nash," *NCF*, 12 (1957), 177–87, and "Gabriel Nash—Somewhat Less Than Angel," *NCF*, 14 (1959–60), 231–39; Lyall H. Powers, "J's *TM*—Ave Atque Vale," *PMLA*, 83 (1958), 270–74, and "Mr. J's Mr. Nash Again," *NCF*, 13 (1959), 341–49; Fujio Murakami, "The Aesthete in *TM*," *Jimbun Kenkyu*, 12 (1961), 95–108; William F. Hall, "Gabriel Nash: 'Famous Centre' of *TM*," *NCF*, 21 (1966–67), 167–84; Ronald Wallace, "Gabriel Nash: HJ's Comic Spirit," *NCF*, 28 (1973), 23–34; and Robert S. Baker, "Gabriel Nash's 'House of Strange Idols' Aestheticism in *TM*," *TSLL*, 15 (1973), 149–66. See also Dorothea Krook, *The Ordeal of Consciousness in HJ*.

24. See *Notebooks*, p. 31, and cf. Cargill, *Novels of HJ*, pp. 192–93, and Edgar, *HJ, Man and Author*, p. 287. James took a very dim view of Wilde as both man and writer, although he was kind to him when he fell into trouble. There is a suggestion of homosexuality in what Miriam says of Nash in Chapter 25, but this may not have been intended. I might add that although it is impossible for us today to read of the fading out of Nash's portrait without thinking of *The Portrait of Dorian Gray*, those who would cite this book as a possible influence on James must be reminded that its date is 1891.

25. Cf., for example, Alan W. Bellringer, "*TM*: The Objective Center," *JAS*, 4 (1970–71), 73–89, and Ernest H. Lockridge, "A Vision of Art: HJ's *TM*," *MFS*, 12 (1966), 83–92. Lotus Snow, however, has some interesting commentary on Miriam in "'The Prose and the Modesty of the Matter': J's Imagery for the Artist in *RH* and *TM*," *MFS*, 12 (1966), 61–82. William R.

Goetz, "The Allegory of Representation in *TM*," *JNT*, 8 (1978), 151–64, provides a careful study of the novel as a whole.

26. *Turn West, Turn East: Mark Twain and HJ* (HM, 1951), p. 201.

27. See Sr. Mary Brian Durkin, "HJ's Revisions of the Style of *R*," *AL*, 33 (1961–62), 330–49.

28. Charles R. Anderson, "HJ's Fable of Carolina," *SAQ*, 54 (1955), 249–57.

29. George Knox, "Reverberations and *R*," *Essex Institute Historical Collections*, 95 (1959), 348–51, argues that the Lowell–Julian Hawthorne affair which James refers to in his preface was important for this story and (unconvincingly, I think) "that the character of George Flack derives directly from Julian."

## 7. TRANSITION

1. Hearst's New York *Journal* reviewed *The Other House* under the heading "Henry James's New Novel of Immorality and Crime: The Surprising Plunge of the Great Novelist into the Field of Sensational Fiction." See Abigail Ann Hamblen, "HJ and the Press: A Study of Protest," *WHR*, 11 (1957), 169–75.

2. Muriel G. Shine, *The Fictional Children of HJ*, pp. 79–81, is excellent in showing how James's imagery "succeeds in establishing the sacrificial nature of the child's role." One of the wildest of Leon Edel's many wild conjectures is that "the little Henry, within the mature artist, felt himself annihilated by the brutality of the audience at *Guy Domville*" and expressed it through the drowning of Effie Bream! *See HJ: The Treacherous Years*, p. 262.

3. This is argued in some detail by David K. Kirby, "*OH*: From Novel to Play," *MR*, 3 (1971), 49–53. See also Ross Labie, "*OH*: A Jamesian Thriller," *North Dakota Quarterly*, 45 (1977), 23–30. The play text is in Edel's *Complete Plays of HJ*.

4.  See Edel, *HJ: The Treacherous Years*, pp. 164–68,
    and his introductions to the play version in the *Com-
    plete Plays* and to the 1947 New Directions edition
    of the novel. Cf. Elizabeth Robins, ed., *Theatre and
    Friendship: Some HJ Letters* (Putnam, 1952). The
    case for *Medea* is argued in "HJ at the Grecian Urn,"
    *PMLA*, 66 (1951), 327–31.

5.  Levy, *Versions of Melodrama*, p. 108. Holland, *The
    Expense of Vision*, p. 102. Charles Palliser has the
    best commentary on Fleda's question to Mrs. Brigs-
    tock in "'A Conscious Prize': Moral and Aesthetic
    Values in *SPo*," *MLQ*, 40 (1979), 37–52.

6.  Alan H. Roper, "The Moral and Metaphorical Mean-
    ing of *SPo*," *AL*, 32 (1960–61), 182–96, thinks
    "Fleda" indicates the girl's tendency toward with-
    drawal or flight. He is supported by Arnold Gold-
    smith, "The Poetry of Names in *SPo*," *Names*, 14
    (1966), 134–42.

7.  Cargill, *Novels of HJ*, pp. 218–19. Tintner, "'The Old
    Things,' Balzac's *Le Curé de Tours*, and J's *SPo*,"
    *NCF*, 26 (1971–72), 436–55; this article also consid-
    ers *Le Cousin Pons*. Bernard Richards, "J and his
    Sources: *SPo*," *Essays in Criticism*, 29 (1979), 302–
    19, attempts to identify originals for both Poynton
    and Waterbath.

8.  See *Notebooks*, pp. 136–38, and the subsequent en-
    tries as pointed out by the editors, all significant for
    the development of the story.

9.  See Arnold Goldsmith, "The Maltese Cross as Sign
    in *SPo*," *Renascence*, 16 (1963–64), 73–74, for an
    elaborate interpretation of the symbolism of the
    cross.

10. See Quinn, "Morals and Motives in *SPo*," *SR*, 62
    (1962), 563–77; Baym, "Fleda Vetch and the Plot of
    *SPo*," *PMLA*, 84 (1969), 102–11; McLean, "The Sub-
    jective Adventure of Fleda Vetch," *AL*, 36 (1964),
    12–30; Reid, "Moral Passion in *PL* and *SPo*," *MFS*,
    12 (1966–67), 24–53; and Schneider, "The 'Full
    Ironic Truth' in *SPo*," *Connecticut Review*, 2, April
    1969, pp. 5–66. Arnold Edelstein, "'The Tangle of

Life': Levels of Meaning in *SPo*," *Hartford Studies in Literature*, 2 (1970), 133–50, tries to hew his way through the tangle of criticism but admits that his own heavily Freudian view may seem too "extreme" to many readers. Philip L. Greene makes a much better job of it in "Point of View in *SPo*," *NCF*, 21 (1967), 359–68, and Emily K. Izsak's "The Composition of *SPo*," *TSLL*, 6 (1965), 460–71, is also a valuable study. Mildred E. Hartsock's "A Light Lamp: *SPo* as a Comedy," *ES*, 50 (1969), Anglo-American Supplement, pp. xxix–xxxvii, has value as pointing out the comic elements, but it does not necessarily follow, as she seems to think, that the novel is essentially comic.

11.  See John C. Broderick, "Nature, Art, and Imagination in *SPo*," *NCF*, 13 (1965–66), 295–312; Thomas G. Hunt, "Moral Awareness in *SPo*," *Discourse*, 9 (1966), 255–62; and Carren O. Kaston, "Emersonian Consciousness and *SPo*," *ESQ*, 26 (1980), 88–99.

12.  Jule S. Kaufman, "*SPo*: In Defense of Fleda Vetch," *AQ*, 35 (1979), 342–56, feels that "more than any other James heroine, she is aware of a man's physical presence."

13.  Edmund L. Volpe, "The Spoils of Art," *MLN*, 74 (1959), 601–08, who admires Fleda, finds her out of character when she sends the telegram but rather gives his case away when he adds, "I do not deny that the portrait of Fleda capitulating to her emotions has the force of psychological truth. It is true to life." Other sympathetic studies of Fleda are provided by James W. Gargano, "*SPo*: Action and Responsibility," *SR*, 69 (1961), 650–60: Akio Namekata, "Some Notes on *SPo*," *Studies in English Literature*, 40, English Number (1970), 17–35; and Charles Thomas Samuels, in *The Ambiguity of HJ*. Since Fleda is the only James heroine who serves as a double confidante, it is not surprising that she should be treated at length by Sr. M. Corona Sharp, *The Confidante in HJ*. So far as I know, this writer stands alone in

believing that Fleda ought to have made Owen's decision for him.

14. See Ward S. Worden, "A Cut Version of *WMK*," *AL*, 24 (1952–53), 493–504, and the same writer's "HJ's *WMK*: A Comparison with the Plans in the *Notebooks*," *PMLA*, 68 (1953), 371–83.

15. J. D. MacFarlane, "A Literary Friendship—HJ and Paul Bourget," *Cambridge Journal*, 4 (1950–51), 144–61; see also Cargill, *Novels*, p. 254. For the Colin Campbell divorce case, see Edel, *Letters*, III, p. 146. Percy Lubbock suppressed the name when he printed the letter in his 1920 edition.

16. *WMK*, New York Edition, Preface, p. ix; also *Notebooks*, p. 236.

17. See Walter Isle, *Experiments in Form*, and J. A. Ward, *The Search for Form*. Isle's is much the best detailed account of how the author supplements and fills out Maisie's perceptions. Ward has a detailed analysis of structure and is especially good on James's subtle and masterly use of parallelism.

18. Compare on this point Joseph Wiesenfarth's excellent chapter on *Maisie* in *HJ and the Dramatic Analogy*.

19. Cf. Leavis, "J's *WMK*," *Scrutiny*, 17 (1950), 115–27.

20. Beale's telling Maisie that this title is "American" has occasioned both mirth and puzzlement, but probably Thomas L. Jeffers has the right explanation in "Maisie's Moral Sense: Finding Out for Herself," *NCF*, 34 (1979–80), 154–72; "Isn't it plain . . . that she is a mulatto South American countess, a titled descendant of someone like Miss Swartz in Thackeray's *Vanity Fair*? There were, e.g., countesses in Brazil before 1889."

21. This may have been intended to have more significance than critics have seen in it; cf. Juliet Mitchell's interpretation of the action of the novel in terms of a game in her "*WMK*: Portrait of the Artist as a Young Girl," in John Goode, ed., *The Air of Reality*, pp. 173ff.

22. *The Fictional Children of HJ*, p. 113.
23. Cf. Wilson, "What Did Maisie Know?" *CE*, 17 (1955–56), 279–82; Cargill, *Novels*; Wasiolek, "Maisie: Pure or Corrupt?" *CE*, 22 (1960–61), 611–16; and McCloskey, "What Maisie Knows: A Study of Childhood and Adolescence," *AL*, 36 (1964–65), 483–512.
24. For an interesting interpretation of the admittedly difficult symbol of the gold Virgin on the church, see Jeanne Delbaere-Garant, *HJ: The Vision of France* (Paris, Societé d'Editions, "Les Belles Lettres," 1976).
25. It should be added that the same question that has been raised about Maisie has also been raised about Mrs. Wix. Both admit that they "adore" Sir Claude from an early stage (see also *Notebooks*, pp. 257, 259), and there are critics who believe that the governess too offers herself to Sir Claude sexually, which on the part of a beetlelike old woman would be as fantastic as distasteful. The crucial passage is in Chapter 24, where the "good lady" with whom Maisie had not previously connected the "faintest shade of any art of provocation, actually, after an upward grimace, gave Sir Claude a great giggling insinuating naughty slap," and in Chapter 30 he asks Maisie, "Then, my dear child, why can't she let me alone?" But there are other passages which give a very different impression. Mrs. Wix's general commitment to decency and her distress over what she considers Maisie's failure to develop a "moral sense" make it very difficult to think of her as shamelessly (and idiotically) offering herself to Sir Claude, especially before the girl, and what she stresses in her frankly expressed desire to go away with them both is that she should be permitted to work her fingers to the bone to make a home for the child. Despite her capacity for developing a "crush" on a handsome young man, I believe Mrs. Wix's decency to be sincere and straightfoward as far as it goes, but she is neither intelligent nor disinterested (Maisie

is her meal ticket). Her morality is a preformulated, rule-of-thumb morality, which is not proof against Mrs. Beale's flattery, and devoted though she is to Maisie, she shows both moral indifference and hardness of heart toward the maid, Susan Ash, whom she does not like. The strongest reasonable statement of the case against her is that of Sr. M. Corona Sharp, but Juliet Mitchell is also pretty hard on her; see especially pp. 169, 184–89 of her essay. The best overall consideration of her character is Lee Ann Johnson's in "J's Mrs. Wix: The 'Dim, Crooked Reflector,'" *NCF*, 29 (1974), 164–72.

26.  Not all the articles that have been published about *Maisie* can be listed here, but the following are all worthy of consideration: James W. Gargano, "WMK: The Evolution of a 'Moral Sense,'" *NCF*, 16 (1961–62), 33–46; Joseph A. Hynes, "The Middle Way of Miss Farange; A Study of J's *Maisie*," *ELH*, 32 (1965), 528–53; Abigail Anne Hamblen, "HJ and the Power of Eros: *WMK*," *MQ*, 9 (1967–68), 391–99; Martha Banta, "The Quality of Experience in *WMK*," *NEQ*, 42 (1969), 483–510; Alfred Habegger, "Reciprocity and the Market Place in *WD* and *WMK*," *NCF*, 25 (1970–71), 455–73; A. E. Dyson, "On Knowing What Maisie Knew, Perhaps," in B. S. Benedikz, ed., *On the Novel* . . . (Dent, 1971); Paul Fahey, "*WMK*: Learning Not To Mind," *Critical Review* (Melbourne), No. 14 (1971), 98–108; Carren O. Kaston, "Houses of Fiction in *WMK*," *Crit*, 18 (1976), 27–42; William L. Nance, "*WMK*: The Myth of the Artist," *SN*, 8 (1976), 88–102; and Jean Frantz Blackall, "Moral Geography in *WMK*," *UTQ*, 48 (1978–79), 130–48. The present writer could do without such specialized "psychological" approaches as those of H. R. Wolf, "*WMK*: The Rankian Hero," *American Imago*, 23 (1966), 227–34; Sam B. Girgus, "The Other Maisie: Inner Death and Fatalism in *WMK*," *AQ*, 29 (1973), 115–22; Paul B. Armstrong, "How Maisie Knows: The Phenomenology of J's Moral Vision," *TSLL*, 20 (1978), 517–37;

Kenny Marotta, "*WMK*: The Question of Our Speech," *ELH*, 46 (1979), 495–508; and M. A. Williams, "The Drama of Maisie's Vision," *HJR*, 2 (1980–81), 36–48. Several writers have compared Maisie's moral development with that of Huckleberry Finn; besides Tony Tanner's *The Reign of Wonder: Naivety and Reality in American Literature* (CUP, 1960), mention may be made of Glauco Cambon, "What Huck and Maisie Knew," *SA*, 6 (1960), 204–20, and John Snyder, "J's Girl Huck: What Maisie Knew," *ALR*, 11 (1978), 109–23. Finally, a salute may be made in passing to Marius Bewley's passionate appreciation of the novel in *The Complex Fate: HJ and Other American Writers* (Grove Press, 1934).

27. See Margaret Walters, "Keeping the Place Tidy for the Young Female Mind," in John Goode, ed., *The Air of Reality*.

28. The magazine articles are described by Hamlin L. Hill, Jr., "'The Revolt of the Daughters': A Suggested Source for *AA*," *NQ*, N.S. 8 (1961), 347–49. The best article on social backgrounds is Elizabeth Owen, "*AA* and the Contemporary English Scene," *Victorian Studies*, 11 (1967–68), 63–82. Marcia Jacobson, "Literary Convention and Social Criticism in HJ's *AA*," *PQ*, 54 (1975), 633–46, argues the possible influence of a number of English dialogue novels, beginning with E. F. Benson's *Dodo*, and of Olive Schreiner's *The Story of an African Farm* and other popular books. Jean Frantz Blackall's "Literary Allusion as Imaginative Event in *AA*," *MFS*, 26 (1980–81), 179–97, is a fascinating piece of detective work, pointing out the possibility of implied references to Goethe, Victor Hugo, Zola, Thomas Nelson Page, and James's own *RH* in a passage toward the end of *The Awkward Age*.

29. There has been considerable discussion as to whether Mrs. Brook's motive is to keep Van for herself or provide for Nanda or both. For different views of this matter see James W. Gargano, "The Theme

of 'Salvation' in *AA*," *TSLL*, 9 (1967–68), 273–87, and William F. Hall, "J's Concept of Society in *AA*," *NCF*, 23 (1968–69), 28–48. I do not find it credible that so devious a creature as Mrs. Brook would ask Mr. Longdon, "Why do you hate me so?" or tell him that "Edward and I work it out between us to show off as tender parents and yet to get from you everything you'll give." As to Nanda's future, I am prepared to consider any hypothesis except that advanced by those who believe that she will some day be Mrs. Longdon (which would make the novel a rerun of *Watch and Ward*), but I should no more go to the barricades to defend the thesis that she will never marry anyone than that Isabel Archer will never leave Gilbert Osmond.

30. Lubbock, *Letters*, I, pp. 324–25.

31. For Wiesenfarth, see his *HJ and the Dramatic Analogy*; for Davidson, "J's Dramatic Method in *AA*," *NCF*, 29 (1974–75), 320–35; and for Isle, his *Experiments in Form*. Francis Gillen, "The Dramatist in his Drama: Theory vs. Effect in *AA*," *TSLL*, 12 (1970–71), 663–74, counts thirty direct author's comments in the novel and other veiled comments. Probably the best summary account of what happens in the novel is in Joseph J. Firebaugh's "The Pragmatism of HJ," *Virginia Quarterly Review*, 27 (1951), 419–35.

32. Some critics have stated that Nanda smokes. This is based on the passage in Book Fifth, Chapter 1, where she plays with and admires Van's cigarette case, but James writes, "She continued to handle the cigarette case, without, however, having profited by its contents." This is a small but annoying example of his incorrigible tendency to avoid clear and definite statement. If the indulgence under consideration were sexual, it would be fair to call the passage sniggering.

33. See also Lotus Snow, "Some Stray Fragrance of an Ideal: HJ's Imagery for Youth's Discovery of Evil," *HLB*, 14 (1960), 107–25; Mildred Hartsock, "The

Exposed Mind: A View of *AA*," *Critical Quarterly*, 9 (1967), 49–59; and Carl Nelson, "J's Social Criticism: The Voice of the Ringmaster in *AA*," *AQ*, 29 (1973), 151–68. Daniel J. Schneider, "J's *AA*: A Reading and an Evaluation," *HJR*, 1 (1979–80), 219–27, offers an interesting interpretation of the novel which differs importantly from mine yet reaches a conclusion much more in harmony with it than might have been expected from what precedes it. He is much less sympathetic toward Nanda than I am and much more so toward Mrs. Brook, and I confess I have no idea why he includes me, in my *Eve and HJ*, among those who find *The Awkward Age* "irritating and tedious and badly made." Jean Frantz Blackall, "The Case for Mrs. Brook," *HJR*, 2 (1980–81), 155–61, is still more friendly toward Nanda's mother; in some aspects indeed her article is a "response" to Schneider.

34.  I am in agreement with Muriel G. Shine's severe judgment of Van in *The Fictional Children of HJ* and not with Joseph P. O'Neill's defense in *Workable Design*. See also Gerald Levin, "Why Does Vanderbank Not Propose?" *UR*, 27 (1960–61), 314–18, and Eben Bass, "Dramatic Scene and *AA*," *PMLA*, 79 (1964), 148–57.

35.  *HJ: The Treacherous Years*, pp. 338–39.

36.  Roger Burlingame, *Of Making Many Books: A Hundred Years of Reading, Writing and Publishing* (S, 1946), pp. 36–37.

37.  Worthington C. Ford, ed., *Letters of Henry Adams, 1892–1918* (HM, 1938), p. 333n.

38.  See Lubbock, *Letters*, II, pp. 407–410; Edel, "Introductory Essay" to the 1953 Grove Press edition of *The Sacred Fount* (reprinted in Lyall H. Powers, ed., *HJ's Major Novels*); and Allan W. Bellringer, "*SF*: The Scientific Method," *EIC*, 22 (1972), 244–64.

39.  James Reaney, "The Condition of Light: HJ's *SF*," *UTQ*, 31 (1962), 139–51, and William F. Hall, "The Meaning of *SF*: 'Its Own Little Law of Composi-

tion,'" *MLQ*, 17 (1976), 168–78. See also James K. Folsom, "Archimago's Well: An Interpretation of *SF*," *MFS*, 7 (1961), 136–44, and Robert L. Gale, "*The Marble Faun* and *SF*: A Resemblance," *SA*, No. 8 (1962), 21–33.

40.  There is an interesting reference to Wagner's patron, Ludwig II, the mad king of Bavaria, in Chapter 13 of the novel. Jean Frantz Blackall makes much of this in her book-length study, using it, as she uses everything else, to disparage the narrator. She builds up a fascinating background study, clearly establishing that the reading public in James's time was considerably interested in Ludwig, but she also seems to me inclined to force a passing allusion to bear more weight than it can be expected comfortably to support.

41.  The quotation is from Maxwell Geismar's *HJ and the Jacobites* (HM, 1963). Holland's study is in his *The Expense of Vision*.

42.  Jean Frantz Blackall, *Jamesian Ambiguity and* SF (Cornell University Press, 1965). The fullest documentation of the book's ambiguity, and one of the best studies of it we have, is in Shlomith Rimmon's chapter on it in *The Concept of Ambiguity*.

43.  Rebecca West spoke for all who are not willing to give the book the attention it demands when she wrote in her *HJ* (Holt, 1916) that the narrator expends "more intellectual force than Kant can have used on *The Critique of Pure Reason* in an unsuccessful attempt to discover whether there exists between certain of his fellow-guests a relationship not more interesting among these vacuous people than it is among sparrows."

44.  Early examples of some of the interpretations alluded to will be found in Wilson Follett, "The Simplicity of HJ," *American Review*, 1 (1923), 315–25, and "HJ's Portrait of HJ," *New York Times Book Review*, August 23, 1926, pp. 2, 16, and in R. P. Blackmur, "SF," *Kenyon Review*, 4 (1942), 328–52. Most of what had been published up to 1965 is listed in

Mrs. Blackall's full and excellent bibliography. Those who wish to sample more recent opinion may consult James J. Kirschke, "HJ's Use of Impressionist Painting Techniques in *SF* and *Amb*," *Studies in the Twentieth Century*, 13 (1974), 83–116; Josephine Harris, "*SF*: The Geometry in the Jungle," *Michigan Quarterly Review*, 13 (1974), 57–73; Joanne Feit Diehl, "'One Life Within Us and Abroad': The Subverted Realist in *SF*," *JNT*, 6 (1976), 92–100; John C. Rowe, "The Authority of the Sign in HJ's *SF*," *Crit*, 19 (1977), 223–40; and Norman Lavers, "Art and Reality: The Theme of *SF*," *Publications of the Arkansas Philological Association*, Vol. 4, No. 2, Spring 1978, pp. 37–44. Dorothea Krook's *The Ordeal of Consciousness*, Walter Isle's *Experiments in Form*, and Philip M. Weinstein's *HJ and the Requirements of the Imagination* all have extensive chapters on *SF*. Bernard Richards's "*Amb* and *SF*: The Artist Manqué" is in Goode's *Air of Reality*. Edel's introduction to the Rupert Hart-Davies edition of 1959 supplements that to the Grove Press edition, cited elsewhere.

45. See, for example, Blackall, pp. 128–31, 141; Rimmon, *The Concept of Ambiguity*, pp. 224–26, and the references both give to earlier studies; also William F. Hall (cf. n. 39); W. B. Macnaughton, "The Narrator in HJ's *SF*," in Robert Falk, ed., *Literature and Ideas in America: Essays in Memory of Harry Hayden Clark* (Ohio University Press, 1975); and Elizabeth Keyser's interesting and ingenious interpretation in "Veils and Masks: *The Blithedale Romance* and *SF*," *HJR*, 2 (1980–81), 101–110, whose principal purpose, however, is to make a minute comparison between the two works.

46. Cf. Max Beerbohm's delightful cartoon, "A Rage of Wonderment," reproduced on p. 360 of *HJ: The Treacherous Years*, in which James is shown on one knee, musing over two pairs of shoes outside a closed bedroom door. There is an amusing bur-

lesque of *The Sacred Fount* in Owen Seaman's *Borrowed Plumes* (Holt, 1902).

47. Elliot W. Schrero's "The Narrator's Palace of Thought in *SF*," *MP*, 68 (1970–71), 269–88, is based on the assumption that some knowledge of the climate of scientific opinion at the time of the book's composition and especially of the philosophical views which Henry shared with William James is necessary for full understanding. Schrero shows that the narrator's methods are completely in harmony with those of the members of the Society for Psychical Research, of which William was president from 1894 to 1896, and with the whole outlook of the pragmatists. Materialistic scientists called the psychical researchers crazy, quite as Mrs. Briss calls the narrator. As James Reaney observes (see n. 39): "If Mrs. Briss is right, then not only the narrator but the whole world of science may be crazy also, for it too consists of a palace of thought reared on just the sort of induction that the narrator is continually making, just his sort of hypotheses that lead to general laws."

48. *The Lucid Reflector*, p. 166.

49. Fred Obert's refusal to back the narrator at the end is perhaps less easy to dispose of than that of Mrs. Briss, but see Sidney Finkelstein's excellent article, "The 'Mystery' of HJ's *SF*," *Massachusetts Review*, 3 (1961–62), 753–76. The narrator's remark toward the end of Chapter 11 proves that he and Obert kept in touch beyond the scope of the book and strongly suggests that the painter may have had more sympathy for the narrator after he had had a chance to think things over. On the narrator's responsibility, see also Bellringer and Reaney, previously cited, and Charles Thomas Samuels, "At the Bottom of the Fount," *Novel*, 2 (1968–69), 46–54. I did not read James W. Gargano's article, "James's *SF*: The Phantasmagorical Made Evidential," *HJR*, 2 (1980–81), 49–60, until after I had finished my own discussion of the novel, but I am completely in agreement with

his interpretation of the characters of both Mrs. Briss and the narrator. I find the attempt of E. A. Sklepowich, "Gossip and Gothicism in *SF*," *HJR*, 2 (1980–81), 112–15, to interpret the novel in Gothic terms unconvincing.

## 8. The Masterpieces, I

1. The Harper edition reversed Chapters 28 and 29, corresponding to Chapters 1 and 2 of Book Eleventh in the New York Edition, where the error was perpetuated. Neither James nor any reader or scholar seems to have noticed this until Robert E. Young, then an undergraduate, published "An Error in *Amb*," *AL*, 22 (1950–51), 245–53; cf. Leon Edel's correction, "A Further Note on 'An Error in *Amb*,'" *AL*, 23 (1951–52), 128–30, and Young's reply, "A Final Note on *Amb*," *AL*, 23, 487–90. Cf., further, Edel, "The Text of *Amb*," *HLB*, 14 (1960), 452–60, reprinted in Albert E. Stone, Jr., ed., *Twentieth Century Interpretations of* Amb (Prentice-Hall, 1969) and S. N. Rosenbaum's comprehensive discussion of "Editions and Revisions" in his Norton Critical Edition of the novel (1964).

2. See three articles by R. W. Stallman, "Time and the Unnamed Article in *Amb*," *MLN*, 72 (1957), 27–32; "'The Sacred Rage': The Time-Theme in *Amb*," *MFS*, 3 (1957), 41–56; and "Time and Mrs. Newsome's 'Blue Message,'" *MLN*, 76 (1961), 20–23. To Stallman, who was committed to the untenable hypothesis that time was the "all-consuming theme" of the novel, it seemed that the identification of the "mysterious article" was "crucial" to the understanding of the work; he made it an alarm clock. Others have conjectured a safety match, a buttonhook, and "a certain undistinguished toilet-article." See also Edel, "Time and *Amb*," *MLN*, 73 (1958), 177–79.

3. *The Notebooks of HJ*, pp. 370–415. A similar, less extensive scenario for *WD* has not survived.

4. See James's preface, pp. v–vi, and Lubbock, *Letters*, I, pp. 375–77. Cargill, *Novels of HJ*, p. 304, points out that the germ anecdote had been anticipated by James in "A Bundle of Letters" (1879). With special reference to *The Blithdale Romance* and *Indian Summer*, Robert E. Long, "*Amb* and the Genteel Tradition: J's Correction of Hawthorne and Howells," *NEQ*, 42 (1969), 44–64, argues that James was more successful in relating his characters to their environment than either of the others and that he gave different values to their experience of Europe.

5. "Balzac's 'Madame Firmiani' and J's *Amb*," *CL*, 25 (1973), 128–35, and "Balzac's Two Maries and J's *Amb*," *ELN*, 9 (1971–72), 284–87. In the first article, Ms. Tintner points out a number of very suggestive resemblances between the works under consideration, but the differences are sufficiently great so that she contents herself by finding influence "not inconceivable." The second article takes its point of departure from the rather odd fact that Miss Gostrey and Madame de Vionnet bear the same given name and rejects the religious interpretations of this fact that have been advanced by others. In "*Amb* and *Louis Lambert*," *MLN*, 75 (1960), 211–13, James W. Gargano gives careful, rather strained consideration to a comparative study of the two works, and in "'High Melancholy and Sweet': J and the Arcadian Tradition," *Colby Library Quarterly*, 12 (1976), 109–21, Ms. Tintner invokes the "Arcadian elegiac tradition" not only for *The Ambassadors* but also for *The Europeans*, *The Portrait of a Lady*, and *The Sacred Fount*. Poirier's essay is in his *A World Elsewhere: The Place of Style in American Literature* (OUP, 1966).

6. Cf. Warren, "HJ," in his *Rage for Order: Essays in Criticism* (UCP, 1948); Wallace, "Comic Form in *Amb*," *Genre*, 5 (1972), 31–48; Chase, "J's *Amb*," in Charles Shapiro, ed., *Twelve Original Essays on*

*Great American Novels* (Wayne State University Press, 1958); Garis, "The Two Lambert Strethers," *MFS*, 7 (1961–62), 305–16; and Knoepflmacher, "'O Rare for Strether!': *Antony and Cleopatra* and *Amb*," NCF, 19 (1964–65), 333–44, reprinted in Stone (see no. 1). Warren also cites Racine, Ibsen, and Maeterlinck in connection with James's "close conversation" and metaphor, and Chase was reminded of Molière, Jane Austen, and James's own *Europeans*.

7. See Cargill, *Novels of HJ*, pp. 306–307, 309, 331–32; Edel *HJ: The Conquest of London*, p. 232, *The Master*, p. 72; *HJ Letters*, III, p. 93, and "Jonathan Sturges," *Princeton Library Chronicle*, 15 (1953), 1–9; Spender, in his *The Destructive Element* (Jonathan Cape, 1935). Quay Grigg, "The Novel in *John Gabriel Borkman*," HJR, 1 (1979–80), 211–18, brings Ibsen into consideration again when he argues ingeniously, interestingly, but inconclusively that *Borkman*, which he believes was the play Strether saw with Maria Gostrey, may have helped him solve some of his problems in *The Ambassadors*.

8. See Lubbock, *The Craft of Fiction* (S, 1921). On stylistic matters, see further William M. Gibson, "Metaphor in the Plot of *Amb*," *NEQ*, 24 (1951), 291–305; John Paterson, "The Language of 'Adventure' in HJ," *AL*, 32 (1960), 291–301, reprinted in part in the Norton Critical Edition; John Q. Reed, "*Amb*: HJ's Method," *MQ*, 4 (1962–63), 55–67; and Richard Chartier, "The River and the Whirlpool," *Ball State University Forum*, 12, Spring 1971, pp. 70–75, which studies water imagery as "the clearest and most lucid unifying element in the novel."

9. See Tilford, "J The Old Intruder," *MFS*, 4 (1958), 157–64, reprinted in Stone (see n. 1); Thomas, "The Author's Voice in *Amb*," *JNT*, 1 (1971), 108–21.

10. Much the best and most detailed study of Maria Gostrey is that of Sr. M. Corona Sharp, *The Confidante in HJ*.

11. *J's Later Novels*.

12. *Turn West, Turn East* (HM, 1951), p. 277.
13. There is a suggestive commentary on one possible extremely subtle expression of Marie's subtlety in Marilyn L. Williamson, "'Almost Wholly in French': The Crisis in *Amb*," *NQ*, N.S. 9 (1962), 106–107.
14. See Elsa Nettels, "*Amb* and the Sense of the Past," *MLQ*, 31 (1970), 220–35, for a fine study of Strether as a "person haunted by the sense that he has not lived, who at a critical point in his life reaches out for the experience he has missed in the past" and of Paris as the ideal setting for this realization.
15. Glenda Leeming, *Who's Who in HJ*, believes that the Gloriani in *Amb* is a different person from the Gloriani in *RH*, but nobody seems to agree with her. Certainly Leon Edel does not, although he wrote an admiring foreword to her useful book (see his *Conquest of London*, p. 96, and *The Master*, p. 74), and Viola Hopkins, "Gloriani and the Tides of Taste," *NCF*, 18 (1963–64), 65–71, not only believes that the same character is presented in both novels and in the short story "The Velvet Glove" but develops the view that the sculptor has grown in fame, authority, and insight since *Roderick Hudson* and that James's more admiring later presentation of him reflects a change in his own tastes in art.
16. *Maule's Curse: Seven Studies in the History of American Obscurantism* (New Directions, 1938).
17. For Forster, see his *Aspects of the Novel* (Harcourt, Brace, 1927). Forster himself qualifies when he says that James's pattern "has woven itself itself with modulations and reservations" foreign to Anatole France. If there is a suggestion of *Thaïs* in *The Ambassadors*, perhaps it might be found in the fact that as Paphnutius's conquest of Thaïs is facilitated by her having had an earlier contact with Christianity, so one element in the appeal of Paris to Strether is his previous visit there. At the opposite extreme from Forster stands Robert Garis (see n. 6), who believes that James changed his mind about Strether after Chapter 29 and that he remains imprisoned in

Puritan inhibitions to the end. For views intermediate between these two extremes, see Philip M.
Weinstein's fine chapter in *HJ and the Requirements
of the Imagination* and D. J. Dooley, "The Hourglass Pattern in *Amb*," *NEQ*, 41 (1968), 273–81.
Christof Wegelin, *The Image of Europe in HJ*, es-
pecially pp. 93ff., comments illuminatingly upon
Strether's achievement of moral pragmatism. Other
studies of Strether's experience, essentially in har-
mony with my interpretation, include Frederick C.
Crews's chapter in *The Tragedy of Manners*; Daniel
J. Schneider, "The Ironic Imagery and Symbolism
of *Amb*," *Crit*, 9 (1967), 172–96; L. Moffitt Cecil,
"'Virtuous Attachment' in J's *Amb*," *American
Quarterly*, 19 (1967), 719–24; and Pauline Fletcher,
"The Sense of Society in *Amb*," *English Studies in
Africa*, 17 (1974), 70–86. Daniel Mark Fogel, "The
Jamesian Dialectic in *Amb*," *Southern Review*, 13
(1977), 468–91, has an elaborate and thoughtful
study in terms of "dialectal ordonnance," similar to
that of "many of the major poetic and philosophical
works of the Romantic age." Joanna A. Higgins,
"The Ambassadorial Motif in *Amb*," *JNT*, 8 (1978),
165–75, supplements my point of view though going
at the problem from another angle, but Judith Wilt,
"A Right Issue in a Tight Place: HJ and Maria Gostrey," *JNT*, 6 (1976), 77–91, has little relevance to
what I have written. There have also been a number
of distinctively religious interpretations of Strether's
experience; see Cargill, *Novels of HJ*, p. 236, and
the references cited there. Quentin Anderson, *The
American HJ*, interpreted James in terms of his father's Swedenborg-influenced philosophy, but
Brian Lee, "HJ's 'Divine Consensus': *Amb*, *WD*, and
*GB*," *Renaissance and Modern Studies*, 6 (1962),
5–24, argues, rightly, I believe, that the novelist was
"a descendant of Emerson, Hawthorne, Thoreau and
the whole Concord School, rather than . . . his father's disciple." See also Austin Warren, "The New
England Conscience, HJ, and Ambassador

Strether," *Minnesota Review*, 2 (1962), 140–61, reprinted in Powers, *HJ's Major Novels*, and David Robinson, "James and Emerson: The Ethical Content of *Amb*," SN, 10 (1978), 431–46. John M. Warner, "In View of Other Matters: The Religious Dimension of *Amb*," *Essays in Literature*, 4 (1977), 78–94, develops a searching critique of both the moral and the aesthetic attitudes toward life, invoking Kirkegaard and Simone Weil and seeing the focus of James's novel as shifting away from "visionary man (whether the moral vision of Woollett or the aesthetic vision of Paris) to man in tune with cosmic reality." See also J. A. Ward, "*Amb* as a Conversion Experience," *Southern Review*, 5 (1969), 350–74, which makes use of William James's *Varieties of Religious Experience*. Frederick C. Crews, already cited, sees Strether achieving "a tolerance that borders on Christian love" and results in a kind of Christian humility, although he "does not love his neighbor for Jesus' sake but for the sake of filling his own consciousness with truth."

18. Susan M. Greenstein, "*Amb*: The Man of Imagination Engaged and Provided For," *SN*, 9 (1977), 137–53, explores, sometimes indirectly, the relationship between Strether and James.

19. See Philip L. De Rosa, "The Experience of Perception: A Reading of *Amb*," *Publications of the Arkansas Philological Association*, 2, Summer 1976, pp. 1–8; Tony Tanner, "The Watcher from the Balcony: HJ's *Amb*," *Critical Quarterly*, 8 (1966), 35–52, a study of Strether's expanding consciousness; and James N. Wise, "The Floating World of Lambert Strether," *Arlington Quarterly*, 2, Summer 1969, pp. 80–110, which emphasizes Strether's passivity with reference to the water imagery in the novel.

20. More articles have been published about *The Ambassadors* than about any other James novel, and they cannot all be listed here. Ronald Wallace, "Comic Form in *Amb*," *Genre*, 5 (1972), 31–48, Sarah Blacher Cohen, "*Amb*: A Comedy of Musing

and Manners," *Studies in American Humor*, 1 (1974–75), 79–90, and Edgar J. Bunde, "*Amb* and the Double Vision of HJ," *Essays in Literature*, 4 (1977), 59–74, all see the work as essentially comedy. Allan F. Stein, "Lambert Strether's Circuitous Journey: Motifs of Intermingled Quest and Circularity in *Amb*," *ESQ*, 22 (1976), 245–53, interprets his experience in the light of "the Medieval quest romance form," and Robert A. Durr, "The Night Journey in *Amb*," *PQ*, 35 (1956), 24–38, in Jungian and mythological terms. Mildred E. Hartsock, "The Dizzying Crest: Strether as Moral Man," *MLQ*, 26 (1965), 414–25, invokes existentialism; her article is a stimulating discussion of Strether's final decision, challenging many simplistic, extremist views previously proferred by other critics. Robert N. Hudspeth, "The Definition of Innocence in *Amb*," *TSLL*, 6 (1964), 354–60, explores the nature of Strether's American innocence and his recovery from it. C. M. Finn, "Commitment and Identity in *Amb*," *MLR*, 66 (1971), 522–31, stresses the open ending. William Veeder, "Strether and the Transcendance of Language," *MP*, 69 (1971–72), 116–32, studies developments with special reference to language. N. I. Bailey, "Pragmatism in *Amb*," *Dalhousie Review*, 53 (1973–74), 143–48, finds Henry lacking in William James's optimism. Elsa Nettels, "Vision and Knowledge in *Amb* and *Lord Jim*," *English Literature in Transition, 1880–1920*, 18 (1975), 181–93, provides a comparative study.

## 9.  THE MASTERPIECES, II

1. *The Notebooks of HJ*, pp. 169–76. On pp. 174–76 the editors comment helpfully on the differences between these notes and the novel.
2. Sr. Stephanie Vincec, "'Poor Flopping Wings': The Making of HJ's *WD*," *HLB*, 24 (1976), 60–93. Cf. Edel, *HJ: The Master*, pp. 108–109.
3. A number of writers have pointed out resemblances

between *The Wings of the Dove* and some of James's short stories, especially "Georgina's Reasons" (1884), in which Mildred Theory has a sister named Kate. See *Notebooks*, p. 61; Edel, *The Master*, p. 100; and Cargill, *Novels of HJ*, pp. 347–48. Both Elizabeth Stevenson, *The Crooked Corridor*, pp. 111–12, and Sr. M. Corona Sharp, *The Confidante in HJ*, p. 202, are reminded of James's own invalid sister, Alice; the latter writes that Milly's "contempt for her disease and rejection of all pity are much more like the jeering attitude of Alice James" than like Minny Temple. James was also familiar with the pathetic circumstances of the illness and death of W. D. Howells's remarkable young daughter Winifred; see Edward Wagenknecht, *William Dean Howells: The Friendly Eye* (OUP, 1969), especially pp. 176–79.

4.  See Ernest Sandeen, "*WD* and *PL*," *PMLA*, 69 (1954), 1060–74. Adeline R. Tintner, "Hezekiah and *WD*; The Origin of 'She Turned Her Face to the Wall,'" *NMAL*, 3 (1979), Item 22, has now shown reason to believe that James was also thinking of 2 Kings 20:2 and Isaiah 38:2.

5.  *The Novels of HJ*, pp. 338–41.

6.  This seems to have been first pointed out by Marius Bewley in *The Complex Fate* . . . (Grove Press, 1954). Bewley did not admire either character, but in his book on Hawthorne, James called Hilda "one of those things that mark the man of genius."

7.  Edel, *HJ: The Master*, p. 115; Matthiessen, *HJ: The Major Phase*, p. 50.

8.  See *HJ: The Master*, pp. 121–22 (cf. Lewis, *Edith Wharton* [Harper & Row, 1975]; Cargill, *Novels of HJ*, p. 380, n. 21; and Harold N. Rypins, "HJ in Harley Street," *AL*, 24 (1953), 481–92. A hilarious footnote to the study of possible James originals was supplied by the adventuress Emilie Busby Grigsby, reputed mistress of the traction magnate Charles T. Yerkes, who tried to pass herself off as the original of Milly Theale because she had red hair, although she never met James until after the novel had been

published. Her pretensions were taken seriously only by the Hearst press, which proclaimed also that James wished to marry her; see *HJ: The Master*, pp. 174–80. Emilie Grigsby *is* the authentic original of Beatrice Fleming in Theodore Dreiser's novel about Yerkes, *The Titan*.

9.   The most elaborate analysis is that of J. A. Ward, *The Search for Form*, who finds the *Dove* structurally James's most difficult novel because it has no "pre-established system of organization" and "represents James's most extreme departure from the high standards of external symmetry that he generally imposed upon himself" but concludes that "the outer disorder reflects an inner order; it is the price James pays for a deeper, integral consistency and coherence." See also Leo Bersani, "The Narrator as Center in *WD*," *MLR*, 6 131–44. In his preface James himself analyzed his structure much more elaborately than usual.

10.  *The Confidante in HJ*, pp. 189–90.

11.  "Mr. HJ's Later Work," reprinted in Dupee, ed., *The Question of HJ*.

12.  *A Rhetoric of Literary Character*, p. 209. Cf. James Grove, "The Neglected Dinner in J's *WD*," *American Notes and Queries*, 18 (1979), 5–6.

13.  Lubbock, ed., *Letters*, I, pp. 399, 403.

14.  *HJ: The Major Phase*, p. 71.

15.  *HJ: The Major Phase*, pp. 70–73. Matthiessen's qualifications were important. He made the point that unlike the symbolist poets, James drew his images from painting and the theater rather than from music and that he made little or no use of mythology and anthropology. See Jean Kimball, "The Abyss and the Wings of the Dove: The Image as a Revelation," *NCF*, 10 (1955–56), 281–300, and Lotus Snow, "The Disconcerting Poetry of Mary Temple: A Comparison of the Imagery in *PL* and *WD*," *NEQ*, 31 (1958), 312–39.

16.  *Strange Alloy*, p. 92.

17.  *The Search for Form*, p. 138.

18. James describes the ravages of sexual passion more fully in connection with Densher than anywhere else in his work. As to the night of love at the beginning of Book Ninth (the only one, alas, the lovers were ever to have), it is both beautiful and terrible. That Kate comes for an ulterior end, in response to an ultimatum, introduces a sordid element of prostitution into it, but it is impossible not to be moved by the "prime afterglow" that the girl leaves behind her for her enraptured lover. "What it came to . . . was that when he closed the door behind him for an absence he always shut her in."

19. See J. A. Ward, "Social Disintegration in *WD*," *Crit*, 2 (1960), 190–203, and Milton Kornfeld, "Villainy and Responsibility in *WD*," *TSLL*, 14 (1972), 337–46, and, for further consideration of Densher, R. W. B. Lewis, "The Vision of Grace: J's *WD*," *MFS*, 3 (1937–38), 33–40; Quentin S. Kraft, "Life Against Death in Venice," *Crit*, 7 (1965), 217–23; R. Christian Brown, "The Role of Densher in *WD*," *Moderna Sprak*, 65 (1971), 5–11; and Sr. Stephanie Vincec, "A Significant Revision in *WD*," *Review of English Studies*, N.S. 23 (1973), 58–61. The most furious attack on Densher is that of Joseph J. Firebaugh, "The Idealism of Merton Densher," *Texas Studies in English*, 36 (1957), 141–54, and the most ardent defense that of George Sebouhian, "The Transcendental Imagination of Merton Densher," *Modern Language Studies*, 5, Fall 1975, pp. 33–45.

20. See especially John Carlos Rowe, "The Symbolization of Milly Theale: HJ's *WD*," *ELH*, 11 (1973), 131–60.

21. Matthiessen, *HJ: The Major Phase*, p. 43; Wilson, "The Ambiguity of HJ," reprinted in Dupee, *The Question of HJ*. Since I am not writing a history of the aberrations of James criticism, I pass quickly over such nonsense as Robert C. McLean's "Love by the Doctor's Direction: Disease and Death in *WD*," *PLL*, 8 (1972), Supplement, pp. 128–45, which sees Milly as ugly, jealous, sexually frustrated, and

free from organic disease, and her death as a suicide, and Judith A. Gustafson's "The Wings of the Dove or, A Gathering of Pigeons," *Gypsy Scholar*, 3 (1975), 13–19, where she appears as a vampire and "James's satiric comment on popular taste in heroines." Stuart Hutchinson's "J's Medal: Options in *WD*," *EIC*, 27 (1977), 315–35, is not vicious in tone, but it is equally wrongheaded.

22. The Bronzino has been identified; it is the portrait of Lucrezia Panciatichi in the Uffizi Gallery; see Miriam Allott, "The Bronzino Portrait in HJ's *WD*," *MLN*, 68 (1953), 23–25, and Plate XIII in Viola Hopkins Winner's *HJ and the Visual Arts* (the picture is also reproduced on a smaller scale in Harry T. Moore, *HJ and his World* [Viking Press, 1974], p. 93). For the use James makes of another painting, Veronese's *The Marriage at Cana*, to mark "the transition to [Milly's] martyrdom with its appropriate imagery," see Cargill, p. 343, and the fuller discussion in Ward, *The Search for Form*.

23. See Alan W. Bellringer, "*WD*: The Main Image," *MLR*, 74 (1979), 12–25. John Goode's own essay, "The Pervasive Mystery of Style; *WD*," in his *The Air of Reality*, and Millicent Bell's "The Dream of Being Possessed and Possessing: HJ's *WD*," *Massachusetts Review*, 10 (1969), are important detailed studies. John Hagan, "A Note on the Symbolic Pattern in *WD*," *CLAJo*, 10 (1966–67), 256–62, finds the stages in Milly's development imaged and foreshadowed in the cliff scene.

## 10.  THE MASTERPIECES, III

1. *Edith Wharton and HJ: The Story of Their Friendship* (George Braziller, 1965), p. 43.
2. *Notebooks*, pp. 130–32, 187–89, 233.
3. Lubbock, *Letters*, II, pp. 15–16, 28, 29–30, 41; Edel, *HJ: The Master*, pp. 173, 219; Cargill, *Novels of HJ*, p. 434.

4. Edel, *HJ: The Master*, pp. 209, 211; Cargill, *Novels of HJ*, pp. 385–86; Mildred S. Greene, *"Les Liaisons Dangereuses* and *GB*: Maggie's 'Loving Reason,'" *MFS*, 19 (1973–74), 531–40; Scott Byrd, "The Fractured Crystal in *Middlemarch* and *GB*," *MFS*, 18 (1972–73), 551–54; and Miriam Allott, *"Romola* and *GB*," *NQ*, 198 (1953), 124–25. For the Keats reference see Book Second, Chapter 1, for the Poe Book First, Chapter I. Adeline R. Tintner has an important commentary on the latter in "J Corrects Poe: The Appropriation of Poe in *GB*," *American Transcendental Quarterly*, 37 (1978), 87–91. See also her "Sir Sidney Colvin in *GB*: Mr. Crichton Identified," *Colby Library Quarterly*, 10 (1974), 428–31; "A Source for Prince Amerigo in *GB*," *NMAL*, 2 (1978), Item 23; and *"GB* and Waddeston Manor," *Apollo*, 104, August 1976, pp. 106–113.

5. Ralf Norman studies "End-Linking as an Intensity Creating Device in the Dialogue of HJ's *GB*," *ES*, 61 (1980), 236–51. For other stylistic commentaries, see H. K. Girling, "The Function of Slang in the Dramatic Poetry of *GB*," *NCF*, 11 (1956), 130–47, reprinted in Powers, *HJ: The Major Novels*; Marianna Torgovnick, "Gestural Pattern and Meaning in *GB*," *Twentieth Century Literature*, 26 (1980), 445–57; and Ruth Bernard Yeazell, *Language and Knowledge in the Late Novels of HJ*, Chapter 5.

6. Adeline R. Tintner, "Maggie's Pagoda: Architectural Follies in *GB*," *MR*, 3 (1973), 113–15, finds the pagoda "a fairly accurate description of existing architectural follies, relics of the oriental craze that swept England in the eighteenth century." Only two survive, one in the Royal Gardens at Kew and the other at Alton Towers in Staffordshire. Both are pictured in the article. "Maggie's pagoda appears to resemble remarkably closely the one at Alton Towers." Ms. Tintner relates the pagoda image to James's similar, though less elaborate, use of "architectural chinoiserie" in other novels. Amy Ling's "The Pagoda Image in HJ's *GB*," *AL*, 46 (1974–75), 383–88, in-

cludes a summary of views previously expressed by others. Other useful studies are Leo B. Levy's "*GB* and 'The Voice of Blood,'" *HJR*, 1 (1979–80), 154–63, and Gabriel Pearson's remarks on the pagoda in his ambitious and highly subjective "The Novel To End All Novels: *GB*," in Goode's *The Air of Reality*.

7. Ruth Taylor Todasco, "Theme and Imagery in *GB*," *TSLL*, 4 (1962–63), 228–40, even sees the bowl as "carrying the aura of the holy grail." Lotus Snow, "'A Story of Cabinets and Chairs and Tables': Images of Morality in *SPo* and *GB*," *ELH*, 30 (1963), 413–35, and James L. Spencer, "Symbolism in *GB*," *MFS*, 3 (1957–58), 333–44, have other elaborate interpretations. For less strained commentaries, see Matthiessen, *HJ: The Major Phase*, pp. 83–87, and Crews, *The Tragedy of Manners*, pp. 101–103.

8. Edith Wharton, *A Backward Glance* (Appleton-Century, 1934), p. 191.

9. Cf., for example, the use made of weather in Book Third, Chapter 4. Matthiessen was probably wrong in seeing James as indifferent to capitalistic abuses in his portrait of Adam Verver, although he certainly lets him off more lightly than the critic would have done. But it is not necessary to go all the way with J. A. Ward, *The Imagination of Disaster*, p. 150: "James's point is that an assimilation between American wealth and European tradition cannot come about without mutual contamination."

10. Mrs. Wharton's remark is in *The Writing of Fiction* (S, 1925), pp. 90–91, quoted in full by Cargill, *Novels of HJ*, p. 438. For more careful definition of the function of the Assinghams see Cargill, pp. 423–24; Segal, *The Lucid Reflector*, pp. 195–210; and especially Sharp, *The Confidante in HJ*. Wegelin's remark is quoted from *The Image of Europe in HJ*, p. 123, and Matthiessen's from *HJ: The Major Phase*, p. 95. Whether James intended the names of the Assinghams as a pun I cannot say. It would seem an unbelievably crude one for him, but it seems equally unbelievable that he could have named them as he

did without being aware of how it might be interpreted. Neither do I have any idea why he made
them so grotesque physically. Cargill, p. 437, n. 40,
shows reason to believe that he may originally have
intended to make the lady Jewish; there are a couple
of passages in the novel that might well be taken as
anti-Semitic.

11. The most exalted view of both Verver and his daughter is that of Quentin Anderson, *The American HJ*.
Francis Fergusson, "*GB* Revisited, *SR*, 63 (1955),
13–28, is in agreement with Anderson, as in some
aspects are R. P. Blackmur, "The Loose and Baggy
Monsters of HJ," *Accent*, 11 (1951), 129–46, and
Crews, *The Tragedy of Manners*, but George Sebouhian, "Adam Verver: Emerson's Poet," *MR*, 7,
Fall 1977, pp. 39–40, turns to the Concord tradition.
Caroline Gordon's article is "Mr. Verver, Our National Hero," *SR*, 63 (1955), 29–47. Caroline G. Mer-
cer, "Adam Verver, Yankee Businessman," *NCF*, 22
(1967–68), 251–69, first summarizes the various
views that have been taken of Adam, and then develops the interesting idea that the character was
colored from the traditional "smart" Yankee in popular American fiction and drama. Mildred E. Hartsock, "Unintentional Fallacy: Critics and *GB*,"
*MLQ*, 35 (1974), 272–88, furnishes a useful corrective to many attitudes expressed up to that date, and
A. R. Gard, "Critics of *GB*," *Melbourne Critical Review*, 6 (1963), 102–109, argues that James's treatment of the Ververs is deliberately ambiguous.
Among the books which comment usefully on
Verver, see Bowden, *The Themes of HJ*, pp. 103ff.;
Holland, *The Expense of Vision*, pp. 352ff.; Maves,
*Sensuous Pessimism*, pp. 126–29; and Mull, *HJ's
"Sublime Economy,"* pp. 138ff.

12. Charlotte has been defended by, among others, F.
R. Leavis, *The Great Tradition* (Chatto & Windus,
1949); Ferner Nuhn, *The Wind Blew from the East:
A Study in the Orientation of American Culture*
(Harpers, 1942); and, most extravagantly, Jean Kim-

ball, "HJ's Last Portrait of a Lady: Charlotte Stant in *GB*," *AL*, 28 (1956–57), 449–67, who sees her as the heroine of the book and argues that her affair with the prince existed only in Maggie's imagination. Elizabeth Owen has an excellent article on "The 'Given Appearance' of Charlotte Stant," in *EIC*, 13 (1964), 264–74.

13. Cf. especially the end of Book Third, Chapter 9, where Charlotte and the Prince leave Lady Castledean's together. It is interesting that in both the *Dove* and the *Bowl* the man should be represented as capable of repentance and redemption and the woman not. Let feminists and antifeminists make what they like of this!

14. "New Reflections on *GB*," *Twentieth Century Literature*, 3 (1957–58), 20–26.

15. The most extreme statements are those of Sallie Sears in *The Negative Imagination* and Joseph J. Firebaugh in "The Ververs," *EIC*, 4 (1954), 400–410. To Ms. Sears "the last part of the book, under Maggie's sponsorship, resembles a sado-masochistic nightmare worthy of the dark dreams of Poe," and Maggie's treatment of Charlotte is "a *tour de force* of masochistic self-manipulation and disguised sadism." Firebaugh brings in philosophical, political, and sociological considerations, viewing the novel as "a criticism of the very basis on which the notion of the absolute stands," with Maggie's wealth also making her a "politioco-economic monster" and a symbol of the "cartelized totalitarian state." Of such absurdities on the one hand and those of Anderson & Company on the other, Walter Wright provides a useful corrective in "Maggie Verver: Neither Saint Nor Witch," *NCF*, 12 (1957), 59–71.

16. James makes the Ververs Roman Catholics (although Adam's Catholicism seems pretty nominal), but the priest who appears at their table does nothing but eat and drink, and it is very clear that Maggie does not consult him about her problem. Cargill, p. 388, connects all this with the use he believes James

made of the work of his friend Paul Bourget and his
desire not to offend that earnest son of the church,
but Michael Gilmore, who reads the novel in the
context indicated by his title, sees James tracing
Maggie's development in terms of Protestant and
Puritan conceptions of sainthood; see *The Middle
Way: Puritanism and Ideology in American Romantic Fiction* (Rutgers University Press, 1977), especially pp. 298ff.

17. David Mogen, "Agonies of Innocence: The Governess [in "The Turn of the Screw"] and Maggie
Verver," *ALR*, 9 (1978), 231–42, studies the ambi-
guities of the two characters and attributes the dislike they sometimes awaken to modern reaction
against Victorian values.

18. See his *The Melodramatic Imagination: Balzac, HJ,
Melodrama and the Mode of Excess* (YUP, 1976).
Other useful studies of the *Bowl* include John J.
Enck, "Wholeness of Effect in *GB*," *Transactions of
the Wisconsin Academy of Sciences, Arts, and Let-
ters*, 45 (1958), 227–40, and Donald D. Kummings,
"The Issue of Morality in *GB*," *AQ*, 32 (1976), 381–
91.

## 11.  ADDENDA

1. The play version of *The Outcry* appears, with an introduction, in Edel, *Complete Plays of HJ*. The letters cited in this paragraph are in Lubbock, *Letters*,
II, pp. 129, 183, 209. Since he was writing Mrs.
Wharton from England, James probably refers to the
sale of the two books there; as we have seen in Chapter 10, *The Golden Bowl* reached its fourth printing
in America before James had returned from his first
visit there. See also Cargill, *Novels of HJ*, p. 444.

2. James made up both names, but in 1912 a correspondent called it to his attention that there had
been a painter named Montavano, whose work was

represented in the National Gallery; see Lubbock, *Letters*, II, pp. 280–81.

3. Lubbock, *Letters*, II, pp. 119, 154; cf. Cargill, *Novels*, pp. 462–65. In his preface to *The Ivory Tower*, Lubbock says merely, "It was composed during the summer of 1914."

4. The quotations are from Matthiessen, *The J Family* (Knopf, 1947); Pelham Edgar, *HJ, Man and Author*, p. 89; and Dupee, ed., *The Question of HJ*, p. 189.

5. *The Crooked Corridor*, p. 14.

6. See Cargill, *Novels*, pp. 468ff., for the most determined effort to discover how James would have developed and concluded his book, including considerable reference to attempts made by other critics.

7. On this point see Alan W. Bellringer, "*IT*: The Cessation of Concern," *JAS*, 10 (1976), 241–55. Other interesting studies of the novel are provided by Peter Buitenhuis, "The Fresh Start and the Broken Link: HJ's *IT*," *UTQ*, 33 (1963–64), 355–68, and Jan W. Dietrichson in *The Image of Money in the American Novel of the Gilded Age* (Humanities Press, 1969).

8. I confess myself unable to fathom what James fancied he gained by making Rosanna an Amazon and a cigarette addict. His harping on her size almost every time she is mentioned strikes me as the most unsubtle thing he ever did. In the first chapter alone we have "a truly massive young person," "the large loose ponderous girl," "his big quiet plain daughter," and "her powerful exposed arm, raised to her broad shoulder, slowly made her heavy parasol revolve."

9. *The Crooked Corridor*, p. 77.

10. The "First Statement" is in *Notebooks*, pp. 361–69; see also p. 299, and in Lubbock, *Letters*, I, pp. 349–51, and II, pp. 426–26. James's 1914 statement to Edith Wharton that he had written thirty-thousand words of his novel fifteen years before supports Lubbock's view that the manuscript originally broke off

in the middle of Pendrel's interview with the ambassador.

11. "Consciousness in J's *SPa*," *Crit*, 5 (1963), 148–72.
Beams further sees Book Fourth as approximating
"William James's studies of dissociated personality
(with a modern explanation in the repressed Ralph
of 1910, rather than William James's physiological
ones); and at the same time an apprehending of the
flux or 'stream' of normal consciousness as it creates
multiple identities in the community of the individual." He also finds "Bergsonian duration and recap-
ture of things present, a deranged Symbolist expression of the inexpressible and finally James's noblest
allegory of the consciousness of the artist who makes
life by making awareness of it."

12. *The Time Machine*, itself influenced by J. W.
Dunne's theories of "serial time," was an important
influence upon the production of many time-travel
novels and plays, especially in England, during the
1930s and 1940s; see my *Cavalcade of the English
Novel* (Holt, 1943), pp. 464–65, and the introduction
to Robert Nathan's *Portrait of Jennie* in my anthol-
ogy *Six Novels of the Supernatural* (Viking Press,
1944).

## 12.   Significances

1. This closing chapter is based on the discussion of
Henry James in the author's *Cavalcade of the American Novel*, copyright 1952 by Henry Holt and Company, Inc., copyright renewed 1980 by Edward Wagenknecht.

2. Percy Lubbock, in the introduction to his edition of
*Letters*. For further interesting discussion of this
point see William Cosgrove and Irene Matthees,
"'To See Life Reflected': Seeing as Living in *Amb*,"
*HJR*, 1 (1979–80), 204–10.

3. Graham Greene in his essay on James in Derek Ver-

schoyle, ed., *The English Novelists* (Harcourt, Brace, 1936); Bernard Smith in *Forces in American Criticism* (Harcourt, Brace, 1930), pp. 207–210.

4. In the Harper symposium *In After Days* (1910), reprinted in F. O. Matthiessen, ed., *The J Family*.

# Suggestions for Further Reading*

Anderson, Quentin. *The American Henry James*. Rutgers University Press, 1956.

Andreas, Osborn. *Henry James and the Expanding Horizon: A Study of the Meaning and Basic Themes of James's Fiction*. University of Washington Press, 1948.

Beach, Joseph Warren. *The Method of Henry James*. Yale University Press, 1918.

Bowden, Edwin. *The Themes of Henry James: A System of Observation through the Visual Arts*. Yale University Press, 1956.

Buitenhuis, Peter. *The Grasping Imagination: The American Writings of Henry James*. University of Toronto Press, 1970.

Cargill, Oscar. *The Novels of Henry James*. Macmillan, 1961.

Cary, Elizabeth L. *The Novels of Henry James: A Study*. Putnam, 1905.

Clair, John A. *The Ironic Dimension in the Fiction of Henry James*. Duquesne University Press, 1965.

* An adequate bibliography of what has been written about Henry James's novels would fill a larger volume than this one. What follows is not such a bibliography but merely a list of books (not articles) in which some of those who have read this volume might like to read further. These works are not all of equal value or importance, nor does the author of this volume like them all equally well. What he thinks of some of them may be inferred from his references to them in the notes, but the usefulness of individual items to individual readers may best be discovered by themselves.

Crews, Frederick C. *The Tragedy of Manners: Moral Drama in the Later Novels of Henry James.* Yale University Press, 1957.

Dupee, F. W. *Henry James.* William Sloane Associates, 1951 (reprinted as a Doubleday Anchor book, 1956).

Dupee, F. W., ed. *The Question of Henry James: A Collection of Critical Essays.* Holt, 1945.

Edel, Leon. *Henry James: The Untried Years; Henry James: The Conquest of London; Henry James: The Middle Years; Henry James: The Treacherous Years; Henry James: The Master.* Lippincott, 1953–1972.

Edel, Leon, ed. *Henry James Letters.* Volumes I–III. Harvard University Press, 1974–1980.

Edgar, Pelham. *Henry James, Man and Author.* Houghton Mifflin, 1927.

Gale, Robert L. *The Caught Image: Figurative Language in the Fiction of Henry James.* University of North Carolina Press, 1964.

Goode, John, ed. *The Air of Reality: New Essays on Henry James.* Methuen, 1972.

Graham, Kenneth. *Henry James: The Drama of Fulfilment.* Oxford University Press, 1975.

Hocks, Richard H. *Henry James and Pragmatistic Thought: A Study of the Relationship between the Philosophy of William James and the Literary Art of Henry James.* University of North Carolina Press, 1974.

Hoffman, Charles G. *The Short Novels of Henry James.* Bookman Associates, 1957.

Holland, Laurence Bedwell. *The Expense of Vision: Essays on the Craft of Henry James.* Princeton University Press, 1964.

Isle, Walter. *Experiments in Form: Henry James's Novels, 1896–1901.* Harvard University Press, 1968.

James, Henry. *The Art of the Novel.* Scribners, 1934. (Collected prefaces, indispensable to readers who do not have access to the New York Edition)

Jefferson, D. W. *Henry James and the Modern Reader.* Oliver and Boyd, 1964.

Kelley, Cornelia P. *The Early Development of Henry*

*James.* University of Illinois Press, 1965 (originally published in 1930).

Krook, Dorothea. *The Ordeal of Consciousness in Henry James.* Cambridge University Press, 1962.

Lebowitz, Naomi. *The Imagination of Living: Henry James's Legacy to the Novel.* Wayne State University Press, 1965.

Leeming, Glenda. *Who's Who in Henry James.* Taplinger, 1976.

Levy, Leo B. *Variations of Melodrama: A Study of the Fiction and Drama of Henry James, 1865–1897.* University of California Press, 1957.

Leyburn, Ellen. *Strange Alloy: The Relation of Comedy to Tragedy in the Fiction of Henry James.* University of North Carolina Press, 1968.

Lubbock, Percy, ed. *The Letters of Henry James,* 2 volumes. Scribners, 1920.

Marks, Robert. *James's Later Novels: An Interpretation.* The William-Frederick Press, 1960.

Matthiessen, F. O. *Henry James: The Major Phase.* Oxford University Press, 1944.

Matthiessen, F. O., and Kenneth B. Murdock, eds. *The Notebooks of Henry James.* Oxford University Press, 1947.

Maves, Carl. *Sensuous Pessimism: Italy in the Work of Henry James.* Indiana University Press, 1973.

McCarthy, Harold T. *Henry James: The Creative Process.* Thomas Yoseloff, 1958.

McElderry, Bruce L. *Henry James.* Twayne Publishers, 1965.

Mull, Donald L. *Henry James's "Sublime Economy": Money as Symbolic Centre in the Fiction.* Wesleyan University Press, 1973.

O'Neill, Joseph P. *Workable Design: Action and Situation in the Fiction of Henry James.* Kennikat Press, 1973.

Perosa, Sergio. *Henry James and the Experimental Novel.* University Press of Virginia, 1978.

Poirier, Richard. *The Comic Sense of Henry James.* Oxford University Press, 1960.

Powers, Lyall H., ed. *Henry James's Major Novels: Essays in Criticism*. Michigan State University Press, 1973.

Putt, S. Gorley. *A Reader's Guide to Henry James*. Thames and Hudson, 1966.

Rimmon, Shlomith. *The Concept of Ambiguity: The Example of James*. University of Chicago Press, 1977.

Samuels, Charles Thomas. *The Ambiguity of Henry James*. University of Illinois Press, 1971.

Schneider, Daniel J. *The Crystal Cage: Adventures of the Imagination in the Fiction of Henry James*. Regents Press of Kansas, 1978.

Sears, Sallie. *The Negative Imagination: Form and Perspective in the Novels of Henry James*. Cornell University Press, 1968.

Segal, Ora. *The Lucid Reflector: The Observer in Henry James's Fiction*. Yale University Press, 1969.

Sharp, Sr. M. Corona. *The Confidante in Henry James: Evolution and Moral Value of a Fictive Character*. University of Notre Dame Press, 1963.

Shine, Muriel G. *The Fictional Children of Henry James*. University of North Carolina Press, 1969.

Springer, Mary Doyle. *A Rhetoric of Literary Character: Some Women of Henry James*. University of Chicago Press, 1978.

Stevenson, Elizabeth. *The Crooked Corridor: A Study of Henry James*. Macmillan, 1949.

Veeder, William. *Henry James—The Lessons of the Master: Popular Fiction and Personal Style in the Nineteenth Century*. University of Chicago Press, 1975.

Wagenknecht, Edward. *Eve and Henry James: Portraits of Women and Girls in his Fiction*. University of Oklahoma Press, 1978.

Wallace, Ronald. *Henry James and the Comic Form*. University of Michigan Press, 1975.

Ward, J. A. *The Imagination of Disaster: Evil in the Fiction of Henry James*. University of Nebraska Press, 1961.

Ward, J. A. *The Search for Form: Studies in the Structure of James's Fiction*. University of North Carolina Press, 1967.

Wegelin, Christof. *The Image of Europe in Henry James*. Southern Methodist University Press, 1958.

Weinstein, Philip M. *Henry James and the Requirements of the Imagination*. Harvard University Press, 1971.

Wiesenfarth, Joseph. *Henry James and the Dramatic Analogy*. Fordham University Press, 1962.

Winner, Viola Hopkins. *Henry James and the Visual Arts*. University Press of Virginia, 1960.

Wright, Walter F. *The Madness of Art: A Study of Henry James*. University of Nebraska Press, 1962.

Yeazell, Ruth Bernard. *Language and Knowledge in the Late Novels of Henry James*. University of Chicago Press, 1976.

# Index of Names

# Index of James's Writings

*Complete list of titles in the series available from publisher on request.*